Eyes Across the Channel

INTERDISCIPLINARY NINETEENTH-CENTURY STUDIES
AIMS AND SCOPES

Co-Editors
Keith Hanley, University of Lancaster, UK
Greg Kucich, University of Notre Dame, USA

Interdisciplinary Nineteenth-Century Studies is a book series designed to address the new and rapidly expanding wave of academic and popular fascination with the nineteenth century's deep, often contested relation to our own time. Representing one of the more compelling developments in recent academic criticism and theory, works in this series trace many of our contemporary notions of self, society, race, gender, class, and nation to their originary (or diversionary) formulations in the nineteenth century. These inquiries bear urgent contemporary relevance to the shaping of current global sites of intense political and military strife, such as Ireland, the Balkans, the Middle East, and the American racial divide. The nineteenth century has never been more alive, and its diversified presence within academic communities and throughout social formations around the world encourages our interdisciplinary approach to its persisting significance.

The present series had derived from an active affiliation with the scholarly organization Interdisciplinary Nineteenth-Century Studies (INCS), which reflects and helps to form innovative ways of encountering the above interests within the academy, and from the journal Nineteenth-Century Contexts: An Interdisciplinary Journal (NCC), which has been produced since 1994 under the same transatlantic editorship. But we aim also for more extensive horizons within and beyond the academic community—to that broader readership made up of all those who share special interests in our topics. Our aim is both to publish interdisciplinary studies written in English from all over the world focused on a specific historical frame, and to theorize that enterprise itself, either separately or within the same work. The editorial board is designed to oversee our drawing on a multiplicity of disciplinary backgrounds, such as anthropology, history, political science, ethnic studies, history of science, musicology, religious studies, art history, philosophy, sociology, economics, literary studies, and women's studies.

Volume 1
Eyes Across the Channel: French Revolutions, Party History and British Writing, 1830–1882
Clare A. Simmons

Eyes Across the Channel
French Revolutions, Party History and British Writing, 1830–1882

Clare A. Simmons
The Ohio State University
USA

harwood academic publishers
Australia • Canada • France • Germany
India • Japan • Luxembourg • Malaysia
The Netherlands • Russia • Singapore • Switzerland

Copyright © 2000 OPA (Overseas Publishers Association) N.V. Published by license under the Harwood Academic Publishers imprint, part of The Gordon and Breach Publishing Group.

All rights reserved.

No part of this book may be produced or utilized in any form or by any means, electronic or mechanical, including photocopying and recording, or by any information storage or retrieval system, without permission in writing from the publisher. Printed in Singapore.

Amsteldijk 166
1st Floor
1079 LH Amsterdam
The Netherlands

British Library Cataloguing in Publication Data
A catalogue record for this book is available from the British Library.

ISBN: 90-5823-048-1
ISSN: 1562-3432

To my husband, Henry Stern

CONTENTS

Acknowledgments		ix
Introduction		1
Chapter 1	Burkean Prophecy and the July Revolution	33
Chapter 2	After Reform: Conservatism and Carlyle	63
Chapter 3	1848: The Threat to Property	99
Chapter 4	Historical Repetition and *A Tale of Two Cities*	135
Chapter 5	Alternative Worlds and the Franco-Prussian War	167
Epilogue	Dreams of a Channel Tunnel	199
References		211
Index		223

ACKNOWLEDGMENTS

I would like to thank the many people and institutions that contributed to this book in ways that ranged from the highly practical to the morally supportive. Many ideas that became part of—or, equally important, were rejected from—the project were first aired at the Interdisciplinary Nineteenth-Century Studies conference, so it is appropriate that the book should appear in the *Interdisciplinary Nineteenth-Century Studies* book series under the editorship of Keith Hanley and Greg Kucich. David Riede and Mark Schoenfield patiently read early drafts of the entire manuscript. Pam, Michael, Hilary, and Annie Simmons collected newspaper cuttings on my behalf. Frances and Joy Simmons accompanied me on a snowy Channel Tunnel excursion. A version of Chapter Two appeared in *Prose Studies*, and a section of Chapter Five in *Studies in Medievalism*; thanks for this, and much else, are due to the editors, Ronald Corthell of *Prose Studies* and Leslie Workman and Kathleen Verduin of *Studies in Medievalism*. The Ohio State University Library proved itself equal to the task of locating the most obscure materials. Support for research was provided by the Ohio State University Department of English and College of Humanities. Others who provided hints, suggestions, and general goodwill include, but are certainly not limited to, James Bracken, Jerome Christensen, Mark Conroy, Laura George, Sebastian Knowles, Peter Manning, Mary McDougall, Ken McNeil, James Phelan, and Herbert Tucker. I am appreciative of comments and kindness from so many more of my colleagues in the Department of English at the Ohio State University that it is hard to single them out, but I would like to recognize particularly both the critical skills and the friendship of those in Nineteenth-Century British literature, Audrey Jaffe, Marlene Longenecker, Richard Martin, David Riede, Cathy Shuman, and Les Tannenbaum. Finally, I thank my husband Henry Stern for his endless patience.

Introduction

Happy England! ... that the wise dispensation of Providence has cut her off, by that streak of silver sea, which passengers so often and justly execrate, though in no way from the duties and honors, yet partly from the dangers, absolutely from the temptations, which attend upon the local neighbourhood of the Continental nations.

(W. E. Gladstone)

A Frenchman must have his revolution.

(W. M. Thackeray)

On October 30, 1990, the French and English sides of a tunnel under their shared territorial waters were linked by a small drill-hole—in the words of *The Times*, "a mousehole through to France."[1] The construction, a challenge both to engineering and to creative financing, promised to ease travel by providing a land-link between Britain and the rest of Europe within the next three years. The media, however, interpreted the significance of the venture not logistically or economically, but historically. "Whether you like it or not," the British Broadcasting Company informed viewers, "Britain will be joined to France for the first time in 8,000 years."[2] By 1993—later postponed "for technical reasons" to 1994—for the first time since the Ice Age, a land-link would be created between Britain and the European mainland. Yet the B.B.C.'s presentation of the event, however humorously intended, depends on what Stuart Hall has called the "shared meanings" of a culture.[3] The joke is not funny unless there is a cultural awareness that at least some Britons will not like the idea of being joined to Europe by what has been significantly described as an "artery" of the European Community's planned high-speed rail network.

Indeed, the day after representatives of French and British workers were shaking hands under the stretch of water known to the French by its geographical shape (La Manche) and to the British by a sense of proprietorship (the English Channel), Britain's Prime Minister Margaret Thatcher, whose government had refused to provide an infusion of money for the "artery," was insisting that Britain would make "no further surrender" to the European Monetary Union.[4]

Thatcher was standing against of model of European development that was federalist and progressivist in order to ensure the survival of British independent identity. The identity of a nation is itself, of course, problematic. In the case of Britain, speaking English is not proof of identity with the nation, since English is the official government language of many nations; as a residue of Empire, even having British citizenship is not proof of Britishness.[5] Britain's island status marks what Britain is, and hence the Tunnel represents the erosion of that form of identity.

In this case of identity, however, the geographic cedes to the historic. Only the previous year, Thatcher had attempted to teach France a history lesson. While in Paris in July 1989 to attend the celebrations of the two hundredth anniversary of the storming of the Bastille, Thatcher had been interviewed on French television. When asked whether she believed that the "rights of man" had begun with the French Revolution, Thatcher replied, "No—pardon me for saying—but I think not." Suggesting that the concept of individual right was part of the Judeo-Christian tradition, Thatcher pointed out that "we" (by which she meant Britain) had proclaimed certain rights in the Magna Carta, the Declaration of Right, and "our quiet revolution of 1688." In contrast, the storming of the Bastille—in which, she pointed out, there were only seven prisoners at the time—led to "the Terror and Napoleon."[6]

After *Le Monde* headed its transcription of the interview "'The rights of man did not begin in France,' Mrs. Thatcher tells us"—France also can be a "we"—Thatcher was booed by the French public. The most common British reaction was that such comments were impolite at best, damaging to European relations at worst; in retrospect, Thatcher herself was prepared to concede in her memoirs that "the French Revolution is one of the few real watersheds in the history of political ideas."[7] At the time, though, Thatcher's attempt to spoil France's party seems to have been motivated both by a conception of history and by a fear that dates back to Edmund Burke and the French Revolution itself. The fear is, I would suggest, twofold, although in British consciousness the two elements are often intertwined. One fear is of the power of the people, and the question of whether their assertion of rights must lead to terror. The second fear is of the influence of

France, and the question of whether Britain must follow where France leads. Thatcher certainly had reason to suspect that the elaborate Bicentennial celebrations, which were followed by an international economic summit, were an attempt by France to strengthen its claim to a leadership role in world politics. But in terms of outright rudeness and unfairness, she could hardly hope to equal Edmund Burke almost two hundred years before, although she had apparently been reading him.

Underlying Thatcher's comments, then, are some important assumptions that she shared with both with Burke and with many Tories of the period of this study, 1830–1882. The relations between Britain and Europe, and particularly between Britain and France, are the product of a long history, and history cannot be forgotten or even considered impartially, because it was bought at the cost of terror. Britain's preservation is its own separate history.

The Channel Tunnel—or, more disturbingly for Britons, the Eurotunnel—is thus not merely a piece of engineering linking two towns, Dover and Calais, that were it not for a shallow stretch of seawater would be closer together than the suburbs of some United States cities. The Tunnel is a symbol of Britain's changing place in history, an end of separation; and yet as it linked France and Britain, newspapers continually referred to Britain's "isolationist" attitude towards Europe, embodied by Margaret Thatcher. On November 2, 1990, Geoffrey Howe, Thatcher's deputy Prime Minister and the last survivor of her 1979 Cabinet, resigned, citing Thatcher's intransigent European policies as his reason;[8] Thatcher's leadership lasted only two more weeks. The long-term Prime Minister's failure to acknowledge Britain's changing relations with Europe—indeed, her interpretation of British identity as dependent on a history of isolationism—was a significant contribution to her rejection by her party so soon after she had declared "no surrender" to Europe.

Britain could, then, live in its past history as the world's greatest power, or it could acknowledge a different world order and seek to be joined with it. Britain's crisis of identity in 1990 is thus symbolically represented by the link with, or breach from, France. Historically, the Channel waters have represented Britain's protection against the threat of invasion by France (notably by Napoleon) or from France (by Hitler), and various news sources reminded the British public that Napoleon had been interested in such a project. On September 16, 1990, for example, the *New York Times Magazine* reproduced a French engraving from about 1803 depicting a scheme by which Napoleon could construct a tunnel under the sea for invading England.

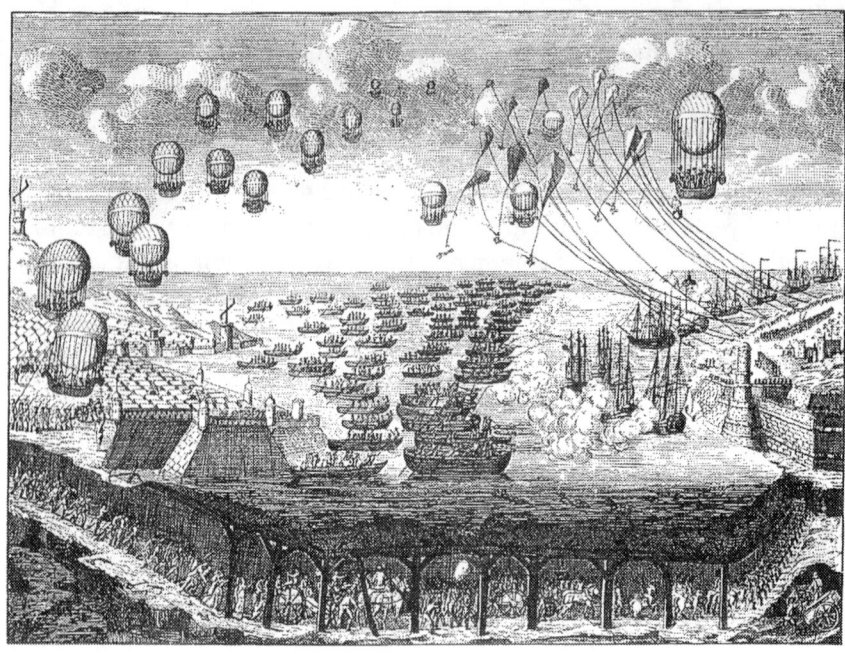

Figure 1. Anonymous French engraving from 1803 depicting a French invasion of England, including through a Channel Tunnel.

Like much of the suspicion between France and Britain explored in this book, the "Napoleonic Threat" was based on inaccurate history. Napoleon listened to Albert Matthieu's idea for constructing a tunnel, but this was in early 1802, after the Treaty of Amiens, when Britain and France were at peace. Donald Hunt has remarked that the "history of the Channel Tunnel has always been a mirror of European history, and particularly of the changing relations between France and Britain";[9] I would go further and suggest that the cooperation needed to undertake such a project dictates that the times when the Channel Tunnel has been most discussed are those when British and French relations have been most cordial. Since an interpretation of this "plan" of invasion was published as a print, it was clearly not a secret military project—and even if a tunnel were technically feasible at this date, a secret one was not. According to Thomé de Gamond, the concept was so far from secret that Napoleon discussed it with the Whig leader Charles James Fox as an example of the "great things" Britain and France could achieve together.[10]

All the same, a tunnel might still represent an aura of threat to Britain's island integrity. The Channel marks the separation of Britain from Europe, the essential preservation of a cherished difference. Even when in 1992, under the more conciliatory John Major, the mainstream British Tories committed themselves (and Britain) to the Maästricht Treaty's call for closer political and economic union, hardline Thatcherite Tories and the political Left formed a strange alliance in voicing doubts about the surrender of national autonomy. France was permitted a referendum on whether or not to approve the Treaty, and Britain was not, but Major promised to take the French result into consideration. Hugo Young, writing in Britain's least conservative national newspaper *The Guardian*, hence asked the most feared historical question of all: whether this would mean "Government from Paris." Suggesting that right-wing Tories might be the true preservers of the discourse of democracy, Young deliberately played on the historic resonances of the opposition between France and Britain:

> In the one [France], where democracy is so unreliable, and parliamentary history so corrupted by the taste for revolution, the people will speak. In the other [Britain], where the genius of de Montfort has prevailed for 700 years, the people must consider their rights well satisfied by being important spectators at a squabble between the Conservative leader and his little band of party troublemakers.[11]

Given this manipulation of the role of history, it is scarcely surprising that the Tunnel is an artifact that works as symbol: in reminding Britain and France of their enforced closeness, it simultaneously draws focus to past differences. The object of this study is to look at this double sense of closeness and difference at a particular historical period from a partial point of view, that constructed by British writers; and to argue that the appeal to history has always been a powerful one in shaping cultural response. British writers—among whom I shall not distinguish between the declaredly "literary" and the political, historical, and occasional—have consistently demonstrated awareness that when comparing France and Britain, the central concerns are, as in the case of the Tunnel, not geographical but historical. In thinking of France, British writers and readers include a historical awareness of all that France has represented over the centuries. Even when discussing recent or current events (people in their twenties at the time of the first French Revolution would only have been in their sixties in 1830), this historical awareness need not be accurate—indeed, a loosely-conceived myth can be more effective than a factually-based one. At its broadest and most deeply significant, it becomes an analogizing force which enables a specific historical event to be read not as a moment in history, but as embodying multiple references to the continuum that is History. In effect, in the literary consideration of what gives experience the status of event, many other parts of history that have already been granted the status of event must simultaneously be recalled.

My goal is therefore to look at British responses to France during the period 1830 to 1882 in a broad spectrum of texts, and to argue that readings of these texts may be significantly informed by two considerations that literary criticism's persistent underplaying of specific historical awareness within a culture has often overlooked. While scholars of cultural trends (Michel Foucault being an obvious example) have argued the centrality of history to the philosophy of the nineteenth century, less attention has been given to the discursive strategies through which writers and readers of this period applied specific knowledge of history to the creation of cultural meaning. That appeals to "history" might serve competing interpretive functions seems obvious; the nature of those functions, however, may be more susceptible to categorization than most analyses have suggested.

By focusing on interpretations of moments when European civilization seemed most in crisis, I hope to demonstrate that the cultural articulation of historical analogy is especially powerful when associated with an ideological, and in some cases physical, attack on tradition through "revolution." I would suggest that responses to revolution reveal significantly different patterns of thinking about history *within a culture* that suggest how much ideology is dependent on constructs of language, and particularly binarisms.

The nineteenth century was an age of many things—even, perhaps, the age in which the naming of ages became important—and I am far from alone in claiming it as an age of history. Foucault, in *The Order of Things*, characterizes the nineteenth century as the beginning of "The Age of History";[12] but sixty years earlier, George Peabody Gooch had examined many approaches to history of this period in his *History and Historians in the Nineteenth Century*, implicitly privileging history as a dominant force of the age.[13] Whereas, though, a historiographer of historiographers such as Gooch only indirectly challenges the nineteenth-century notion that history may be "true" and "scientific," modern theorists have stressed the literary nature of history. A. Dwight Culler, for example, refers to the "habit" among Victorian writers "of drawing analogies between their own their own age and various historical periods in the past and attempting to understand their problems, and their place in history, in terms of those analogies."[14] To acknowledge nineteenth-century history as a form of discourse is to recognize that history may not be cast-iron, but rather wrought-iron, a flexible and consciously-crafted artifact: my particular interest is in the social and cultural uses to which a literarily constructed history may be put.

Before discourse, however, history does not exist, which presents this project with certain difficulties of language. What is the material reality[15] upon which history is based *before* it becomes history? To call it an "event" or "occurrence" is already to grant it a beginning and an end, and to isolate it from the continuum of human experience, inevitably, as Raymond Williams observes, with the effect of serving specific cultural ends.[16] For want of a better term, I shall call the matter from which history is formed an "event," since until it can be formulated in language and time in this way, it cannot become history. David Ferris wrestles with this problem in *Theory and the Evasion of History* and reaches the conclusion that "history is what will have happened in order to know what was not known as an occurrence";[17] if only the recording of experience in words creates history, this "defines the present as a temporal or spatial gap."[18] What is remarkable about British responses to loci of historical potential in France during the period 1830–1882 is how rapidly this present becomes history, through a process that Ferris perhaps underemphasizes: the analogy of other events already enshrined as history, most notably the first French Revolution.

Foucault has remarked that "From the nineteenth century, History was to deploy, in a temporal series, the analogies that connect distinctive organic structures to one another."[19] The same approach, that of deducing origins from remains, would be applied to economics, natural science, and linguistics. But if, as J. W. Burrow has noted, a connection is made between all the disciplines "concerned with the reproduction of states no longer directly observable,"[20] history could provide its own analogies. That is, one or more historical events can supply the pattern of classification needed for interpreting actions in time as event, and hence as potential history. In the case of history as science, however, the part not "directly observable" that could only be understood by analogy with known states was not the past but the present and future.

Consequently, as Britons observed the series of revolutions in France during the nineteenth century, they applied to their readings of these events a series of analogies that for British readers had powerful associations, and that created a partial—that is, a personally interested—response. First, as Gerald Newman and Linda Colley have argued, France was seen as Britain's historic "natural enemy," the country against which Britain had fought most of its wars, and which in its laws and religion presented a touchstone by which Britain could at least negatively define itself.[21] That some elements of this sense of enmity survive in the late twentieth century suggests the longevity of a vague historical memory, but for Britons in, for example, 1830, war with France was only fifteen years distant and within the memory of all adults. The nineteenth-century French revolutions reminded Britons of the state of France in 1789–1795 that had brought them into a series of wars, and that had by 1830 become the French Revolution, the starting-point being the fall of the Bastille, and the end being seen as either the fall of Robespierre or the rise of Napoleon.[22]

This led to a more reified history. Barton Friedman has suggested that:

> The historical record, so called, is the outgrowth of a largely unwitting collaboration between those who, after the fact, sought to order and understand the materials of its making, to give them form, and later generations who have interpreted the texts their predecessors' understanding produced, and have fit that understanding into their own frames of reference.[23]

Friedman hence envisages history taking time in the making. In the middle years of the nineteenth century, British writers and readers interpreted events in France almost immediately as history, and hence in giving them form, they were compelled to construct an interpretive model from earlier historical analyses available to them.

In trying to read occurrences in France between 1830 and 1882 as history, they therefore consistently applied the touchstone event of *the* French Revolution. Yet in addition, they applied analogies from British history, including Magna Carta, the Great Rebellion leading to the Civil War of the 1640s, and the so-called "Glorious Revolution" of 1688—the same events as cited by Thatcher in 1989.[24] The comparisons provided some means for British readers to consider French affairs in the form of a simile: the past and native (the familiar) provides the means of reading the present and alien (the unfamiliar). But this, I would argue, is not the total force of the analogy. The Tunnel, like the Channel, represents a sense of difference. Yet the possibility arises not merely that French developments may be analogous to events in past history, but that they may also be analogous to contemporary or future events in Britain. Here the analogy becomes more disturbing.

During the period covered by this study, France experienced a revolution, a constitutional monarchy, another revolution, two brief republics, a coup, an empire, an invasion and a further revolution, and the untidy establishment of another republic. During the same period, Britain had experienced some unrest, but appeared to have had no revolution and to have grown in influence and prosperity. The French, the British have repeatedly asserted, are different—or, as I have previously argued, self-definition requires opposition, the British being seen as different from the French.[25] Still, the fear of historical analogy may remain: if similar events and circumstances may lead to similar outcomes, then the French present may become the British future.

From the British point of view, then, the French Revolution is never read in a disinterested way, but always in a partial way as a metaphor for its own national concerns. Yet even within the category of metaphors of self-interest, differing interpretations are possible. Here Hayden White's distinction between metonymy and synecdoche in historical interpretation may be useful. White defines metonymy as the form of metaphor by which "one can simultaneously distinguish between two phenomena and reduce one to the status of a manifestation of the other." At the same time, however, a metonymy can also be synecdoche: "the essentially *extrinsic* relationship that is presumed to characterize the two orders of phenomena in all Metonymical reductions can by Synecdoche be construed in the manner of an *intrinsic* relationship of shared *qualities*."[26]

An example from British readings of the French Revolution which, like the Tunnel question, involves an artifact that becomes a symbol, may demonstrate the possibilities of White's distinction. At the time of the outbreak of the French Revolution, writers such as Edmund Burke consciously used metonymy in referring to "lamp-posts." The Paris lamp-posts upon which alleged enemies of the Revolution were hanged become a metonymic expression of mob-rule. When taken as metonymy as defined by White, the limited applications of the image could be reassuring. Britain did not have such lamp-posts: indeed, in her *Historical and Moral View of the French Revolution*, Mary Wollstonecraft considered it necessary to explain to British readers that French lamp-posts were different and strong enough to serve as a gallows.[27] If hanging a person on a British lamp-post was not physically possible, British readers could feel secure that this emanation of mob-rule was exclusively a French phenomenon. As Seamus Deane observes in his valuable study of British intellectual responses to the first French Revolution, seeing "the Revolution as an essentially French phenomenon allowed it to be understood as alien to English circumstances and inclinations."[28]

When interpreted synecdochically, however, the lamp-post becomes a microcosm of all the possibilities of mob-rule. In Burke's words:

> It is said, that twenty-four millions ought to prevail over two hundred thousand. True; if the constitution of a kingdom be a problem of arithmetic. This sort of discourse does well enough with the lamp-post as its second ... .[29]

In connecting the (personified) lamp-post with the general theory of the "constitution of a kingdom," Burke suggests that the image may indeed have an application to the British situation—and that it is a serious cause for alarm.

This one example of the variation in metaphorical use applied to the analogy of history suggests that the relationship between French revolutions and Britain, even when read analogously, might be open to multiple interpretations. Indeed, the number of variables creates a broad spectrum of readings. Inevitably, the word "revolution" itself had some positive and some negative connotations. Perhaps it is appropriate that one of the best-known British descriptions of the French Revolution written during this period calls it both "the best of times" and "the worst of times."

My goal in this study is to illustrate that although multiple interpretations of history are possible, all history is "partial." This is not a new claim: François Furet has noted that "There is no such thing as 'innocent' historical interpretation, and written history is itself located in history, indeed *is* history, the product of an inherently unstable relationship between the present and the past ..."[30] and I am aware that this study too is not "innocent." Any historical reading is only a part of the continuum of History, and must be construed in its relation to past, present, and future. Philosophically, revolution might appear a theoretical construct: if a number of hypothetical conditions are fulfilled, then an event might be called a revolution. Historically, however, revolution can only be defined as such through written or voiced association with other revolutions. Like history itself, revolution would thus appear ultimately a product not of action as much as of discourse.

Yet once an event is granted the status of a revolution, the question remains as to how to interpret its significance. And here I would suggest that whereas all historical interpretation is partial, that this partiality might be shaped to preexisting cultural meaning, not merely in declaredly political discourse but even in imaginative literature such as the novel when history has a thematic role, has been insufficiently recognized. In the case of Britain, ideology in the form of party politics became the basis for historical theory; in a two-party political system, the result is two histories that even when considering the same historical information, oppose and contradict each other, yet that may still in significant respects be read as parts of the same history: as opposing discourses, they indeed rely on the existence of each other.

To give these discourses party labels is something of a fiction, but probably the only practicable one, given that "whig" has already been applied to one of the two. Herbert Butterfield first used the term "the 'whig' interpretation of history" in 1931, and more recent writers have generally accepted that in the mid-nineteenth century, this "whig" approach to history predominated at least in the form of what J. W. Burrow calls "confidence in the possession of the past."[31] Even those who have recast the declaredly political model in the form of discourse—Foucault, De Certeau—assume that in spite of its pretensions to science, nineteenth-century history takes the form of story, the aspect of "whig" history that Butterfield found most disturbing in its construction of the past as a narrative to validate the present. Discourse analysts, who tend in any case to be examining history from a broader European perspective, do not, however, specifically connect structural readings of history with party, and in consideration of British history, this is a loss. In party history in the years after 1830, writers come close to acknowledging what late twentieth-century discourse analysis has rediscovered: that historiography requires the adoption of a position where recording of literal truth—if such a thing exists—may be secondary to interpreting the facts in accordance with a specific ideology. Doubtless, some British historians of the nineteenth century believed that they were entirely right, and that those who disagreed were entirely wrong. Given the political framework of their discussion, however, many must have realized that history, like politics, is open to choice for those who have the right to choose.[32] Once the choice is made, however, the chooser is pledged to a specific model of history. For British historiography, Hayden White's distinction between the "metonymic" and "synecdochic" might alternatively be read as a political one: between a "whig" reading of history that recognizes a part of history as a representation of the whole while preserving a sense of difference; and the opposing use of historiography to discover deep-structured resemblances through the metaphor of history.[33] One model suggests a linear progress, towards a higher civilization, but the other, I shall argue, is not merely traditionalism or a denial of progress, but, as Karl Mannheim recognized in the 1920s, a "style of thought" leading to a mode of interpretation of history in its own right.[34] The focus given to the "whig" model of history in nineteenth-century Britain has caused the place of party and the literary implications of this second form of historical interpretation to be overlooked, but if the now-traditional label of the first as the "whig" form, then this second should logically be called the "tory."[35]

Party History

The British Parliamentary system was more clearly dominated by two parties during the middle years of the nineteenth century than at any other time. Much as historians traced the origins of party to the English Civil War,[36] at that time the principal opposition had been between Parliament and the Court, rather than within the House of Commons itself. For the next two centuries, the fortunes of the factions known in hindsight as "Whigs" and "Tories" rose and declined largely in proportion to their relative favor with the monarch, rather than as a measure of the extent to which their principles and policies were favored by a body of voters. During the wars with France following the execution of Louis XVI in 1793, "Whigs" and "Tories" began to present themselves in oppositional terms in the House of Commons under the leadership of Charles James Fox and William Pitt the Younger. Yet only when the election following the death of George IV in 1830 brought in a reform-minded Whig government who expanded the electorate through the passing of the First Parliamentary Reform Act in 1832 were the two parties truly a Parliamentary construct. The monarch still asked an individual to form a government; in effect, however, the only person able to form a government was the leader of the Parliamentary majority created by the voters. Thus Britain, while retaining the form of a monarchy, became governed by a system theoretically representative of the wishes of the nation—or to be more accurate, the empowered part of it.

During the period of this study, then, Tories and Whigs, or Conservatives (as the Tories called themselves from 1830) and Liberals (as the Whigs named their party after the Conservative split over the repeal of the Corn Laws in 1847),[37] alternately held power. A linguistic binarism was only established in the later 1820s, when the phrase "His

Majesty's Opposition" was first used to describe the party not in power; while initially it implied opposition to the government ruling by the will of the monarch rather than opposition to a party, the phrase "the Opposition" was used familiarly in *The Times* by 1827.[38] As in any political parties, the apparently simple division disguised many variations of opinion, but in the mid-nineteenth century, the Parliamentarians identifying themselves by these two labels constituted the only real political force. (A few Members of Parliament, such as John Stuart Mill, designated themselves "Radicals," yet they were either obliged to ally themselves with the Whigs in order to have a share in government, or to be classed as eccentric outsiders.) Soon afterwards, in the 1880s, the enfranchisement of even poorer men, the rise of the Labor Movement through Trades Unions and finally the emergence of the Labour Party changed the dynamic from a two-party system to one in which two parties have generally retained the status of "Government" and "Opposition," but in which other political groups have remained significant. Although the British Parliament since the end of the First World War has again been dominated by two parties, Conservative and Labour, the principle distinctions between parties are easier to define, notably in respect of economics and attitudes towards individual and group responsibility.[39]

Nineteenth-century Whigs and Tories thus represented a binary opposition of party unique in British history—yet the nature of that opposition is a problematic one. The actual origins of political party in Britain are less important to this study than how those origins were perceived. Some historians of the time, notably the French liberal Augustin Thierry, traced the origin of British political party back to the Norman Conquest, when the Normans became the "Tory" landowners and the Saxons the "Whig" populace.[40] In fact, this distinction was the product of an age when the Tories were the landowners and the Whigs the merchants and industrialists, and would not even have made sense a century earlier to David Hume, who in his 1742 essay "Of the Parties of Great Britain" explained the origin of the Whigs as in the "Country" party—for him, Whigs represented the rural landowners, and Tories the "Court" and the city.[41] Hume was nevertheless aware that the actual use of "Whig" and "Tory" as oppositional terms emerged only at the time of the Revolution of 1688, when those who remained loyal to James II after his Roman Catholicism became known were called by the Irish name of "Tory"; and those who maintained that England was by definition a Protestant monarchy and who thus supported the claims of James's daughter Mary and her husband William of Orange were called by the Scots name of "Whigs."[42]

Hume's history of party points to a problem in Tory identity: if the loyalty of the court party is both to the monarch and to the state Church, such loyalty must be self-conflicting if, as in the case of James II, the monarch repudiates the national religion. Only three years after this essay was published, the invasion of Charles Edward Stuart ("Bonnie Prince Charlie") on behalf of his father, the disputed son of James II, tested the loyalty of the Tories to the Stuart line. The Roman Catholic Prince's failure to win support from Protestants suggested that the Tories now accepted "the Protestant succession" above strict dynastic succession, and that some other definition of party must emerge.

Party might therefore simply be defined by degree: to keep Hume's original distinction, Tories stressed monarchy, and hence authority, above liberty, while Whigs stressed liberty above monarchy. Hence in the American War of Independence, Whigs tended to be more sympathetic to the colonists, and Tories to the King. In retrospect, some historians conceded that the distinction between the two parties was not fundamental. In the January 1833 *Edinburgh Review*, writing when party friction was still at its height following the first Parliamentary Reform Act, Thomas Babington Macaulay argued that the parties defined themselves relatively against each other. In his account of events of the reign of Queen Anne, the Tory historian Lord Mahon, whose ancestors were Whigs, had observed "how much the course of a century has inverted the meaning of our party nicknames, how much a modern Tory resembles a Whig of Queen Anne's reign, and a Tory of Queen Anne's reign a modern Whig."[43] Macaulay agrees that a modern Tory resembles an old Whig, but this is because "the worst things of one age often resemble the best things of another." Because society is "constantly advancing in knowledge … though a Tory may now be very like what a Whig was a hundred and twenty years ago, the Whig is as much in advance of the Tory as ever." For Macaulay, the Whigs are the party of progress, "the leaders of their species in a right direction," and the Tories the party of tradition. As a result, in Macaulay's reading, history defines policy: the Whigs will continue to bring about cautious change, and the Tories will ensure that the changes are not too sudden. Although as we shall see, this effect of history on policy was not systematically invoked, the fact that it could be—and indeed can be—invoked makes history an integral component of party politics.

In this essay published soon after the Whigs had fought the first Parliamentary Reform Act through Parliament, Macaulay states that Whigs are "best" and "right," Tories "worst" and by implication, wrong. By the time that Macaulay was writing his *History of England* in the 1840s, his tone is more moderate—indeed, more like Hume's. In discussing the Earl of Chatham, he states that each party is "representative of a great principle, essential to the welfare of nations. One is, in an especial manner, the guardian of liberty, and the other of order. One is the moving power, the other the steadying power of the state."[44]

Nevertheless, in the course of the nineteenth century, major innovations—for example, Robert Peel's repeal of the Corn Laws, which fractured the Tory party; or the Second Parliamentary Reform Act, passed only in 1867 by the Conservative Disraeli when almost all of the Whigs of 1832 were dead, suggested that Tories were capable of pragmatic politics, and that Whigs were less committed to progress than to the belief that their major reform to the Parliamentary system was permanent—or perhaps, as Patrick Brantlinger observes, a belief in natural progress avoids the need for any imposed reform.[45] Lord John Russell, by this time Earl Russell, had begun his political career dedicated to political change, but had now earned the nickname of "Finality Jack."

It might be argued that all political labeling is a fiction, and that parties only define themselves against each other, their nature being dictated not by policy, but by the concept of opposition. Certainly, Whigs and Tories had a shared interest in maintaining property ownership; much of their policy was hence dictated by what each saw as the best way to defend private property, the only difference being in how that they believed this might best be achieved. Especially after the emergence of socialism in the 1840s, the most immediate enemy of property was seen to be revolution, and adherents of both parties looked to patterns of revolution to predict the effect on property. Neither the "Glorious Revolution" of 1688 nor the American Revolution were read historically as having their basis in enmity between those with property and those without, and thus in an age of socialism they did not provide a suitable model of revolution. Only France's 1789 Revolution posited a modern and coherent pattern of what might happen to security of property in the case of revolution.

Given the centrality of the emphasis on security of property, Whigs and Tories might thus be expected to have similar interpretations of revolution. But here a significant philosophical distinction—perhaps by this time the only real philosophical distinction—between parties emerges, and that is in the conception of the function of history.

Samuel Taylor Coleridge claimed in 1829 that a universality among "civilized men, acknowledging the rights of property" was that "the two antagonist powers or opposite interests of the state, under which all other state interests are comprised, are those of PERMANENCE and of PROGRESSION."[46] And neither "permanence" or "progression" have meaning without historical comparison.

For political reformists (a broad category ranging from moderate Whigs to radical republicans), history consists of conscious human acts to advance or prevent the progress of civilization. Herbert Butterfield defined the view of history that predominated in nineteenth-century England as "Protestant, progressive, and whig."[47] In *The Whig Interpretation of History*, Butterfield made the doctrine seem simple: whig history divides the world into "the friends and enemies of progress."

Yet Butterfield avoids the question of the source of this progress—which, as we shall see, was often called "improvement" by whig historians and "innovation" by tories. Perhaps he is justified in that whig historians themselves, unlike the German historians whose ideas they sometimes appear to echo, showed little interest in philosophy. The Whig supporters of the first French Revolution failed to resolve this problem. The only way to find a consistency in the whig reading is to assume a belief in the natural right of all people to be free, and then to relegate history to the mode that creates the consciousness that natural right has been violated.[48]

History thus provides the steps by which the present has been created: it is crucial as an aid to our understanding of the present, but to abstract moral lessons would be to underestimate the specifics of every age and social context. For the whig historian, human beings do not make their age, but are made by it; their actions as formed by their historical context, however, shape ages to come. The Channel Tunnel would conform with this pattern of an awareness that society needs to change as history progresses.

This might suggest that the opposite, tory history, is simply antiprogressive, or to use Karl Mannheim's word, "traditionalist" in its fear of change.[49] In fact, tory history stresses evolution (the natural changing of the polity over time) as opposed to revolution (human imposition of change). Tory history is clearly indebted to the classical historical tradition represented by such works as Plutarch's *Lives*, in which the fortunes of great men provide moral examples. The influential Tory thinker Lord Bolingbroke reemphasized this moral construct in his *Letters on the Study and Use of History*, notably in his much-repeated phrase "History is philosophy teaching by examples," for which he claims a questionable classical source.[50] While the focus on the great implies a human universality, later tory historians, especially after 1793, applied this universal moral lesson not merely to individuals, but to societies and institutions. Drawing on the philosophical tradition perhaps best represented by David Hume, tories assumed a consistency of "nature." As James K. Chandler observes, the word "nature" applies to more than one concept.[51] "Nature" in its vaguest sense may suggest an order to the universe: a hierarchical and morally-based structure that Revolution attempts to violate. Edmund Burke was not alone in maintaining an association between natural order and property, according to which he could describe the French Revolution as "a strange chaos" in which "everything seems out of nature."[52] Yet particularly for tory historians, "nature" suggested "human nature." In his *History of England*, just as in his philosophical writings, Hume had proceeded on the assumption that a general consistency in moral feeling underlies human nature. Behavior might vary from individual to individual (King John, for example, was a less moral person than Henry I), and by the opportunities presented by circumstance; yet Hume never suggests, as other historians had done, that as a whole the people of one era were more or less virtuous than those of another; or as whig historians tended to do, that actions were shaped by the spirit of the age.[53]

Although Hume's account of the origin of moral feeling dispenses with the necessity of a deity, such a reading of history was not incompatible with a Christian sense of original sin. For traditionalists who chose to combine such philosophies, "human nature" is fallen from an originally morally-pure state: this cannot be reclaimed, but the arrest of "innovation" may provide the means of preventing the world from becoming worse. Unfortunately, given similar circumstances and opportunities, "human nature" will cause people to respond in similar ways. In other words, the dangers of mob-rule seen in histories of previous ages would inevitably be repeated (The *Quarterly Review*'s July 1831 article on "The Subversion of Ancient Governments" in ancient Athens and Rome, for example, seems merely to provide the occasion to discuss contemporary implications of democratic movements). Tory history, then, implies a recognition of history's metaphorical force: its example is one that given human and cosmic consistency, may be infinitely replayed.

In its most extreme form, the analogy in tory history thus resembles biblical typology, with which, as George P. Landow has shown, the nineteenth-century reader could reasonably be expected to be familiar.[54] In typological readings of biblical texts, the historical truth of the Old Testament stories is not disputed in the sense of reducing them to allegory; their literal meaning remains significant. Their place as history, however, is supplemented by a dispensing providence that makes them simultaneously prefigurations of the histories of the New Testament (notably the life, death, and resurrection of Christ) and possibly also representations of universal truths concerning the life of the soul. In the case of history, the typological application is, like Biblical typology that privileges the Gospel "antitype" over the Judaic "type," often an assertion of cultural superiority, or at the least, of ethnocentricity. As explained by the Scots theologian Patrick Fairbairn in his *Typology of Scripture*, many events of the Old Testament, while as much history as those of the New Testament, were thus designed by God "to foreshadow and prepare for the better things of the Gospel."[55] A nationally-centered reading of history makes similar assumptions: the historical actuality of French Revolutions may not be in dispute, but from the perspective of British commentators, the events themselves are less important than their application to moments in British history, or as types of universal patterns in human behavior. If the whig sense of the future can be modeled by the Tunnel, the tory sense of the future is represented not by the French Revolution as a whole, but by the Terror.

The whig idea of progress is more materially-based than its tory counterpart, since material advances provide the means by which all progress can be judged. Indeed, just as whigs assume human perfectibility, the best that tory history can hope for is the perfection of the state. In terms of human action, tory history tends to imply moral regression: since human nature is essentially consistent (and essentially fallen), technological advances increase opportunities for human wickedness. In the French Revolution, the lamp-post is replaced by the guillotine, a state-sanctioned means of moral detachment from the act of judicial murder.[56]

The polarities of whig and tory history are amply represented in two works published just prior to the French Revolution of 1830, Robert Southey's *Sir Thomas More; Or Colloquies on the Progress and Prospects of Society* (1829), and Macaulay's review of the book in the January 1830 *Edinburgh Review*.[57] While self-evidently Southey's and Macaulay's positions are respectively opposed to social and political change and enthusiastically in favor of such change, this division oversimplifies the theoretical attitudes towards history that each embodies.

Southey himself is of interest as a radical who had welcomed the 1789 French Revolution, but who by 1830 was a staunch Tory. The *Colloquies* were Southey's response to the question of Roman Catholic emancipation, debated in the years 1828–1829, and hence take the tory position that interference in the natural order of government is a danger to the nation.

Southey's chosen wise man, the ghost of Sir Thomas More, proves to be a true tory historian in some significant respects. First, More explains that from the detached stance of paradise, he and his fellow-spirits are able to use the lessons of history to predict likely outcomes. Hence while unable to prophesy, "having a clearer and more comprehensive knowledge of the past, we [spirits] are enabled to reason better from causes to consequences, and by what has been, judge of what is likely to be."[58] More's discussions with a narrator who appears to be Southey but calls himself Montesinos[59] are hence filled with historical illustrations, many from his own age, but also from other important events in human history. As More remarks:

> the sum and substance of historical knowledge for practical purposes consists in certain general principles: and he who understands those principles, and has a due sense of their importance, has always, in the darkest circumstances, a star in sight by which to guide his course directly. (*Colloquies* 2:262–263)

Although More's point is to argue that principles are more important than specifics of historical knowledge, among the examples illustrating these principles, the French Revolution is repeatedly cited as the event which "for its complicated monstrosities, absurdities, and horrors, is more disgraceful to human nature than any other series of events in history" (*Colloquies* 1:38). Rejecting Whig-Radical ideals, More calls those Britons who welcomed the French Revolution "blockheads" (1:35). More was a famed punster, yet given the mode of his departure from life, he would hardly wish to associate heads and blocks, and Southey seems to be speaking directly through More here.

More is also a tory historian in believing that while theoretically, humans may overall be slowly progressing in accordance with the will of a benign deity, British society is not: technological advances have outstripped morality (2:324), and for the poorer classes of society have increased human misery. "Wickedness," says More, "is ever the same" (2:321); but the so-called "progress" of the manufacturing system has given more scope for selfishness. Britain's willingness to abandon the ideal of a state centered on a national church is proof of "the sinfulness of the nation" (2:324). More's (and of course Southey's) conclusion is that Britons were happier before the age of "commerce"—that is, the coming of a capitalist system based on manufacturing. Southey has thus used historical comparison to argue the need for Britain's moral regeneration.

Macaulay's response to the arguments that Southey puts in the mouth of Thomas More is better-remembered than the work that inspired it, the topicality of the *Colloquies* rapidly passing once Roman Catholic emancipation was recognized as final. Twenty-nine when he wrote this essay, Macaulay was able to consider the events of the French Revolutionary era from a more detached position: whereas Southey had lived through the hopes and fears of the 1790s, to Macaulay, they were history, and he did not sympathize with the process by which Southey had become "a violent Ultra-Tory."[60]

Macaulay proceeds to contradict Southey's position by practical demonstration. Citing examples of how standards of living and conditions of society have improved in Britain and other nations, he argues that "history is full of the signs of this natural progress of society" (*Complete Works* 7:499). Through the advancement of human reason, and consequently of social structures and material goods, human happiness can be demonstrated to have advanced, resulting in an increased sense of security from disease and civil unrest, and greater material advantages to all classes of society: "the improvements of machinery have lowered the price of manufactured articles, and have brought within the reach of the poorest some conveniences which Sir Thomas More or his master [Henry VIII] could not have obtained at any price" (7:491). An explanation of the source of progress is finally given. Macaulay, who is "at a loss to conceive in what sense religion can be said to be the basis of government" (7:477), notes that he, like Southey, relies "firmly on the goodness of God." The difference is that Macaulay's deity manifests goodness in "those general laws which it has pleased him to establish in the physical and in the moral world. We rely on the natural tendency of the human intellect to truth, and on the natural tendency of society to improvement" (7:499). The "signs of the times" hold forth possibility that Southey's God may choose to punish the nation for its wickedness (especially, it is implied, meddling with the divinely-constructed relationship between Church and State). In contrast, Macaulay's deity has established a benevolent order that, even if human beings temporarily make what appear to be wrong choices, is ultimately progressive towards perfection through the instrumentation of the human instinct for improvement.[61] History itself proves the lesson: "on what principle is it," Macaulay asks, that when we see nothing but improvement behind us, we are to expect nothing but deterioration before us?" (7:502).

Ironically, Macaulay's question captures both the fundamental distinction between whig and tory history, their reading of human progress; and the essential likeness: in each the role of history is to use the past to understand the present, and thereby to model the future.[62] Yet in the whig instance, understanding is a sufficient goal, the greatest, or possibly the only, error for which earlier ages should be condemned being resistance to progress. For the tories, in contrast, looking at the past enables certain futures to be avoided, and thus a correct reading of whether events or individuals in history were admirable or not is a moral imperative. Thus for a whig historian, outrage at the bloodshed of the French Revolution should not be allowed to mask the *Ancien Régime's* original error of resisting natural progress; for a tory, be it Southey or More, the bloodshed is a direct consequence of allowing a form of progress in violation of natural order.

Also illustrated by the disagreement between Southey and Macaulay is that while both historical models are shaped by a concern for the material, the preservation of property, the role of the material is in each instance different.[63] Macaulay measures progress by technological advances that have physically improved the standard of living. Southey does not deny technological advances, yet argues that in the establishment of the manufacturing system, morality has been overlooked. Tory history argues from the basis of human morality abstractly considered, although observed in individuals. Whig history, influenced by Utilitarianism, assumes that human morality is inseparable from social progress, since that social progress is the determiner of what, within the given circumstances, is deemed to be moral.

In consequence, the whig historian can describe the past as the means of explaining how the present came into being, but cannot be shocked by it. If the standards of human morality and civilization are improving, to apply one's own moral values to the barbarity, cruelty, or oppression of other ages is to apply higher standards than were then historically possible: hence Macaulay's assertion that the whigs of the past become the tories of today. For the tory historian, in contrast, outrage at the errors of the past is first, an acceptance of human universality, and second, a means of ensuring that they are never repeated. Whereas the whig focus on the larger historical plot prompts the overlooking of individual human suffering, tory history continues to ask questions about how history affects the individual: the point of the

Colloquies, after all, is to show that the English Reformation is vital to British identity, yet the history is presented by a human victim of that Reformation.

Southey's *Colloquies* and Macaulay's response show whig and tory readings of history as consciously opposed. This study seeks to examine ways in which they are finally alike. In both cases, the overall metaphorical use of the idea of the French Revolution is in self-definition: a means of explaining the state of Britain. For both whig and tory readers, history provides a means of understanding the road on which not France but Britain was traveling, be it to prepare the way for freedom, or merely, to quote a commentator of 1830, to "macadamise the road to tyranny."[64]

Yet although whig and tory readers need not be members of the Whig and Tory parties, a history that defines itself by means of party must be "partial" in another respect: that of limiting the concerns and self-interest of history to only a part of the population. Between 1830 and 1882, party-politics were the domain of only a small proportion of the British people. Although the 1832 Reform Act enfranchised much of the middle class, the working class was still excluded from participation in the party system. Further expansion of the electorate did not come until 1867, and even then, the poorest working males (and also, of course, non-working males) were excluded. Women had no place in politics at all, John Stuart Mill's support for equal voting rights for women in the 1860s being simply a source of amusement to publications such as *Punch*.[65] Thus to link history with party was to exclude the poor and women from historical consideration, and a clear part of the social threat presented by revolution was that it provided the opportunity for women and the poor to claim a part in history. Even though Dorinda Outram and others have demonstrated that in fact women had low visibility during the French Revolution, and moreover, that the image of the frenzied mob around the guillotine is itself suspect,[66] women and the mob become disturbing images of disorder in nineteenth-century depictions.[67] The threat of anarchy is hence repeatedly embodied in texts through the poor and through dangerous women who attempt to usurp a role in history by challenging the domain of the propertied (and thus enfranchised) male: on a significant number of occasions, the "mob" is further alienated from the British middle class by some level of identification with Britain's perpetual outsiders, the Irish. The symbolic recreations of the "mob" and the "maenads" of the first French Revolution constitute the ultimate threat against which even opposing parties must finally unite themselves.

But even if until the end of this period the deepest threat is almost constantly analogized in terms of gender and class, treatments of the topic of French Revolution are immensely varied, particularly when stimulated by contemporary revolutionary activity in France. In the chapters that follow, examinations of the impact of the three major revolutionary moments in French history during this period, the Revolutions of 1830, 1848, and 1871, frame—and more significantly, separate—chapters discussing the two most privileged British texts concerning French Revolution, Carlyle's *The French Revolution: A History* and Dickens's *A Tale of Two Cities*. The trajectory is from the immediacy of creating events as history as the Revolution of July 1830 unfolded, to a restructuring of history as narrative in the novel, to a conscious use of history to establish identity and even to predict the national future.

I first explore responses to the July Revolution of 1830, and the competition in the periodical press to assume the prophetic role of Edmund Burke in interpreting the significance of French revolution for Britain, a process in which Burke himself becomes mythologized. Chapter Two places Thomas Carlyle's *The French Revolution: A History* within the context of those tory readings of history that provide a counterbalance to the apparent victory of liberalism in the 1830s. The third chapter explores notions of political, economic, and personal property as affected by the revolutions of 1848 in both novels and histories of that year, including Thackeray's *Vanity Fair* and Macaulay's *History of England*. Chapter Four turns back to Carlyle to challenge the reading of Dickens's *Tale of Two Cities* as a historical repetition and to reclaim it as a product of 1859. I conclude with an examination of why British reactions to the Franco-Prussian War of 1870–1871 should have taken a futurist or fantasy form in works such as Lord Lytton's *The Coming Race* and other texts that consciously link language and identity, and a brief epilogue on the fate of the 1882 Channel Tunnel project.

Some of these works are mixed (or even muddled) in their approach to history. In all cases, however, I hope to demonstrate a level of self-interest: we shall see repeatedly how Britons only cast eyes across the Channel only when seeking a parallel with events at home, overcoming their customary insular myopia at key moments when their historical vision needed guidance. The topic is hence not merely French revolution, but also British self-definition: by detection of differences and similarities, French revolution provides a means of using a multiple historical perspective to understand Britain's history, and from this, to predict Britain's future. Alfred Cobban has suggested that in the debate arising from the first French Revolution were laid "the theoretical foundations of British political progress in the nineteenth century": in Cobban's opinion, this was Britain's "last real discussion of the fundamentals of politics."[68] Perhaps Cobban slightly overstates his case, but certainly, during the nineteenth century, the French Revolution provided a vital means of focusing debate, both in avowedly political discussion and in a variety of other literary works consciously or casually informed by ideological readings.

Although this study centers on the literary interpretation of a specific series of events at a precise historical moment, the implications are, I believe, broader. From the field of human experience events are granted a significance that shapes the reading of other events—and, indeed, that can be used to determine the political and intellectual future of a nation. In Britain's case, the manipulation of historical analogy, and especially that of French revolution, contributed both to the passing of the first Parliamentary Reform Act in 1832, and very probably to the delay before the passing of further reforms.

With the benefit of hindsight both literary and historical—Southey's fears, for example, that Roman Catholic emancipation would be the end of English national identity proved to be unfounded—present-day readers of nineteenth-century literature may too readily imagine themselves on the side of the reformers. Perhaps we would not have been Macaulays, but we can envision ourselves sympathizing with a Wollstonecraft, or a Chartist, or perhaps a John Stuart Mill. So, to cite some notorious instances, the literary academy's response to the later Wordsworth, or Thomas Carlyle, or even George Eliot when discussing who should be enfranchised and who should not, may take the form of embarrassed silence or moral indignation. This book asks the reader to reimagine the responses to key political incidents as they occurred, and by acknowledging the prominence of history in British national consciousness to try to understand (which is not necessarily to endorse or sympathize with) the processes of thought behind those responses.

To consider the relation between revolution and reform prompted by the events of 1830 within their context, however, some preliminary examination is required of the inheritances of whig and tory history from the first French Revolution, and especially an assessment of the role of the writer who had most influence on the generation of 1830, Edmund Burke.

Notes

1. *The Times*, November 1, 1990, p. 29 (by David Brewster).
2. Quoted in the *Washington Post* October 31, 1990, p. A38.
3. See Stuart Hall, ed., *Representation: Cultural Representations and Signifying Practices* (Sage, 1997), particularly pp. 2–4. For a definition of culture, see Raymond Williams, *Culture and Society* (Columbia University Press, 1958, 1983), pp. xvi–xviii.
4. In a babel of acronyms, on October 6 the Chancellor of the Exchequer John Major had announced Britain's entry into the European Exchange-Rate Mechanism (the ERM). Thatcher's resistance at the end of the month was to the European Monetary Union (the EMU) and especially the European Currency Unit (the Ecu). See *The Times*, October 31. Britain was to drop out of the ERM again after a massive fall in the value of sterling in September 1992, and to date, has refused to adopt the Euro.
5. Under Thatcher's administration, the definitions of "Britishness" were narrowed by creating different classes of citizenship. I am assuming that "identity" is itself culturally constructed within a field of discourse; on the problem of cultural identity, and in particular its oppositional nature, see Stuart Hall and Paul du Gay, eds., *Questions of Cultural Identity* (Sage, 1996), pp. 2–5.
6. *The Times*, July 12, 1989; *Le Monde*, July 13, 1989; see also Margaret Thatcher, *The Downing Street Years* (HarperCollins, c. 1993), pp. 752–754. Presumably partly because of translation, none of these three sources agrees as to Thatcher's exact words.
7. Thatcher, *The Downing Street Years*, p. 753.
8. The Tories had, of course, other reasons for discontent with their leadership, notably their phenomenal loss of popularity over the replacement of local property taxes ("the Rates") with a per-head "Community Charge" ("the Poll-Tax"). Within the party, however, European policy was cited as the main cause of division.
9. Donald Hunt, *The Tunnel: The Story of the Channel Tunnel 1802–1994* (Image Publishing, 1994), pp. 17–18.
10. Joseph-Aimé Thomé de Gamond, *Étude pour l'Avant-Projet d'un Tunnel Sous-marin entre l'Angleterre et la France* (Victor Dalmont, 1857), p. 4.
11. Young claims to be in favor of progress towards European union, but not at the expense of democratic process. *Manchester Guardian Weekly*, September 13, 1993, p. 3.
12. Michel Foucault, *The Order of Things* (Vintage Books, 1973), pp. 217–218.
13. George Peabody Gooch, *History and Historians in the Ninteenth Century*, 2nd ed. (Beacon Press, 1959). A danger, though, may be that in thus characterizing a not insubstantial portion of the human experience, we of the late twentieth century may in our turn become "whig" historians. Whig historians can overlook moral and intellectual shortcomings in previous ages by

noting progress since that point, and staying secure in a sense of the moral superiority of the present: whereas "they" did not, in fact could not, know better, "we" do. Although Nancy Armstrong and Leonard Tennenhouse do not use the phrase "whig" history, they point out that even Foucault's insistence on viewing cultural developments "retrospectively" coopts him into its narrative tendency of using the past to explain how present-day culture emerged Nancy Armstrong and Leonard Tennenhouse, "History, Poststructuralism, and the Question of Narrative," *Narrative* 1 (January 1993), p. 49.

14. A. Dwight Culler, *The Victorian Mirror of History* (Yale University Press, 1985), p. vii. Among works which discuss the figurative nature of historiography, see, for example, Hayden White's *Metahistory* (Johns Hopkins University Press, 1973) and "Historicism, History, and the Figurative Imagination," in *Tropics of Discourse* (Johns Hopkins University Press, 1978); various writing of Michel De Certeau, notably "The Historiographical Operation" in *The Writing of History* (English version, Columbus University Press. 1988); Timothy Bahti, *Allegories of History: Literary Historiography after Hegel* (Johns Hopkins University Press, 1992). Barton Friedman's *Fabricating History: English Writers on the French Revolution* (Princeton University Press, 1988) also applies formalist analysis to nineteenth-century writings on the French Revolution. While all these writers recognize that discourse and ideology are inextricably intertwined, their primary focus is not on the nineteenth-century political consciousness.

15. Even though many of the facts discussed in this book were and frequently remain in dispute, I wish to stay at least as materialist as to proceed on the assumption that certain facts have a material reality; my concern, though, is less with what "really happened" then with the process of observing and reporting happenings as discourse.

16. Williams's observations about "tradition" obviously assume a longer time between experience and the construction of discourse concerning that experience than many of the examples in this study, but his discussion of selection from a position of cultural power is nevertheless applicable: "From a whole possible area of past and present, in a particular culture, certain meanings and practices are selected for emphasis and certain other meanings and practices are neglected or excluded. Yet, within a particular hegemony, and of one of its decisive processes, this selection is presented and usually successfully passed off as 'the tradition' ..." Raymond Williams, *Marxism and Literature* (Oxford University Press, 1983), p. 115.

17. David Ferris, *Theory and the Evasion of History* (Johns Hopkins University Press, 1993), p. 168.

18. Ibid., p. 174.

19. Foucault, *The Order of Things*, pp. 217–218.

20. J. W. Burrow, *Evolution and Society* (Cambridge University Press, 1966), p. 109.

21. See Linda Colley, *Britons: Forging the Nation 1707–1837* (Yale University Press, 1992)and Gerald Newman, *The Rise of English Nationalism: A Cultural History 1740–1830* (St. Martin's, 1987); also Jeremy Black, *Natural and Necessary Enemies: Anglo-French Relations in the Eighteenth Century* (Duckworth, 1986).
22. The label "Revolution" had been used from a very early stage, but until 1830, the general reading seems to have been that the Revolution was part of a longer historical phenomenon, from the National Convention of 1788 to the fall of Napoleon. Hence two of the earliest historical narratives of the French Revolution appear as parts of the life of Napoleon, in Sir Walter Scott and William Hazlitt's biographies of Napoleon, published in 1827 and 1828 respectively.
23. Friedman, *Fabricating History*, p. 9.
24. To some extent, of course, they also considered the American Revolution, but with more general agreement that in this case the analogy was inapt. This was because despite their historic differences in how they responded to the American War of Independence at the time, both the Whig and Tory parties believed that stability was based on the security of property. America was still regarded as a land of unlimited potential, and therefore European limits on property (that there was only so much property available, and that the empowerment of the unpropertied classes would endanger the sanctity of ownership) did not apply. Indeed, only radical extremists such as Thomas Paine, who affected a disdain for the rights of property, would argue the parallel. See, for example, John Fullarton's 1832 *Quarterly Review* article on "The Progress of Misgovernment" (p. 583).
25. Clare A. Simmons, *Reversing the Conquest: History and Myth in Nineteenth-Century British Literature* (Rutgers University Press, 1990), p. 12. See also Colley's argument that the British "defined themselves against the French as they imagined them to be, superstitious, militarist, decadent, and unfree" (p. 5).
26. White, *Metahistory*, p. 35.
27. Mary Wollstonecraft, *Historical and Moral View of the French Revolution*, 2nd edition (1795; Scolar Reprints, 1975), p. 197.
28. Seamus Deane, *The French Revolution and Enlightenment in England 1789–1832* (Harvard University Press, 1988), p. 1.
29. Edmund Burke, *Reflections on the Revolution in France*, edited by L. G. Mitchell, in *The Writings and Speeches of Edmund Burke* volume 8 (1790; Clarendon, 1989), p. 103. The image was sufficiently powerful for Burke's opponents to feel a need to comment on the lamp-posts. Thomas Paine chooses to deny the lamp-post stories, and thereby demonstrate the lack of truth of Burke's view of France as a whole. See Thomas Paine, *Rights of Man*, 6th edition (1791), p. 46. Catherine Macaulay regards the use of the lamp-post as a means of execution as the effect of a barbarous society, and preferable to the judicial equivalent of being broken on the wheel. See

Catherine Sawbridge Macaulay, "Observations on the Reflections of the Right Hon. Edmund Burke" (1791), p. 11.

30. François Furet, *Interpreting the French Revolution* (Cambridge University Press, 1981), p. 1.

31. J. W. Burrow, *A Liberal Descent: Victorian Historians and the English Past* (Cambridge University Press, 1981; rpt. 1983), p. 3. Burrow recognizes the potential complications of Whig (he capitalizes the word) history, but argues nevertheless that in the flourishing period of narrative history in the mid-nineteenth century, "the abiding spirit of liberty" prevailed (pp. 1–3). Similarly, John Clive accepts Butterfield's "pudding-mold" without proposing any alternative model. John Clive, *Not By Fact Alone: Essays on the Writing and Reading of History* (Knopf, 1989), pp. 124–125.

32. In 1833, for example, Benjamin Disraeli, choosing revolution as the appropriate topic for a modern epic, depicted human history as a contest between "Feudalism" and "Federalism," the forces of order and the forces of freedom. Feudalism and Federalism tell their own versions of the development of civilization, and thus function as tory and whig historians. Disraeli's *Revolutionary Epick* remained unfinished as he entered the actual world of politics and was obliged to make a commitment to the party prepared to elect him. I would suggest that in its recognition of merits in both the dominant political positions, this work represents a moment in Disraeli's career where he might have committed himself to either party.

33. This form of history is related to typology, discussed by George Landow in *Victorian Types, Victorian Shadows* (Routledge, 1980); and to the explication of the force of history as allegory by Timothy Bahti. My focus is, however, on how this is linked to party principles.

34. Mannheim's essay "Conservative Thought," which predates Butterfield's "Whig Interpretation of History" by four years, concentrates on the development of conservatism as a "style of thought" in Germany following the French Revolution. Many of his observations also apply to the British situation, notably the fundamental concept of *quieta non movere*, the emphasis on parts rather than system, and the fear of the loss of rationalism as a guiding principle. Less applicable is his suggestion that conservative thought constructs itself in opposition to a theory of natural law, since although whig history has a loose assumption that human consciousness prompts progress towards an equal (presumably free) civilization, in fact tory history makes more direct appeal to the "laws of nature."

35. In *Not By Fact Alone*, John Clive notes that A. J. P. Taylor has playfully applied the label "Tory History" to the style of Sir Lewis Namier to mark those historians "more interested in what made institutions actually work than in movements of ideas" (p. 283), but my use is somewhat different in suggesting that tory history does amount to a coherent position. Since my opposition is indebted to Butterfield, who does not capitalize "whig" when it refers to ideology, I shall in this study not capitalize "whig" or "tory" when

the words refer to historical interpretation, but shall capitalize when referring to the actual political parties or members of them.

36. Lord Bolingbroke, for example, denies that the Roundheads and Cavaliers were Whigs and Tories, but still sees the origin of division in the dissenters and members of the State Church after the Civil War. Henry St. John, Lord Bolingbroke, *A Dissertation Upon Parties*, in *Works* (Carey and Hart, 1841) 2:37.
37. John Wilson Croker seems to have been the first to speak of a "Conservative party" in early 1830; the label was rapidly adopted. In contrast, the phrase "Liberal party" only entered into use following the Conservative split over the repeal of the Corn Laws in 1847.
38. Lord Broughton (Byron's friend John Cam Hobhouse) claimed the credit for inventing the phrase "His Majesty's Opposition" in a Commons speech in 1826; see his *Recollections of a Long Life* (John Murray, 1909–1911) 3:139–130. Thus Macaulay, for example, is applying it retrospectively when in his 1844 essay on Chatham he discusses a "constitutional Opposition" in Chatham's time; Thomas Babington Macaulay, *Complete Works* (Longmans, 1898) 8:373–375.
39. Labour takes, although most notably in its least pragmatic and least successful moments, a different attitude from the Conservatives in respect of property. The Conservative Party has, of course, expanded its definition of private property from property of individuals or families to include property of corporations. The Labour Party recognizes all these forms of property, but has traditionally placed cautious emphasis on the concept of state-owned property.
40. Augustin Thierry, *History of the Conquest of England by the Normans*, translated by William Hazlitt the Younger (Bohn, 1856) 1:xiii.
41. David Hume, *Philosophical Works* (Black and Tait, 1826) 3:68. The seventeenth-century Court party, who became the Tories, were closely allied with the King and the state Church; the Country party tended to be dissenters and saw Parliament as their means of expressing freedom of opinion.
42. Hume thus argues that since the Revolution of 1688, "A TORY …may be defined, in a few words, to be a *lover of monarchy, though without abandoning liberty, and a partisan of the family of Stuart*: As a WHIG may be defined to be *a lover of liberty, though without renouncing monarchy, and a friend to the settlement in the Protestant line*" (3:75, emphasis in original).
43. Macaulay, *Complete Works* 8:302–303.
44. Macaulay, *Complete Works* 2:361.
45. Patrick Brantlinger, *The Spirit of Reform: British Literature and Politics, 1832–1867* (Harvard University Press, 1977), p. 5.
46. Samuel Taylor Coleridge, *On the Constitution of Church and State*, edited by John Colmer (Princeton University Press, 1977), p. 24.
47. Herbert Butterfield, *The Whig Interpretation of History* (1931; Norton, 1965), p. 3.

48. Thomas Paine would probably not have articulated his use of history in this way, but his examples in *The Rights of Man*, particularly those associating the oppressive Normans with the rule of George III, are calculated to provoke indignation in the thinking reader: Paine is even prepared to argue that kings themselves are a Norman invention. Thomas Paine, *The Rights of Man*, 6th edition (1791), p. 69.
49. Karl Mannheim, *Essays on Sociology and Social Psychology*, edited by Paul Kecskmeti (Routledge and Kegan Paul, 1953, rpt. 1969), p. 102.
50. Bolingbroke, *Letters on the Study and Use of History*, in *Works* 2:177.
51. James K. Chandler, *Wordsworth's Second Nature: A Study of the Poetry and the Politics* (University of Chicago Press, 1984), p. 67.
52. Burke, *Writings and Speeches* 8:60.
53. Hume's presentation of Elizabeth I provides a good instance of his relation of human consistency to history. She was an authoritarian monarch, but "it was not natural for her to find fault with a form of government by which she herself was invested with such unlimited authority ... . Few examples occur of princes who have willingly resigned their power." David Hume, *History of England* (1754; Washbourne, 1841) 6:271.
54. Although in *Victorian Types, Victorian Shadows* Landow focuses on the elaborations of typological theory developed in the Victorian period and as applied to literature and art rather than political history, as Christina Crosby has noted, typology "can be understood as not so much mystical allegory as 'historicized' metaphor, a figurative mode which stresses the dialectical process of representation." Christina Crosby, *The Ends of History: Victorians and the "Woman Question"* (Routledge, 1991), p. 123.
55. Patrick Fairbairn, *The Typology of Scripture*, 2nd edition (T. and T. Clark, 1854) 1:59.
56. Even this requires historical inexactitudes: contrary to common belief among Britons at the time, Guillotin did not invent the guillotine, nor was it distanced from British tradition by being an exclusively French machine, similar beheading devices having been used in Britain centuries previously.
57. Coleridge's *On the Constitution of Church and State* (1829) discusses the same question, but is not as classic an example of tory history as Southey's book because Coleridge characterizes traditionalism as the appropriate form of evolution towards the ideal state.
58. Robert Southey, *Sir Thomas More; Or, Colloquies on the Progress and Prospects of Society*, 2nd edition (John Murray, 1831) 1:55. Subsequent references are cited in the text.
59. This seems an unwise choice on Southey's part; it may have suggested to him the "mountains" of the Lake District where the disucssions take place. Montesinos was a hero of medieval romance, but more British readers would be likely to associate the name with Don Quixote's preposterous account of his adventures in the Cave of Montesinos (*Don Quixote* Part 2, chapters 22–23), or unreliable history.

60. Macaulay, *Complete Works* 7:458; subsequent references are given in text by volume and page-numbers. Interestingly, Macaulay strongly attacks Southey for advocating some policies that would now not be considered characteristically "Tory," such as high taxation, a large commitment to nationally-funded projects, and the claim that the government is responsible to the unemployed.
61. In his *History of England*, a subject which he characterized as "eminently the history of physical, of moral, and of intellectual improvement," Macaulay explained the Utilitarian element of human progress more clearly by ascribing it to self-interest: "In every experimental science there is a tendency towards perfection. In every human being there is a wish to ameliorate his own condition ... . there is constant improvement precisely because there is constant discontent" *(Complete Works* 1:217). The actual origins of the instinct for progress remain mysterious, but perhaps not more mysterious than the process of adaptation in Darwinian evolutionary theory.
62. Mannheim's statement that where "the progressive uses the future to interpret things, the conservative uses the past" (*Essays* p. 111) seems to me too simple a dichotomy: the progressive can only construct the future through viewing the past as narrative, and the conservative's interest in the past is driven by concern for the future.
63. Raymond Williams's analysis suggests that tory commentators such as Southey may often be closer to the radical or socialist critique of capitalism than their liberal or whig counterparts (*Culture and Society*, pp. 20–26).
64. "Political Conditions and Prospects of France," *Quarterly Review* 43 (May 1830), p. 224.
65. See, for example, John Tenniel's cartoons, *Punch* March 30 and June 1, 1867.
66. Dorinda Outram, *The Body and the French Revolution: Sex, Class and Political Culture* (Yale University Press, 1989), p. 115. Outram further argues that in comtemporary depictions, the Ancien Régime was often feminized to emphasize the new Stoic masculine virtues of the new Republic (pp. 41, 87). See also Lynn Hunt's exploration of the projection of male public images under the Republic.
67. See Linda Shires's "Of Maenads, Mothers, and Feminized Males: Victorian Readings of the French Revolution," in *Rewriting the Victorians*, edited by Linda M. Shires (Routledge, 1992), pp. 147–148.
68. Alfred Cobban, *The Debate on the French Revolution 1789–1800* (Nicholas Kaye, 1950), p. 31.

Chapter 1
Burkean Prophecy and the July Revolution

Why had France had a Revolution in the late eighteenth century, while Britain had not? At least in literary terms, by the early 1830s, this complex question had an almost standardized answer. Whereas Britain had initially reacted favorably to the French Revolution, Edmund Burke had correctly forecast its imminent dangers in his *Reflections on the Revolution in France*, published in November 1790. Burke's reading of the historical significance of the Revolution in this and later writings had alerted Britons to its perils, and common sense had saved the nation. Thus although by birth an Irishman, Burke became a champion of the British state.

I wish to suggest, though, that this conception of Burke as savior of the nation evolved in hindsight. In 1817, only two years after the defeat of Napoleon, Coleridge asked why "the speeches and writings of EDMUND BURKE are more interesting at the present day, than they were found at the time of their first publication," while those of his contemporaries were largely forgotten. Coleridge concludes that

> Edmund Burke possessed and had seduously sharpened that eye, that sees all things, actions, and events, in relation to the *laws* that determine their existence and circumscribe their possibility. He referred habitually to *principles*. He was a *scientific* statesman; and therefore a *seer*. For every *principle* contains in itself the germs of a prophecy; and as the prophetic power is the essential privilege of science, so the fulfillment of its oracles supplies the outward and (to men in general) the *only* test of its claim to the title.[1]

Coleridge therefore suggests that without hindsight—the knowledge that Burke's reading of history had come true—Burke's ideas could not be fully appreciated. At the same time, Coleridge commingles the scientific and the mystical: the correct reading of laws will seem oracular to "men in general."[2]

1830, though, was to give a new relevance to Burke's ability to read events. James K. Chandler presents a cogent illustration of the evolution of the myth of Burke as prophet in his examination of the changing views held by a particularly influential British voice, William Wordsworth. Probably in the 1820s, and certainly by 1832, Wordsworth had revised his autobiographical epic to include a tribute to the "Genius of Burke," so that by the final revision of *The Prelude*, Burke is the man who awes "the younger brethren of the grove" as he

> ... forewarns, denounces, launches forth,
> Against all systems built on abstract rights
> Keen ridicule ... .[3]

Even by the time of the 14-Book Prelude which according to its editor W. J. B. Owen was written out during the 1820s and then revised in 1832, the lines I quote are not complete. Book Seven, 526–527 had earlier read "His younger brethren of the grove. Who sits/ Listening beside thee?"[4] The line containing the word "forewarns" was inserted subsequently, as if Wordsworth came very late to the concept of Burke as prophet—possibly, indeed, after the July Revolution of 1830. The retrospective nature of this view of Burke as one who "forewarns" is disguised by the present tense: Chandler points out that in the early 1790s, Wordsworth—like Coleridge—had opposed Burke's reading of the Revolution,[5] and seemingly only came to admire his prophetic force much later.[6]

Wordsworth and Coleridge were not alone in revising their judgments of Burke. The myth of the prophetic Burke only became widely accepted as historical truth when the question of revolution became topical again in 1830, and Britons reconsidered the impact of the literary on history. Developments of the early 1830s were to enshrine the power of the written word to create a reading of politics. Hence both Tories and Whigs tried to assume the role of Burke the patriotic savior by claiming to be able to interpret the present and the future on the basis of their reading of Britain and France's past. Simon Schama states that in 1830, the "French Revolution" became a "transferable entity," and was "no longer a finite series of events":[7] only the second

Revolution provided the means of seeing the first as a whole, and completed the process of enshrining Burke as prophet.

Burke, Past and Future

The myth of the prophetic Burke has been so powerful that even today, Burke remains an icon of conservative thought—as we have seen, in 1989, Margaret Thatcher's interpretation of the French Revolution was openly derived from Burke's reading of history. Burke might, however, have been surprised to find himself characterized not merely as a good reader of history, but as a prophet, and more specifically, a Druid who worshiped in sacred woods, as Wordsworth's reference to the "grove" suggests.[8] In 1757 he had begun *An Essay towards an Abridgment of the English History*, in which he set out the ideas that he then held concerning historical progress, especially the progress of law; the fragment remained unpublished until after his death. In this work, Burke has a surprising amount to say about Druids, because for him they symbolize the barbarous nature of Britain's past. The essay is neither tory, as Hume's history is in emphasizing the consistency of human nature; nor radical, in attempting to reclaim a golden age in which the English were free. Instead, it is a prototypical whig history in finding its hero in the progress of civilization, which for Burke is virtually synonymous with law. In such a reading, humanity in its primitive state is not free, not necessarily because humans do not have an innate right to freedom,[9] but because individuals in an undeveloped society are at the mercy of crude and superstitious systems of rule such as that of the Druids. According to Burke, the Druids ruled by assuming control of the learning, religion, health, and government of the Britons. Following Roman sources, he believes that they practiced human sacrifice, sometimes by immolating large numbers of people in wicker figures:

> They frequently inclosed a number of wretches, some captives, some criminals, and, when these were wanting, even innocent victims, in a gigantic statue of wicker-work, to which they set fire, and invoked their deities amidst the horrid cries and shrieks of the sufferers, and the shouts of those who assisted at this tremendous rite. (*Works* [1866] 7:186)

Burke and seemingly all of his contemporaries believed that the Druids had built Stonehenge. In his "Salisbury Plain" poems composed in the French revolutionary era, the young Wordsworth mentions the practice of killing victims in "wicker men," but in his earliest version of the poem at least, he associates Druids not with prudent foresight, but with the superstition of the old order:

> ... pursue your toils, till not a trace
> Be left on earth of Superstition's reign,
> Save that eternal pile which frowns on Sarum's plain.[10]

Similarly, the Burke of *English History* sees nothing useful in Druid prophecy, remarking:

> Futurity is the great concern of mankind. Whilst the wise and learned look back upon experience and history, and reason from things past about events to come, it is natural for the rude and ignorant, who have the same desires without the same reasonable means of satisfaction, to inquire into the secrets of futurity, and to govern their conduct by omens, dreams, and prodigies. (*Works [1866]* 7:186)

Druids, then, fulfill a need to know what will happen in the future, and in an advanced culture they can be replaced by an awareness of history. In recounting the Roman invaders' confrontation with the Britons, Burke is particularly shocked by the female Druids:

> On every side of the British army were seen bands of Druids in their most sacred habits surrounding the troops, lifting their hands to heaven, devoting to death their enemies, and animating their disciples to religious frenzy by the uncouth ceremonies of a savage ritual, and the horrid mysteries of a superstition familiar with blood. The female Druids also moved about in a troubled order, their hair dishevelled, their garments torn, torches in their hands, and, with an horror increased by the perverted softness of their sex, howled out the same curses and incantations with greater clamor. (*Works [1866]* 7:195–196)

This account of the Druids may be useful in understanding why Burke should be so hostile to the French Revolution. In *English History*, Burke traces England's developments in government from "savagery" to Magna Carta, paying particular attention to times that had the greatest impact upon law, such as the reign of King Alfred, the Norman Conquest, and Magna Carta itself. Yet unlike the radicals of his time, Burke pointedly does not grant any one of these events the status of the foundation of English rights and freedoms. For Burke, the laws of a nation are built on the basis of a tradition of historic right. His *English History* ends with a fragment "Towards a History of the Laws of

England," in which he asserts that nothing can be more instructive than "to observe the first principles of RIGHT springing up, involved in superstition and polluted with violence, until by length of time and favorable circumstances it has worked itself into clearness ..." (*Works* [1866] 7:475). Above all, Burke insists that the origins of law are not lost in prehistory, but can be traced by reasoned investigation into their traditions.

In contrast, in the *Reflections*, the French Revolutionaries seem to him to be rejecting a tradition of historic right; he describes them as leading the people as the Druids led the Ancient Britons, without a regard for history, reason, or the appropriate roles of the sexes. In attempting to create a form of government that is outside previous human experience, they are refusing to learn from history.[11] Burke's description of the French Assembly bears some resemblance to his accounts of the Druids, since he claims that the Assembly delegates

> act like comedians of a fair before a riotous audience; they act amidst the tumultuous cries of a mixed mob of ferocious men, and of women lost to shame, who, according to their insolent fancies, direct, control, applaud, explode them; and sometimes mix and take their seats amongst them ... .[12]

The French Revolution was thus in Burke's reading an attack on history itself, and history merited his defense.

Burke did not originate the practice of understanding an event by reading it against other events already granted the status of history, yet he perfected it. In one of many examples of insular myopia that we shall see in this study, the first events of the French Revolution do not seem to have particularly interested him. Carl B. Cone, for instance, describes Burke's initial response to Charles Jean François DePont's enthusiasm for developments in his home country as "mild."[13] What apparently prompted a change in Burke's attitude was Richard Price's sermon on the anniversary of the revolution that Burke himself was to call "glorious," 1688; the changes in Paris were here construed not merely as a French, but also as a British concern. In the concluding remarks to his "Discourse on the Love of Our Country," Price drew historical parallels between England's political choices and actions in 1688 and those of France in 1789. To strengthen the propitiousness of the omen, Price dated the French Revolution not from the taking of the Bastille in 1789, but from the political developments of 1788: France was merely a century behind England.[14] Stanley Ayling observes that Burke saw Price's sermon in mid-January 1790, and "probably did not plan a full-length book upon events in France much, if at all, before that date." Following this, Ayling adds, the book was "written in a passion, and at speed."[15] Price had provided a way to understand the present through historical precedent. History gave current political negotiations in France the status of events that could no longer be considered as an intellectual curiosity, but were rather matters on which patriotic Britons needed to take a stand.

Although ostensibly Burke is addressing a French audience, the *Reflections* are directed at British readers, as the opening discussion of historical parallels makes clear. Burke himself does not object to the constitutional "principles of the glorious revolution,"[16] yet denies that these create the rights described by Price. Immediately appealing to his readers' nationalist sense of history, Burke suggests that even this has been distorted by Price and his supporters:

> These gentlemen of the Old Jewry, in all their reasonings on the Revolution of 1688, have a Revolution which happened in England about forty years before, and the French Revolution, so much before their eyes, and in their hearts, that they are constantly confounding all the three together. (8:66)

Yet although Burke adds, "It is necessary that we should separate what they confound," once the association has been made, this is becomes a mental impossibility: the historically-aware cannot help making comparisons between events. The best that Burke can do is to attempt to substitute one analogy for the other, and to argue that the French Revolution of 1789 parallels not the English Revolution of 1688, which, he asserts, established no new constitutional principles, but the Rebellion of 1642, which in Burke's opinion overthrew the constitution with catastrophic results. Price is therefore compared to Hugh Peters, who in 1648 preached what was essentially a regicide sermon in the Royal Chapel (*Writings* 8:61).

It is on the basis of the parallel with the English Civil War era that Burke predicts the future. Historical precedent suggests that if 1642 is the model, the French Revolution will result in a democracy giving way to anarchy, military tyranny, and the death of princes.[17] Although in *An Appeal from the New to the Old Whigs* (1791) Burke claimed that the other Whigs had changed, while he had not, in his reading of history, an alteration is apparent: he is more clearly aligning himself with "tory" insistence on the preservation of existing structures, and with the idea that orchestrated change is against "nature." In both the *Appeal* and the *Reflections*, then, Burke primarily deploys history in the tory mode, as part of an implied extended analogy between France and Britain that involves a tory definition of "nature" and a tory sense of moral outrage. Burke therefore would not wish to be a Druid. He would insist that his vision of "futurity" was based upon historical analysis and practical experience. The fact remains, however, that about the time of the French Revolution of 1830, Burke was being recreated not simply as historical analyst, but also as prophet.

The role of the prophetic Burke needs further scrutiny. In the *Reflections*, Burke establishes the reasons why the French Revolution will lead not to free government, but to anarchy. Moreover, in his "Letter to a Member of the National Assembly" (1791), Burke makes the pronouncement remembered many years after his death as an accurate forecast of events: "they will assassinate the king when his name will no longer be necessary to their designs, but not a moment sooner. They will probably first assassinate the queen ..."[18] For historical precedent, Burke may have had in mind the death of Charles I during the English Civil War, suggesting that France will go further towards the breakdown of law by killing not only the king but also his consort. On the other hand, the word "assassinate" implies a lack of legal authority. The French Revolutionaries were careful to give both king and queen trials, and to assert the authority of their law to execute them as criminals and traitors. In the case of Charles I, those who denied that Parliament could legally execute the monarch might in theory have referred to his execution as an assassination, but this does not seem to have been the case, words like "beheading" and "martyrdom" being more common among those who wished to avoid the legal implications of "execution." I suspect that by the word "assassinate," Burke had in mind a lynching such as those currently reported in Paris, or a prison murder such as that suffered by, for example, Edward II or Richard II, rather than a public execution. Burke also feared that the queen would die first. While these might seem minor distinctions, it is upon such loose interpretations of meaning that Burke's reputation as a prophet depends.

Yet Burke left both whig and tory would-be historians a powerful legacy. First, of course, he established the precedent of analyzing one event on the basis of another; in this way, then, Burke was not merely appealing to history, but helping to define what constituted history. But Burke also fixed in the British mind tropes that were to recur throughout later readings of French revolution.

Among these images, Burke contrasts "nature" and "monstrosity." As we have already seen, Burke chooses not to address the question of "natural law"; by the early 1790s, however, he he was insisting upon "natural order." In *An Appeal from the New to the Old Whigs* (1791), Burke answers his critics by claiming to be true to traditional Whig principles of the careful preservation of ancient rights: the 1688 Revolution and the American Revolution were thus "defensive" actions to preserve the constitution.[19] In contrast, the "new principles of Whiggism, imported from France" maintain that a constitution is yet to be formed (*Works [1866]* 4:120). While challenging Rousseau's doctrine of natural right ("In a state of *rude* Nature there is no such thing as a people" (4:169)), Burke continues to claim that the idea of a "people" is a "natural" one, an idea that he had held since the time of the Essay on English history, when he suggested that the power of the Druids was sustained by the people's need for law. Where Burke's ideas seem to have changed is in assuming that "order" itself is "natural":

> ... when you break up this beautiful order, this array of truth and Nature, as well as of habit and prejudice—when you separate the common sort of men from their proper chieftains, so as to form them into an adverse army—I no longer know that venerable object called the people in such a disbanded race of deserters and vagabonds. (4:176)

The critique is said to be of the Parliamentary Whigs, yet this response, particularly in the discussion of the constitution, is also directed at radicals such as Thomas Paine, whose *Rights of Man* is quoted almost verbatim. In making this connection, Burke implies that the Whigs have become radicals, coining "for themselves Whig principles from a French die" (4:215): in other words, they have changed, whereas he has remained constant. Yet at the same time, in making the assertion not merely that order is natural, but that *specific* forms of order (pre-revolutionary France, the England of his day) are natural, Burke shows his new alignment with tory history.

An important image in Burke's portrayal of the destruction of natural order is the reversal of the natural roles of the sexes. Burke's famous appeal to the past epitomizes tory history's fear of the loss of tradition and its insistence that individuals should not be sacrificed to system. At the same time, it suggests that civilization, in which women are treated with respect, is dying. (While civilization might seem the reverse of nature, in its treatment of women, civilization apparently respects women's "natural" qualities, at least as Burke imagines them.) Recalling Queen Marie Antoinette at Versailles some sixteen years before, and the failure of contemporary France to come to her aid, Burke laments:

> ... the age of chivalry is gone.—That of sophisters, economists, and calculators, has succeeded; and the glory of Europe is extinguished forever. Never, never more shall we behold that generous loyalty to rank and sex, that proud submission, that dignified obedience, that subordination of the heart, which kept alive, even in servitude itself, the spirit of an exalted freedom. (*Writings* 8:127)

Burke had already expressed a fear of women as political leaders in his account of the Druids, and from the perspective of a generation later, it was easy to blur together Burke's different pronouncements concerning women and revolution. If a sign of an aberration of nature was the abuse of women, another might be to associate women with aberrations of nature. After the "Terror" was supposedly over, in his 1796 *First Letter on a Regicide Peace*, Burke claims that:

> out of the tomb of the murdered monarchy in France has arisen a vast, tremendous, unformed spectre, in a far more terrific guise than any which ever yet have overpowered the imagination, and subdued the fortitude of man. Going straight forward to it's end, unappalled by peril, unchecked by remorse, despising all common maxims and all common means, that hideous phantom overpowered those who would not believe it was possible she could exist.[20]

This feminized image of a monstrous regicide republic was by later writers reimposed on women of the period of the Terror, with significant literary effect.

Finally, Burke envisaged the French Revolution as more than a threat to domesticity; it was a threat to the structure of property-ownership itself. In suggesting that the threat is to property, Burke might appear to be appealing to a reasonable fear of loss of order; yet in characterizing property as home, Burke ensures that reason and emotion are intertwined. As we shall see in Chapter Three, his imagery relating nation to home was developed further by later writers. To cite one example, when explaining why the French Revolution should be regarded as relevant to British concerns, Burke writes in the *Reflections*: "Whenever our neighbour's house is on fire, it cannot be amiss for the engines to play a little on our own" (*Writings* 8:60). On the eve of the July Revolution, in May 1830, the *Quarterly Review* justified the amount of attention that it was giving to contemporary French concerns in an elaborate and casually brutal reworking of Burke's metaphor that sets up a disturbing contrast between private and public:

> If our neighbour [in the street] merely beats his wife and children, and regulates his personal concerns in the worst way possible, we have no right to complain; but if he gets intoxicated, and flings about firebrands, so as not only to set his own house on fire, but to threaten the destruction of the whole parish, we are compelled, in spite of our love of quiet, to take a lively interest in the proceedings.[21]

As an "outrage on all the rights of property," the result of revolution is not freedom, but the potentially "most dreadful arbitrary tyranny ever known in any nation."[22] Such sweeping assertions did not go unchallenged; radicals and progressivists were quick to pen replies to Burke's writings on France. Pronouncements such as that "the age of chivalry is dead" depend on a sense of history that is simultaneously powerful and vague. Sir James Mackintosh quickly pointed out that a "caviller might remark that ages, much more near the meridian fervour of chivalry than ours, have witnessed the treatment of queens as little gallant and generous as that of the Parisian mob"[23]: the mistreatment of women, then, is not evidence of the decline of civilization. Mackintosh might be expected to go on to criticize all constructions of historical parallel: he asserts, after all, that "Society is inevitably progressive." In an even more iconoclastic move, he also rejects the myth of Teutonic freedom:

> It is not because we *have* been, but because we have a right to be free, that we ought to demand freedom .... It would be the same absurdity to assert, that we have a right to freedom, because the Englishmen of Alfred's reign were free, as that three and three are six, *because* they were so in the camp of Genghis Khan .... Let us hear no more of her [freedom's] Saxon, Dane, or Norman ancestors ...[24]

In this, Mackintosh echoes the more radical supporters of the French Revolution and opponents of Burke. Radicalism in fact claims to reject the authority of history in that change need not be justified on the grounds of historical precedent, a particularly iconoclastic stance in England, where law itself is based on the tradition of precedent. In *The Rights of Man*, for example, Thomas Paine attacked the Revolution of 1688 on the basis that William III was merely the lesser of two evils, and that the legislators of 1688 were not entitled to create the enduring precedents claimed for them either by Burke or by Price: they could not set up principles for all ages to come because "Every age and generation must be as free to act for itself *in all cases* as the ages and generations which preceded it."²⁵

Another republican respondent to Burke, Catherine Macaulay, perhaps articulated the historical problem better than either Paine or Mackintosh:

> We can gain no light from history; for history furnishes *no example* of any government in a large empire, which, in the strictest sense of the word, has secured to the citizen the *full* enjoyment of his rights. Some attempts have indeed been made of this kind; but they have hitherto failed, through the *treachery* of leaders, or by the *rash folly* of the multitude. But though these circumstances will prevent cautious persons from giving a *decided* opinion on what may be the event of things, yet they do not so *benight* the understanding as to deprive the mind of hope. They do not prevent it from feeling that the present complexion of things in France has something of a different aspect from what history, or the state of other countries, presents to our view.²⁶

Macaulay, who died in 1791 while the French Revolution could still be claimed by the disciples of reason, argued that the progress of civilized thought was such that the parallel with 1688 was largely unfounded, a point with which Mackintosh, with his faith in the progress of human reason, concurred.

Yet even while claiming that natural human rights did not require the precedent of history, these writers could not bring themselves entirely to reject the force of both historical analogy and historical precedent. Each text makes use of significant historical moments in constitutional development. As Burke pointed out in the *Appeal*, Thomas Paine, while denying the material existence of the constitution, is indebted to a loose reading of constitutional history in which the person of William the Conqueror represents the imposition of tyranny. Macaulay, in the seemingly anti-historical passage quoted above, clearly alludes to what she regarded as the great tragedy of English history, the failure of republican democracy in the seventeenth century through the opportunism of Oliver Cromwell. Similarly, Mackintosh's main focus is on the period of his own never-completed history of the Revolution of 1688. Eli Halévy notes this confusion in the case of Mackintosh and sees it as a radical-liberal dilemma between natural right and the philosophy of "utility."²⁷ This is appropriate for Halévy's purpose, which is to trace the Benthamite tradition in nineteenth-century thought, but Mackintosh's confusion may be more fundamental than this. Mackintosh's declaration that Britons should be free "not because they *have been* but because they *ought to be*" asserts a doctrine of natural right that is ahistorical. The theory of utility, however, requires a sense of historical progression: as circumstances and social attitudes change, so legislation should change to ensure that the greatest number of citizens are made content not for all times, but for a specific point in history. Even when Mackintosh, Macaulay and Paine deny the parallel with the history, a contrast simultaneously creates a mode of comparison, and the net effect is to reassociate the events of 1688 with those of 1789.

Hence even the proponents of radical reform of society could not escape the need for placing their arguments in a historical framework. In Britain, the assertions of 1790 to 1791, especially those of radicals, were soon largely forgotten. What was left for liberals in 1830 was a sense of embarrassment: the Revolution did appear to have turned out as Burke had predicted, and moderate philosophical liberals such as Mackintosh lived to recant their pro-Revolutionary assertions of the early 1790s. How could another French Revolution be justified? In fact, for the liberals of 1830, the whig philosophic tradition of Mackintosh was to prove useful. From the perspective of 1830, a broader conception of the events of 1789 to 1794 was possible. Mackintosh had posited that the relation between 1688 and 1789 was not simply analogous, but also organic:

> The Revolution of 1688 deserves more the attention of a philosopher from the indirect influence on the progress of human opinion, than from its immediate effects on the government of England ... . From this progress of opinion arose the American Revolution; and from this last, unquestionably, the delivery of France.[28]

Both whig and tory historians were similarly to argue direct influence in their consideration of 1830. From the whig-reformist point of view, the success of the July Revolution suggested that political change in Britain need not be destructive to property: the July Revolution was thus not merely a point of comparison, but also an incentive. For tory-conservatives, this was part of its danger. Not unreasonably, though, nobody wished to be a new Mackintosh,[29] renouncing his initial enthusiasiam for revolution as misplaced faith, if they could be a new Burke, preserving the essence of the nation through his writings. If language could indeed have this effect on history, the periodical writers of 1830, both Whigs and Tories, were eager to emulate Burke's success.

Burke in 1830

The French Revolution of July 1830 presented two historical possibilities for Britain: analogy and influence. Whether the French situation was interpreted as tory history in providing a warning of what to avoid, or as whig history in the form of encouragement towards a positive goal, the representatives of the British people would justify their subsequent actions by their reading of it. The problem, of course, was that only time could tell who was to be the new Burke and read the signs of history correctly.

Events of 1830 certainly supported Burke's contention that the European states could not be considered entirely in isolation, but as providing warnings and inspiration to one another. In 1815, the Treaty of Vienna had attempted to reverse Napoleon's restructuring of Europe by returning power to those who had possessed it before the wars of the Revolutionary period. In effect, the restored hereditary rulers of Europe, and particularly the Bourbons in France, were declaring that the French Revolution had no permanent historical impact, and was merely a temporary deviation from the divinely-appointed tradition of monarchy.

Yet despite these attempts at denial, Europe had changed. The territorial divisions created under Napoleonic rule showed a greater acknowledgment of nationalism than the return to the rule of petty princes, particularly in the German and Italian states. Moreover, the Napoleonic era had created a new sense that government should not be based on the authority of individuals alone, but on a constitution. Ripples of unrest were apparent in the period around 1820, but the restored hereditary rulers of Europe reasserted themselves. The year 1830, however, proved different.

In Britain, the wars with France had been used as a justification for resisting demands for Parliamentary reform. Even at the outbreak of the French Revolution, it had become obvious that the inequality of representation in Britain was a difficulty. The two central inequities were that the medieval distribution of seats meant that the new industrial towns were insufficiently represented; and a franchise qualification that varied from borough to borough.[30] This begged the question of whom or what members of Parliament were actually representing. Tories might glorify the state—monarch, lords, commons, people—as one of checks and balances that direct intervention would destroy, but the only philosophical basis that could be argued for such a random structure was that of a divine but apparently disorganized Providence.

The distribution of votes and the important factor of the will of the monarch had skewed power in favor of the Tories for many years before 1830. Then on 26 June 1830, George IV died, the law requiring a general election within six months of the death of the monarch. Parliament was still in session, but preparations began to be made for an election after the summer recess.

Parliament was officially dissolved on July 24; the following day, the situation in France suddenly changed. Louis XVIII, the restored Bourbon monarch, had died in 1824, to be succeeded by his brother Charles X. When Charles X's government under Prince Polignac had sensed that they were losing control to an increasingly determined opposition of moderate liberals, republicans, and Bonapartists, they imposed four ordinances revoking constitutional rights. This was July 25; on July 27, in defiance of the ordinances, some Paris newspapers published the news, and the rebellion spread to the streets. As British commentators observed, the reaction of the king's troops was incompetent; on August 2 Charles X abdicated in favor of his grandson, but the leaders (if such they can be called) of the Revolution had already made a compromise choice. The new government would be a constitutional monarchy under the son of the Duke of Orleans who had supported the 1789 Revolution, who would take the new title of Louis Philippe, King of the French.

From the British point of view, once again, just as they had done on Bastille Day 1789, the French had asserted their passionate nature by starting a revolution at a time when rational beings were taking a summer vacation.[31] Nevertheless, the July Revolution initially won widespread approval as long as it was seen as an exclusively French concern. *The Times* welcomed the change of government, asserting that French had "vindicated their rights and those of all mankind":

> the conduct of the French people in their melancholy drama has been justly honoured by every noble mind in Europe; for such promptitude in decision, such courage in execution, such moderation in victory, are scarcely parallelled by any passage in the history of mankind.[32]

Even in the House of Commons, the Tory Sir Robert Peel was prepared to concede that in the case of France, "resistance might be justifiable."[33]

The difficulty was whether or not this was a good example for Britain to emulate. By the time that a British general election was called in mid-September the French appeared to have established their new government. Nor was this all: on August 25, Belgium had risen in revolt against Dutch rule, which seemed to suggest that once more France was setting a revolutionary example to the rest of Europe. Still, the majority of British voters apparently did not consider these changes a threat to their constitution, and elected a reform-minded Whig government that assembled in mid-October.

In opting for a constitutional monarchy, France seems to have caused Britons to reconsider whether their own monarchy was truly as constitutionally-based as they had traditionally asserted. Opponents to British Parliamentary Reform could, however, argue that the changes in Europe were unproven. The revolts of the Poles and Italian Carbonari in the later months of the year, for example, could be construed as signs not of an organized, constitutionally-based Europe where class distinctions continued much as before, but of impending anarchy. The question can be summarized as this: had Europe changed since the era of the French Revolution, or was Europe merely about to replay it? And if so, could Britain preserve its separate status?

As the actions of 1830s began to be read historically, widespread approval was replaced by divisions along party lines. Tory critics of the July Revolution were quick to cast ridicule on the new government as the product of collusions between the new industrialists and the press—the formulation of a new bourgeois ruling class. In January 1830, number of leading liberals including Armand Carrel, the future minister Adolphe Thiers, and the banker Jacques Lafitte, had founded *Le National* as a mouthpiece for their opposition to Charles X and his chief minister Prince Polignac. The July Revolution itself gained momentum through protests at the reimposition of strict controls of the press, and the offices of banned newspapers became rallying-points for formulating the new direction for French government.

British papers were aware of the high impact of journalism upon the Revolution. Earlier in July, *The Times* had reported the "amusing" information that the London paper had been accused by the French liberals of taking bribes from Polignac to voice support for him, and of taking counter-bribes to modify its response.[34] Such an accusation assumes something now familiar but which is only a form of empowerment in a society with representative government: that the press has a direct effect upon public opinion.[35] During the following month, *The Times* derived much of its information about developments in France from the Paris journals. On July 28, for example, *The Times* reported that *Le Moniteur* quoted Prince Polignac's remark that "a thick cloud raised by the journals conceals the truth." The ordinance curtailing the powers of the press was also printed. In future issues, British readers were presented with the text of Charles X's abdication letter, and the new King Louis Philippe's initial address to the nation, all reprinted from French journal sources.

Just as the newspapers were praised or blamed for bringing about the July Revolution, so the British periodical press took on the role of persuading Britain whether or not to accept reforms to its own political system. At this time, the two major critical reviews, both based in Edinburgh, divided strictly according to party. The *Edinburgh Review*, founded in 1802 by a group of Whig lawyers and writers including Francis Jeffrey and Henry Brougham, was literally covered with the party colors of blue and yellow; the *Quarterly Review* was consciously founded in 1809 with the support of Tories such as Walter Scott to represent the Tory position,[36] and might actually claim the credit for having invented the phrase "the conservative principle."[37] Obviously, each journal wanted its party in power; moreover, Whig and Tory goals were much the same in wishing to limit the power to those two parties by the association of political with material property. Now each took on the role of the organ of public opinion that would save the nation.

Such a belief in the authority of journalistic advocacy was not entirely new, yet at this moment, when public opinion seemed more important than ever before in British politics, it had a fresh urgency. In each case, the journals argued for the place of history as the measure of appropriate response to current events. The imperative of party journalism, then, was to shape the interpretation to conform not so much to different ideologies as to different senses of the significance of history. Yet one shadow hung over their readings, one which seemed to give more advantage to the anti-Reformers than the pro-Reformers: the legacy of Edmund Burke. Whigs and Tories, especially through the *Edinburgh Review* and the *Quarterly Review*, both took on the task of convincing Britons that its reading of France and its relevance to Britain was correct, each faction striving to assume the mantle of Edmund Burke, and, as Elishas to his Elijah, to bring the power of political prophecy to history once again.

It may seem only consistent that the *Edinburgh* should approve of the July Revolution in France and that the *Quarterly* should oppose it, yet Tory horror at the July Revolution is notably less in evidence before the introduction of the Whig government's Reform Bill in March 1831 than it is after it. While in theory, Tories might lament the downfall of ancient monarchies, few were prepared to defend the régime of Charles X. Only when the events began to seem applicable to the British situation did the July Revolution seem threatening. In the first major reform debate, Lord Gower stated the moderate Tory position clearly:

> He entertained great respect for the French people, and wished them all possible success in the endeavour rationally to reform their constitution, but he was not favourable to any project of theirs which might render France an emblem of discord, or the focus of revolution throughout Europe.[38]

From this time forward, the degree of passion involved, and the length of the debate, suggests that both parties, and consequently the *Edinburgh* and the *Quarterly*, were responding to more than a matter of foreign politics in which they would maintain their usual positions of moderate reform as opposed to resistance of all political "innovation."

Even before the July Revolution, the *Quarterly Review* had published a article, probably by Basil Hall,[39] arguing that France was approaching a crisis. At the present time, under Charles X and Polignac, the French had, "in point of fact, few or no grievances to complain of—the whole of the outcry now being raised about matters of moonshine."[40] The Reviewer expresses his shock that Cotta, the French author whose work he is reviewing, believes "that as there was nothing very extraordinary—at least according to the nature of his own countrymen—in the horrors of the revolution, so no one need be in the least surprised, should the same scenes be re-enacted upon the first fitting opportunity." Free institutions, the Reviewer argues, are not necessarily appropriate for the French, whose historical record suggests the need for firm control. Indeed, without due care, their boasted institutions will "merely contribute to macadamize the road to tyranny, by breaking down the established usages of the country, and leaving it open for any despot to ride over it at what rate he pleases."[41]

Although written by a different hand from most of the *Quarterly*'s subsequent pieces on France, this essay is significant in establishing the general attitude towards French politics. Given the national character of the French, another French revolution must inevitably lead along the same road as the first, although technological advances may make the (anti-) progress more rapid. Moreover, quoting Napoleon's comment, "a revolution in France is a revolution in Europe," the essay states its Burkean purpose as being the wish "to make our countrymen feel the full importance of the political and moral advantages which they possess over their neighbours."[42] The *Quarterly*'s most ambitious new Burke, however, was another Irishman, John Wilson Croker, who both before and after the First Parliamentary Reform Act of 1832 used his knowledge of French affairs to stand firm against whiggism and anarchy.

Croker against the Whigs

The *Quarterly*'s leading writer on French history was John Wilson Croker, who lost his long-term position at the Admiralty Office to the new Whig government during the Reform era. Croker decided that journalism, rather than parliamentary debate, was the best way to combat the dangers of anarchy—probably the only point on which he agreed with the government of France. Like Burke and like the man whom he considered to be Britain's other champion against French revolution, his friend the Duke of Wellington, Croker was Irish. He never found enough time to write his own history of the French Revolution, although he amassed a remarkable collection of documents in preparation for writing one.[43] Seamus Deane, who not without justification claims that Croker was the greatest authority on the French Revolution in England, has suggested that interpretation of the data required a more flexible and less exact mind than Croker's, and that he had "nothing to offer on the significance of the Revolution other than what a rank, vindictive anti-French feeling would lead one to expect."[44] Yet Croker did have a coherent historical position, albeit an alarmingly narrow one.

Croker, who was fifty years old in 1830, is probably best remembered to literary history as the man who killed Keats. Keats's friends and admirers maintained that the *Quarterly*'s hostile review of *Endymion* in April 1818 caused his illness and death.[45] It may seem more surprising that Croker himself should affect to believe that he had a share in Keats's end, and that Keats had indeed died not of consumption but of criticism, yet in his review of Tennyson's 1833 collection of poems, Croker offers an apology for not having found in *Endymion* "the same merit that its more clear-sighted and prophetic admirers did," and promises not to give the same treatment to Tennyson.[46] For Croker to admit that he prophesied inaccurately is out of character for the new Burke, and he may have another motive beyond apology: to remind the readers of what happened to Keats is to remind them of the power of the *Quarterly*. In attacking Keats, Croker had been using criticism as a weapon against national degeneracy, and as a critic (almost all of Croker's writing takes the form of the review), he continued to expose cultural and political threats to his ideal of Britain. Yet the attack epitomizes Croker's social role as always fighting a rearguard action—to kill Keats, after all, was not to kill Romanticism. And the major rearguard action of his life was his response to the 1830 Revolution and the Reform period.

In retrospect, Croker maintained that he had only been obeying the editors' wishes in using the *Quarterly* so openly as a political organ during the Reform years.[47] Croker and his friends believed that the July Revolution demonstrated the power of journalism to make or break revolutions.[48] In continuing to use his writing to oppose the principle of reform, he was, he believed, performing an important national duty.

Like most Tories, Croker was not opposed to reform of any kind but a constitutional evolutionist, believing that some redistribution of parliamentary seats was appropriate to reflect the growth of the industrial cities. Yet he strongly opposed the Whigs' extensive reform measure, believing that like the concessions made by Louis XVI before 1789, constitutional change would lead to disaster. Before the Reform Bill passed, Croker was only one of a number of writers for the *Quarterly* who forecast calamity on the scale of the first French Revolution: Robert Southey also condemned what he interpreted as the Saint-Simonian doctrines of the new French government, and observed that "the attack on property" of the first French Revolution was being "renewed under the cover of a new religion."[49] Similarly, John Fullarton, in an article ominously titled "Progress of Misgovernment," warned that the new French regime demonstrated "how utterly incompatible with the interests and pursuits of peaceful industry are all violent changes in the political condition of a country."[50]

Fullarton's observation illustrates the *Quarterly*'s rhetorical complexity—or possibly, its confusion. He appears to be discussing contemporary France, but his only means of understanding the present is through the known outcome of the first French Revolution. The comment on the effect on industry, however, is more applicable to Britain. The anti-Reformers' difficulty was that the July Revolution was largely as *The Times* had approvingly characterized it: notable not for its violence, but for its moderation.[51] The lamp-posts, Burke's symbol of mob-rule, had been pulled down at the beginning of the revolution, as if to state that the violence of citizen against citizen would this time be unacceptable.

Whereas the events of 1830 had helped create a clearer historical perspective for those of 1789, they were too close themselves to be seen in a broader framework, except by assuming Burke's powers of prophecy. This Croker seems to have intended to do. Even after Reform was passed in summer 1832, he continued to illustrate the dangers of following the way of the French. He refused to sit in the reformed House of Commons, and instead devoted his energies to editing and to studies of French history and literature. In Croker's opinion, modern French literature was proof of the corrupting influence of the July Revolution, an effect not even limited to France itself. Although the material was immoral, it was therefore his duty to explore it in order once again to warn Britain of the dangers of following France's example: "The habit of *labelling* vials or packets of POISON with that cautionary description may, though, very rarely, have prompted or facilitated a suicide or murder—but how many ignorant or heedless persons has it not saved from destruction!" Some of these volumes, Croker points out, "might get into *ladies' book clubs*."[52] The very danger of the French was their persuasive power over the classes—and the sex—less capable of critical discrimination through the understanding of history than the legitimately enfranchised.

Croker's most important pieces, though, appeared in 1834–1835, when he was once again considering writing a full-length history of the French Revolution.[53] In "The Present State of France," published in August 1834, Croker still doubted both the lasting success of the July Revolution and of British Reform. What success the French had achieved was "as disgraceful to the good sense and honour of the French people, as the tyranny of Robespierre was to their good feelings and humanity."[54] Repetition of the first French Revolution might still lie ahead: "some future demagogues," Croker observes, reminding his readers of Louis Philippe's revolutionary past, "will naturally show less respect to the blood of Louis Philippe than he did to that of Louis XVI" ("State of France," p. 286).

Ironically, by this time, France might be seen by Ultra-Tories as providing a positive example to post-Reform Britain's expansion of the franchise to the less responsible middle classes. Following the 1830 Revolution, the French franchise had been strictly limited—Croker notes that in Paris 14,000 electors chose sixteen representatives, whereas in London, six times that number chose eighteen ("State of France," p. 284). Croker also claims credit for the *Quarterly* in having influenced the French minister Thiers's decision to impose dramatic censorship. Yet in both France and England, Croker concludes, following Burke's example in comparing the constitution to a building: "All is doubt, disorder, and dismay. We are in a moral earthquake, and what portions of the social edifice may survive the shock, or what shelters the unhappy survivors may find among the ruins, no mortal eye can foresee" ("State of France," p. 290).

Croker's other two major pieces on France of this period create an interesting pairing: one is on Louis Philippe, and one on Robespierre. By the time that he reviewed B. Sarrans's *Louis Philippe et la Contre-Revolution de 1830* in November 1834, Croker's personal opinion of the citizen-king whom he had earlier termed a "usurper" had improved. Louis Philippe is presented as the only reason why the initial prophecies of doom and disaster had not come to pass. Even then Croker asserts that Sarrans's book proves that the current French régime is "more convulsed, more bloody, more despotic, than any similar period in the whole half-century of revolution, the Reign of Terror hardly excepted" and that this is "the just price and inevitable punishment of rash revolt and blind innovation."[55] Croker concludes, in the style of Burke, with a prophecy, again based upon the precedent of history:

> France must again pass through a despotism—a republic—or a restoration—and probably all those—before she can settle down into an constitution which shall command the undivided respect and rational obedience of the nation. Neither the *sovereignty of the people*, nor the *power of the sword*, can ever be the basis of a permanent government![56]

In this article, the parallels with Britain are subdued, but Croker was more explicit in his study of Robespierre. Croker begins by associating the Reign of Terror with Gothic—literary—terror: Robespierre is, he asserts, "the most prominent, yet the most mysterious, figure in the *phantasmagoria* of the French Revolution."[57] The Gothic connection is important, because although Robespierre is monstrously villainous, he is simultaneously a type: his excesses are extraordinary, but not necessarily unrepeatable if someone of a similar character were given a similar chance to abuse power.

Croker's more reconciliatory attitude towards the current French régime is again in evidence in his emphasis that the work that he is ostensibly reviewing, a Life of Robespierre by "a young republican, of the name of Laponneraye," was written to glorify the first French Revolution upon the realization that the Revolution of 1830 was not truly radical ("Robespierre," p. 517). Yet Robespierre's character, as much as it can be reconstructed, reveals permanent dangers. Croker refuses to draw many conclusions from the conflicting evidence of the early life of "the most wholesale murderer that, we believe, the world ever produced" (p. 524), but suggests that a society that allows members to formulate their own moral standards is inevitably doomed. Croker's characterization of the Girondists, indeed, who were prepared to compromise with the mob and went to the scaffold declaring their patriotism, seems to hold a prophetic warning for the Whigs of his own age. France had given way to political and religious "maniacs," but perhaps Britain of the 1830s could interpret the lesson correctly: the lesson is finally not that of one individual, Robespierre, but of a whole generation. The analogy is made explicit:

> Happy for US—to whose present condition much of what we have related bears a fearful analogy—happy for US if we could be taught prudence by such lessons—to see that when a people departs suddenly and violently from its ancient ways, there is no limit to error, extravagance, crime, and misery—that under the frenzy of a revolution, the original dispositions and intentions of *no man* can be depended on ...

Most significantly for Croker, the historical pattern depicted here is not culturally limited: Britain can claim no moral superiority over "the once gay and good-natured people of France." The essay ends with a concluding flourish evidently intended to recall Burke, but in its parallelisms ironically reminiscent of Macaulay:

> Let us, then, endeavour to curb the curiosity of innovation—to restrain the frenzy of presumption—to humble the arrogance of self-confidence—to control by constitutional checks the extravagances of political ambition and popular fury—and to endeavour to maintain—through our ancient and approved institutions—the respect and reverence of our people for their laws, their king, their church, and their God. ("Robespierre," pp. 579–580)

Croker seems sincerely to have believed that the ancient constitutional form was forever lost—beheaded, as it were, by the whig Girondists.

In contrast, the *Edinburgh*, as a self-proclaimed reforming journal, welcomed the changes in France in 1830 both as evidence of the progress of civil structures towards freer government and as an example to Britain, now embroiled in reform debates. Brougham declared in October 1830: "we take it to be abundantly manifest, that the battle of English liberty has really been fought and won at Paris."[58] The English people, he asserted, "have suffered their delight at the late Glorious Revolution to burst forth ... . The cause of the French is the cause of all freemen." By giving the July Revolution the name usually ascribed to the English Revolution of 1688, Brougham was proclaiming its safety and reason. While for the Tories, Brougham's article, by making revolution seem reasonable, presented a danger, Brougham himself took a delight in the possibility of example:

> the honest and generous emulation, which has ever made the two greatest nations in modern Europe run the same race of rivalry in improvement, will now help us in the amendment of whatever defects exist in our institutions. The people of England will not long brook any marked inferiority to their neighbours ... France has now a freer government than England. The truth must be told.[59]

Such claims left the Parliamentary Whigs vulnerable to the Tory response that the reforming faction had also welcomed the revolution in 1789, and many of its supporters had afterwards regretted their initial enthusiasm. The question put to the Whigs was therefore how to reconcile the events of the first French Revolution with their reforming, progressive view of human history.

Whig historical writers turned to two main solutions: a moral-exemplary reading and a Utilitarian reading. In the case of the former, certain lessons of the French Revolution could be read in a typological—almost, indeed, in a tory—mode, as a warning of what might happen in England. The distinction was that in the whig historical reading, the warning was not to the pro-reformers but to the anti-reformers. While constitutional change would not necessarily lead to the excesses of the first French Revolution, *not* granting such change certainly might. This approach was used by Lord John Russell in a work published in 1832, *The Causes of the French Revolution*. Russell's name was not on the book, but his authorship was publicized by Lord Mahon's critique of it in the *Quarterly Review*, which recognized the work's association with the interests of reform.[60]

In terms of historical value, Russell's book is one of the poorest treatments of the subject, more than half its length being devoted to a retelling the lives of Voltaire and Rousseau from well-known sources. Yet that during the year of reform Russell devoted time to writing a book on the first French Revolution is revealing in itself—as is the implied rejection of Burke's role as the lone voice of reason that warned Britain not to follow suit. Moreover, that Russell could in effect use some tory strategies of argumentation to support the whig principle of reform demonstrates the interdependency of the two historical models.

Russell argues, as Tocqueville was to argue twenty-four years later, that the French Revolution was the result of a number of factors that in combination were unique to France. France's despotic monarchy in combination the authority of the Roman Catholic Church had prevented the development of a tradition of freedom. By implication, then, Burke did not prevent revolution in Britain, since Britain's situation was different. At first sight, this defuses the potential danger of historical analogy: whereas Burke's parallel depends upon inexactitudes, a closer examination suggests that the parallel is artifically-constructed. On the other hand, Russell recreates the parallel when he hints that the failure of the aristocracy to grant timely concessions caused their ultimate downfall. "It was the fatal error of the French rulers," Russell notes, "that they permitted wealth and knowledge to increase without attempting to adapt their institutions to the altered state of the nation." Apologizing for the irreligious writings of Voltaire and Rousseau, Russell asks, "But what shall we say to the government which, by a timely reform, might have prevented almost the existence, certainly the prevalence, of such fatal notions?"[61] While the overall combination of contributory factors is presented as unique to France, by such remarks, Russell draws parallels with Britain's situation, and the opportunity still open for "timely reform."

Russell and some of his fellow-reformers repeatedly used this approach in parliamentary debate. The chief advantage was that while avoiding identification with the radicals by firmly stating that the Reign of Terror was an aberration, the Whigs were able to use it as a final warning just as the Tories did, yet with the reverse goal of demonstrating the necessity for change, rather than the need to oppose it. The threat of the Reign of Terror made the first French Revolution a more rhetorically persuasive analogy than the comparatively mild 1830 Revolution, yet at least before Reform was passed, the Whigs were anxious to present their policies as an avoidance of all revolution. When the Tory Sir Robert Inglis cited the instance of contemporary France, for example, Lord Althorp replied that

> was it not, then, the duty of those who looked after the welfare of the nature to take measures to prevent such a revolution here? ... [The middle class] desired no change which could fairly, as the hon. Baronet called it, be denominated Revolutionary—no change which was likely to bring with it any destruction of property, or produce any of those frightful scenes which were witnessed in the first French Revolution.[62]

In particular, Russell's position had the parliamentary support of Thomas Babington Macaulay, who agreed with him that all revolutions—1688, 1789, 1830—were caused by the failure to make concessions.[63] The association, though, was one of analogy, not of actual influence: in Macaulay's words, "the excitement which the late French revolution produced in England, was not the cause but the effect of that progress which liberal opinions had made amongst us."[64] Macaulay hence proceeded to warn the House of Lords, who were inclining once again to veto the Bill:

> I trust, Sir, that the innate spirit and honour of the Peers of England require no admonition from the learned Gentlemen [of the Commons], and no lessons from foreign examples; but if such examples were becoming or necessary, I, too, should venture to implore the House of Lords to contemplate with awful attention the conduct and the calamities, the mistakes and misfortunes, of the nobility of France.[65]

Macaulay's historically-based admonition was too much for Croker, who responded again on historical terms, but carefully changed the nature of the parallel: Macaulay, Croker stated, believed that "that frightful period" of the first French Revolution "bears some resemblance to our present circumstances," and although Croker agreed, his "inferences" from this were completely different. Croker proceeded to give his own historical account of the calling of the *Tiers État*, and to conclude that it was the grant of power to a democratically-inclined body that led to the excesses of the French Revolution. Croker's argument is probably stronger from a historical point of view, but given the level of unrest in Britain at this time, the Whig party's claim that timely concessions were appropriate had more weight. In truth, Croker himself had to admit that some concessions were necessary.

Yet this was only part of the whig reading of the French Revolution. The second, Utilitarian-influenced, view stated that in accordance with the greatest happiness principle, an event which might cause misery to individuals might nevertheless be of gain to a larger unit—in this case, all of civilization. Hence during the period of the French Revolution, the long-term human advantages might admittedly be unclear. From the perspective of a few years afterwards, however, once the events even of the most bloody period could be seen as part of a historical process rather than as simply monstrous.[66] Macaulay was thus able in 1834 to find a consistency in Sir James Mackintosh's approach to the

French Revolution that had eluded Mackintosh himself (Mackintosh had died in the Reform year of 1832). Mackintosh had first welcomed the Revolution in a rebuttal of Burke that Macaulay calls "manly"—

> yet he never, in the season of warmest enthusiasm, proclaimed doctrines inconsistent with the safety of property and the just authority of governments. He, like almost every other honest and enlightened man, was discouraged and perplexed by the terrible events which followed. Yet he never in the most gloomy times abandoned the cause of peace, of liberty, and of toleration.[67]

Macaulay's goal is to explain Mackintosh's rejection of his initially pro-Revolutionary position as in keeping with the whig opinion is that "the French Revolution, in spite of all its crimes and follies, was a great blessing on mankind." In a veiled criticism of Burke and those who seek to emulate him, Macaulay concludes that "A man who had held exactly the same opinion about the Revolution in 1789, in 1794, in 1814, and in 1834, would have been either a divinely inspired prophet, or an obstinate fool."[68] Significantly, Macaulay omits the year 1830. Whatever the first French Revolution represents, it is not the same as the July Revolution, and the July Revolution is the appropriate analogy for British parliamentary reform.

The debate on the nature of reform and revolution was not over when Macaulay penned this essay, but the sense of national urgency was greatly diminished. Croker and his *Quarterly Review* colleagues had begun as the Burkes of their generation, but finally, their oratory and their prophecy had little effect in restraining the forces of change. As Croker continued to fulminate against France and reform, Sir Robert Peel was conceding on behalf of more moderate Tories that change was inevitable. Nevertheless, Burke had created a pattern of images by which revolution might be perceived as history, and later analyses of revolution both past and present were able to make powerful use of these images' logical and emotional associations.

Notes

1. Samuel Taylor Coleridge, *Biographia Literaria*, edited by James Engell and W. Jackson Bate (1817; Bollingen, 1983), pp. 191–192.
2. A claim that oracles are "scientific" dates back at least to the Stoics, who defended the reading of omens on the basis that everything is part of a chain of causation, the skill lying in perceiving the connections. Coleridge may possibly have had this in mind.

3. William Wordsworth, *The Prelude*, Book 7 lines 521–522; edited J. C. Maxwell (Penguin, 1986).
4. William Wordsworth, *The Fourteen-Book Prelude*, edited by W. J. B. Owen (Cornell University Press, 1985), pp. 786–789.
5. Chandler, *Wordsworth's Second Nature*, pp. 25–27.
6. Wordsworth's interrelations with the concept of revolution have been explicated not only in Chandler's *Wordsworth's Second Nature* but also in Alan Liu's *Wordsworth, The Sense of History* (Stanford University Press, 1989). Both books share an important assumption with this study: that the literary does not merely reflect history; rather, through articulation, literature creates a sense of history.
7. Simon Schama, *Citizens: A History of the French Revolution* (Knopf, 1989), p. 6.
8. Burke records the Druids' respect for oaks and forests in general in his *English History*, in *Works* (Little, Brown, 1866) 7:183; subsequent references to this edition are cited in the text as *Works (1866)*. Druids are associated with the Britons, displaced to Britain's Celtic fringes, and hence Wordsworth's metaphor may also delicately suggest Burke's Irishness; Burke himself, of course, as an Irish Protestant, would deny being a Celt.
9. The extent to which Burke saw freedom as an innate right in the tradition of John Locke has been the subject of considerable debate. Leo Strauss sees an important philosophical departure in Burke's thought in the replacement of a doctrine of natural right by historical right; others (B. T. Wilkins, for example) have insisted that Burke did believe in natural rights. See Leo Strauss, *Natural Right and History* (University of Chicago Press, 1953), p. 304; B. T. Wilkins, *The Problem of Burke's Political Philosophy* (Clarendon, 1967). Burke's *English History* does not contradict the possibility that humans have the right to be free, but since laws are contractual, in a barbarous state of society, individuals must surrender these freedoms to survive. In the *Reflections*, Burke notes, "Government is not made in virtue of natural rights, which may and do exist in total independence of it." In *Writings and Speeches* (Oxford, 1989) 8:110.
10. William Wordsworth, *The Salisbury Plain Poems*, edited by Stephen Gill (Cornell University Press, 1975), p. 38.
11. Some of the French delegates at least, notably the Girondists, would have denied that they disregarded history, claiming a precedent for their ideas in the ancient Athenian and Roman republics.
12. Burke, *Writings and Speeches* 8:119.
13. Carl B. Cone, *Burke and the Nature of Politics: The Age of the French Revolution* (University of Kentucky Press, 1964), p. 298.
14. Richard Price, "A Discourse on the Love of our Country" (1790), pp. 39–40.
15. Stanley Ayling, *Edmund Burke, His Life and Opinions* (John Murray, 1988), pp. 197, 204.
16. Burke, *Writings* 8:54. Following references to the *Reflections* are cited in the text.

17. This parallel does not withstand close scrutiny. England had not been a democracy in Commonwealth times, and had never become an anarchy. Imposed upon Burke's British historical model, then, would appear to be a reading of the collapse of the Athenian and Roman Republics. England moreover had been developing a powerful, organized army before the execution of Charles I; although spasmodically at war with the rest of Europe, France did not strictly speaking become a military state until the rise of Napoleon, several years after the execution of Louis XVI.
18. Burke, "Letter to a Member of the National Assembly," in *Writings* 8:309.
19. Edmund Burke, *An Appeal from the New to the Old Whigs*, in *Works (1866)* 4:97–101. Following references in the text are to this edition.
20. Edmund Burke, *First Letter on a Regicide Peace*. In *Writings and Speeches* 9:190–191.
21. "Political Conditions and Prospects of France," *Quarterly Review* 43 (May 1830), p. 239. Burke himself may have been influenced by Price's address to the "friends of freedom," "Behold, the light you have struck next, after setting *America* free, reflected to *France*, and there kindled into a blaze that lays despotism to ashes, and warms and illuminates *Europe*!" Price, "Discourse," p. 40.
22. Ibid., pp. 104, 106.
23. Sir James Mackintosh, *Vindiciae Gallicae*, 3rd edition (1791), p. 195.
24. Ibid., pp. 305–306.
25. Paine, *Rights of Man*, 2:192; 1:12.
26. Catherine Macaulay, "Observations," pp. 35–36.
27. Eli Halévy, *The Growth of Philosophic Radicalism* (1928; Kelley and Millman, n.d.), p. 184.
28. Mackintosh, *Vindiciae Gallicae*, pp. 327–328.
29. Thomas Babington Macaulay was to be closest to a new Mackintosh, but only after 1832, when Reform was safely achieved in Britain and Mackintosh was dead.
30. Manchester, with the coming of the factory age now the second largest city in Britain, was not represented at all. Other areas, notably Cornwall, where the Crown was the largest property-owner, had several boroughs and a comparatively small population. This example is addressed by Burke in his *Reflections*, where Burke's constitutional justification is that the king and the lords are several and joint "securities for the equality of each district ... the very inequality of representation, which is so foolishly complained of, is perhaps the very thing which prevents us from thinking or acting as members for districts" (*Writings* 8:235). Burke assumes that the needs of individuals are subsumed in the interests of the nation as a whole, yet by 1830, the interests of those whose income derived from industry and those from property were diverging. The Whigs were in a strong position to argue the reverse of Burke: that the interests of the Tory-dominated House of Commons no longer coincided with the interests of the nation.

31. Henry Brougham makes a particular point of this in his first major assessment of the "Late Revolution in France," *Edinburgh Review* 52 (October 1830), p. 5.
32. *The Times* (August 3, 1830), leader.
33. *Hansard's Parliamentary Debates*, 3rd Series, (December 20, 1830), p. 1388.
34. *The Times* (July 20, 1830).
35. Habermas dates the years before the French Revolution as the point in British cultural development when the public sphere began "casting itself loose as a forum in which the private people, come together to form a public, readied themselves to compel public authority to legitimate itself before public opinion." Jürgen Habermas, *The Structural Transformation of the Public Sphere* (MIT Press, 1989), p. 25.
36. The *Edinburgh* and *Quarterly* thus replicate Mannheim's observation that the French Revolution polarized progressive and conservative thought, and that the conservative position of necessity creates itself in response to progressivism. Mannheim, *Essays*, p. 79.
37. The phrase is capitalized in John Fullarton's essay "Parliamentary Reform," *Quarterly Review* 44 (February 1831), p. 595.
38. Francis Levison Gower, *Hansard* (March 1, 1831), p. 1150.
39. *The Wellesley Index to Victorian Periodicals* attributes the article to the travel and miscellaneous writer Basil Hall on the basis of statements in personal correspondence.
40. "Political Conditions and Prospects of France," pp. 215–216.
41. Ibid., p. 224.
42. Ibid., p. 240.
43. Even before the Battle of Waterloo Croker was in France collecting materials for a history. In 1816, John Murray offered him 2500 guineas for a three-volume study; Sir Robert Peel also encouraged Croker to write such a work in the 1830s. See *The Croker Papers*, edited by Louis J. Jennings, 2nd edition (John Murray, 1885) 1:57; 1:93; 2:276.
44. Deane, *The French Revolution and Enlightenment in England*, p. 36.
45. The most notable examples are Shelley's Preface to "Adonais" and Byron's "Who killed Jack Keats?" Neither knew at the time that Croker was the author of the *Quarterly* piece. In fact, Lockhart's attack on *Endymion* in *Blackwood's Magazine* was more sustained, and this may explain why at one time the Tennyson review was wrongly attributed to Lockhart.
46. John Wilson Croker, "Poems by Alfred Tennyson," *Quarterly Review* 49 (April 1833), p. 82.
47. See *The Croker Papers* 2:229.
48. In October 1830, for example, he wrote to the editor of another publication generally sympathetic to the Tory cause, William Blackwood, to request that *Blackwood's Magazine* show more solidarity with the Tory leaders Wellington and Peel (*Croker Papers* 2:72–73).
49. Robert Southey, "Conspiracy de Babeuf," *Quarterly Review* 45 (April 1831), p. 209.

50. John Fullarton, "Progress of Misgovernment," *Quarterly Review* 46 (January 1832), p. 599.
51. See, for example, *The Times*, August 4, 6 and 9, 1830.
52. John Wilson Croker, "French Novels," *Quarterly Review* 56 (April 1836), pp. 65–66, italics the *Quarterly*'s.
53. See Archibald Alison, *My Life and Writings* (Blackwood, 1883) 1:314–318.
54. John Wilson Croker, "The Present State of France," *Quarterly Review* 52 (August 1834), p. 266. Cited henceforward in the text as "State of France."
55. John Wilson Croker, "Sarrans's Louis-Philippe et la Contre-Révolution de 1830," *Quarterly Review* 52 (November 1834), p. 567.
56. Ibid., p. 569.
57. John Wilson Croker, "Robespierre," *Quaterly Review* 54 (September 1835), p. 517. Following references are cited in the text as "Robespierre."
58. Henry, Lord Brougham, "The Late Revolution in France," *Edinburgh Review* 52 (October 1830), p. 1.
59. Ibid., pp. 23–24.
60. Lord Mahon, "Russell's Causes of the French Revolution," *Quarterly Review* 49 (April 1833), p. 152.
61. Lord John Russell, *The Causes of the French Revolution* (Longmans, 1832), p. 201.
62. *Hansard* (March 1, 1831), p. 1142.
63. E.g. Macaulay: "We drive over to the side of revolution those we shut out from power (*Hansard* 2:1193, March 1, 1831); Russell's assertion on March 22 that Charles X was expelled because he failed to make concessions (*Hansard* 3:801).
64. *Hansard* (September 20, 1831), p. 305.
65. Ibid., p. 310.
66. This point had been made by William Hazlitt even before the 1830 Revolution in his *Life of Napoleon Buonaparte*; Hazlitt maintained that in fact the Terror itself might have been avoided had foreign governments, including Britain, been less determined to oppose France (Hazlitt, *Works* [Dent, 1933–35] 13:111; 13:164–165).
67. Macaulay, "Sir James Mackintosh," in *Works* 8:433.
68. Ibid., 8:431.

Chapter 2
After Reform: Conservatism and Carlyle

At first sight, Croker and the other would-be Burkes of the post-Reform period were fighting for a lost cause, the traditional tory view of the historic consequences of human nature seeming out of place in the world of progressive improvement of the Whig party of 1832. In the eighteen months after the passing of the First Parliamentary Reform Act, the Whigs enacted legislation that demonstrated that they were a party with clear political goals. The abolition of slavery in British territories, the first Factory Act restricting the employment of children, and the first state education grant all declared that the Whigs were prepared to make matters which had previously been seen as those of individual conscience a national responsibility.

This sense of national responsibility extended to history. In 1830, Sir Harris Nicolas had published his "Observations on the State of Historical Literature," in which he lamented the state of British historical records. Nicolas succeeded in winning Whig support for his cause, the result being the establishment of the Public Records Commission in 1836 under the chairmanship of Charles Buller, whose tutor had been the young Thomas Carlyle.[1] In the long term, this aided the cataloguing and preservation of British historical records that enabled later historical study to become more systematic. More immediately, it contributed to a growing sense that serious history was based upon documentation, and British writing on the French Revolution in the 1830s reflects this belief that history could not, as in the era of Burke, be dependent on imprecise parallels, but should be founded on material evidence.

Before the establishment of the Public Records Commission by the Whigs, however, the Tories had a brief taste of government. By the end of 1834, the Whigs were unable to maintain the unity of vision that pushed through Reform, and Conservative commentators gleefully noted that the new Girondists, with all their good intentions, had led their country on the same course to destruction as their French forerunners: if the Tories were now the Conservatives, a popular expression ran, the Whigs were the Destructives.[2] With the Whigs in disarray, the King asked Sir Robert Peel and the Conservatives to form a government.

As Peel shrewdly realized, if the Tory party was to continue to play a role in a political climate where progress was promoted as a moral virtue, some acknowledgment of change was imperative. Tory history thus required reconsideration of the argument that all political change inevitably leads to revolution. Accepting the King's invitation to form a government in December 1834, Peel announced that he considered "the Reform Bill a final and irrevocable settlement of a great constitutional question, a settlement which no friend to the peace and welfare of this country would attempt to disturb either by direct or by insidious means."[3] Peel's language ("settlement" replaces "revolution") is carefully chosen to suggest that by this time, any attempt to reverse reform is the course more likely to spark a revolution. Moreover, as Croker pointed out, that Peel felt it necessary to justify his personal position to his constituents at all was evidence that the dynamics of party politics were changing, and representatives becoming accountable to their constituents.[4]

Some Tories, including "Ultra-Tories" who continued to oppose all forms of constitutional change, continued to read history as a battle against the corruption of progress. Others, however, including Peel himself, as he told his friend Croker soon after this ministry collapsed in Spring 1835, were interested in reanalyzing the first French Revolution.[5] Was its course of events inevitable, or the product of certain historical accidents? At first consideration, the latter option is, for a tory historian, almost blasphemous: if history is the product of an ordered universe, then accident cannot be a part of it. At the same time, if the goal of tory history is to prevent the recurrence of specified patterns of events—and this surely is the goal of even the most declaredly Ultra-Tory history, that of Archibald Alison—then human agency, with all its weaknesses, remains a force to be reckoned with. If one human link in the unfolding of the French Revolution—for example Louis XVI, or Marie Antoinette, or Robespierre, or, as was especially argued during the 1830s, Mirabeau—had been different in action or character, would or could the entire outcome of events be different?

Given this philosophical concern, I shall in this chapter discuss Thomas Carlyle's *The French Revolution, A History* as a form of tory history. This is not to suggest that the political creed of the work can be aligned with Tory party politics of this period, but rather, I attempt to explore the historical problem with which Carlyle wrestles in this text, that of inevitability. To dismiss Carlyle's view of history either as patterned entirely by fate, predestination, or the higher powers, or alternatively as simply idiosyncratic is, I believe, to ignore the resonances of the place of history in the Britain of the 1830s. Especially in the new debate over the role of Mirabeau, Carlyle neither submitted unquestioningly to the concept of an all-ruling destiny, nor divorced himself from contemporary concerns. Nevertheless, in what is perhaps the most significant British work on the French Revolution of the entire period of this study, Carlyle was to present the historian as a new kind of prophet: not merely repeating Burkean messages of doom and fragmentation, but also, by visualizing history an analogy to the contemporary world as well as part of the essential continuity of the human spirit, creating a sense of what was lacking. Once it is noted that Carlyle's was not the only full-length study of the first French Revolution during this period, the full impact of its historical and philosophical ambition may be better appreciated. The traditional tory history of Sir Archibald Alison provides a means of seeing Carlyle's reading of the French Revolution in perspective.

The Ultra-Tory Version

After the Reform Bill was passed in 1832, most Tories followed Peel's lead in accepting Reform as irreversible. The *History of Europe* of Sir Archibald Alison (1792–1867) was an exception in continuing to argue the immediacy of the problem of revolution. The difference in tone may be seen by contrasting Alison's version with a slightly earlier history of the French Revolution by a prominent Scottish Tory, the introductory chapters of Sir Walter Scott's *Life of Napoleon Buonaparte*.

Scott's massive book falls outside the scope of the study both in terms of time (it was published in 1827) and in emphasis (here Napoleon will be discussed only as an emanence of revolution, rather than as treated by Scott and his direct contemporary William Hazlitt, where the French Revolution is a prelude to Napoleon). Scott's view of the Revolution nevertheless deserves some comment. Scott takes the typical approach of the tory historian in conceding that some reforms were necessary in France, but argues that the failure of Louis XVI and his ministers and army to act with "firmness" before losing all authority led to the excesses of the Terror. He seems uncertain, however, that events in France are directly relevant to events in Britain. In Scott's depiction, France, both under the *Ancien Régime*, when the court was at the mercy of powerful women, and during the Revolution, when women also played a prominent role, is not "manly." Louis XVI, who received no "manly defence" from his subjects was saintly but unassertive, while Jacobins such as Robespierre were dastardly cowards.[6] Britain, it would seem, is more appropriately "manly," and Scott cautiously implies that France's lack of manliness is caused by lack of respect for traditional authority and especially by the Roman Catholic religion (the book was published while Roman Catholic emancipation was being debated). Hence even the classic tory dictum that the French Revolution should be regarded as "one of those dreadful prodigies by which Providence confounds our reason, and shows what human nature can be brought to, when the restraints of morality and religion are cast aside"[7] does not entirely remove the impression that France is very different from Britain.

Writing five years later, Archibald Alison never suggests such distinct cultural separation. While analyzing French revolution, Alison simultaneously presents British political reform as a threat not just to tory ideals but to the entire concept of the British constitution. Alison was to continue his history to the end of the Napoleonic era, but my focus will be on the first part originally published in 1833, the section that, like Carlyle's version, covers the French Revolution up to the year 1795. In both research and presentation, Alison's account of the French Revolution is inferior to Carlyle's. To dismiss it on the basis of the first edition alone, however, would be to underestimate its impact. In his conviction that his message to Britain was just as urgent as Burke's had been in his time, Alison constantly reworked his book, revising the text many times as he came upon new sources, and substantially improving on the documentation of his first edition. The result was a popular, although not a critical, success.[8]

In his autobiography, posthumously-published as *Some Account of My Life and Writings* (1883), Alison recalls the nation's ever-growing "passion for innovation" when he began writing his history on January

1, 1829. The continuing discussion of constitutional changes had "awakened gloomy presentiments in my mind. I saw that a revolution was approaching in Great Britain, and that the means of resisting it did not exist in the nation."[9] Alison portrays himself, then, as being forced by a sense of moral duty into Burke's role of interpreting the French Revolution for his compatriots.

This account moreover places Alison's commencement of his project exactly one week after he had been actively involved in the Crown's prosecution of the new threat to social order, William Burke.[10] Like Edmund Burke, William Burke was an Irishman. With his partner William Hare, he murdered numerous poor Edinburgh residents in order to sell their bodies for dissection. Ironically, Alison states that he learned from the second Burke that even the worst humans are not merely "monsters." Personally observing the mass-murderer's concern for his common-law wife, Alison realized that even Robespierre might have had redeeming features, and that "'characters of imperfect goodness' constitute the great majority of the human race."[11] Thus the French Revolution was not an isolated monstrosity, but one that the strengths and weaknesses of human nature could repeat.

In 1831–1832, Alison wrote a series of papers on Parliamentary Reform and the French Revolution for *Blackwood's Magazine*. The evolving focus of these papers as the series developed exemplifies the blurring in historical perspective adopted by British commentators on French Revolutions. The first two papers in the series discuss the "Late French Revolution" (the July Revolution) within the context of its broader historical significance. The recent events in France were proof, Alison wrote in his January 1831 statement of the principles of tory history, "that the experience of the past is totally lost both upon individuals and nations."[12] In his first articles, Alison stresses not the bloodiness of the first French Revolution, but rather the initial lack of blood—his point being that the July Revolution, and British Parliamentary Reform, might at first appear under control, but would in time give way to "democratic ambition." "Human nature," Alison notes in a phrase recalling More in Southey's *Colloquies*, "is still the same" (*Blackwood's* 29:37).

These first two papers were published when the matter of Parliamentary Reform had clearly become a pressing one, but before the introduction of Lord John Russell's Reform Bill on March 1, 1831. As early as February, Alison asserted that "Neckar" (Louis XVI's minister the Swiss financier Jacques Necker) had caused the French Revolution by persuading the king to permit the widening of the franchise (*Blackwood's* 29:177–178). When the question of reform became more urgent, however, Alison changed his focus from the 1830 Revolution to the parallels between the first French Revolution and the progress of Reform: indeed, the editorial title of the series changed to "On the French Revolution, and Parliamentary Reform," until establishing itself in the second half of 1831 with the emphasis of most significance to the readers of the period, "On Parliamentary Reform and the French Revolution." The warning is a terrible one: Britain, in its "slavish imitation of French democracy," is following an example which led to "the prostration of thirty millions of men under the guillotine of the Convention" (*Blackwood's* 30:284). Alison metaphorically depicts the entire nation as being under the guillotine, but the superficial impression may be given that he is being literal, and thirty million people died.[13] When Alison moves his arguments without warning from the Reform Bills to the July Revolution to the English Revolution to the Reign of Terror the effect is often confusing, but the merging of one event into another coincides with his theory of history: that the consistency of human nature and natural law cause the same decisions to lead to the same results.

Alison's historical theory is simple: political change creates social instability, which in turn causes a total disregard of traditional morality, and finally results in anarchy. The French Revolution demonstrates this pattern in its most monstrous form. The way to avoid a similar fate is to accept existing structures as the work of providence, and not interfere.

This does not necessarily imply that no human change at all is possible: many convinced Tories were prepared to consider some reform in parliamentary representation justified on historical grounds, provided that the goal was to restore traditional balance that had been lost through changes in demographics. Identifying with the Ultra-Tories, Alison was less certain about conceding even this historical premise, but his book nevertheless contains some reference to long-term change. Given Alison's fear of what he terms "the terrible evils of precipitate innovation," his belief in evolution may at first sight appear anomalous, more in accord with the whig view of history as progress. A generation before Darwin's *Origin of Species*, Alison reveals a faith in evolution, as opposed to revolution:

> It is by slow degrees, and imperceptible additions, that all the great changes of nature are accomplished. Vegetation, commencing with lichens, swells to the riches and luxuriance of the forest; continents, the seat of empires, and the

abode of millions, are formed by the deposit of innumerable rills; animal life, springing from the torpid vitality of shell-fish, rises to the energy and power of man. It is by similar steps, and as slow a progress, that the great fabric of society is formed.[14]

Evolution, for Alison, means a world ordered at Nature's pace. Just as the world undergoes changes over long periods of time, so the body-politic must be allowed to develop. Human intervention in forcing such change is a sin against divine order, and, as Alison attempts to show in his study of the French Revolution, incurs divine justice.[15]

Having emphasized the slow process by which "the habits of freedom" are acquired, Alison suggests that France is in this particular respect different from Britain. Like Burke, he commences his history by refuting the parallels between the Glorious Revolution of 1688 and the French Revolution of 1789. While, he argues, human nature is essentially consistent, English history, in the form of key events including the revolutions, Magna Carta, and particularly the institution of Protestantism, has caused its citizens to evolve an idea of freedom which includes "veneration for antiquity" (*Europe [1841]* 1:41). In contrast, French history has not given the same opportunity to the people of France, who have only partially overcome "the slavish habits of Roman servitude" (1:61), and for whom any change would involve not respect for history, but rather "innovation."

Alison nevertheless has a problem. Since he concedes that "the reign of Louis XV is the most deplorable in French history" (1:76), some change would appear to be necessary. He thus argues that the initial error was not in conceding the necessity of change, but in dividing political power from property, a symbolic guillotining of the nation. The meeting of the *Tiers État* on May 5, 1789 is labelled "the first day of the French Revolution" (1:95). Alison points out that the representatives were mainly enthusiastic young men who in Britain would be outside the party system since they lacked "the only restraints on human passion—knowledge, age, property, and children" (1:99).

Having demonstrated the effects of broadening the franchise, Alison proceeds to show how the hopes created by this change in the structure of power led to the storming of the Bastille, the National Convention, the execution of the monarch, and the Reign of Terror. Yet even though the *Tiers État* might seem to provide a parallel with a potential reformed House of Commons, Alison further suggests that the more well-intentioned and philosophical leaders of this period provide a warning to Britain. The goals of the initial leaders of the Revolution were, he stresses, philanthropic. The Girondists in particular should prompt caution in his more idealistic British readers. Inspired by "philanthropic principles" and "patriotic feeling," they had violated those "laws of Nature" dictating that once the structure of society has been overturned, those restrained by principle will inevitably succumb to those who have no moral values and spur on the mob, until these too cause their own downfall: "A horse, maddened by terror, does not rush more certainly to its own destruction, than the populace, when excited by revolutionary ambition. It is this law of Nature which provides its slow but certain punishment" (*Europe [1841]* 2:1–2). Alison thus presents the fall of the Girondists, and subsequently of the Dantonists, as part of this process of disintegration, the former group being particularly significant in presenting a parallel with the intention of the British Reformers.

To demonstrate the inevitable course of the laws of Nature, Alison dwells on the gorier aspects of the Revolution, in which the body of the state is portrayed not as expiring of natural causes, but as torn apart. The forlornness of the hope that the body-politic of the *Ancien Régime* might be resuscitated is seen perhaps most effectively in Alison's description of the desecration of the corpses of the old French monarchs,[16] symbolic of the radical rejection of history:

> It seemed as if the glories of antiquity were forgotten, or sought to be buried in oblivion. The tomb of [the crusader knight] Du Guesclin shared the same fate as that of Louis XIV. The skulls of monarchs and heroes were tossed about like footballs by the profane multitude; like the grave-diggers in Hamlet, they made a jest of the lips before which nations had trembled. (*Europe [1841]* 2:45)

In the early 1830s, the threat of a similar destruction of history and tradition in Britain clearly seemed real to Alison, and consequently he emphasizes its typological significance. The French Revolution has

> conferred a lasting blessing on mankind by exposing the consequences of hasty innovation, and writing in characters of blood the horrors of anarchy on the page of history. Let us hope that the dreadful lesson has not been taught in vain. ... (1:138)

Even after his own prophecies concerning British Parliamentary Reform had been ignored, Alison refused to accept the whig doctrine of historical progress that assumed that the French Revolution was inevitable. Refuting the claims of Adolphe Thiers, F. A. Mignet and others that the French Revolution was a necessary phase in such progress, Alison argues that it could have been avoided. The inevitability is not in the connection between necessary change and revolution, but between human nature and moral law: "the moral law of nature, whether in nations or private men, is made to work out [vice's] deserved punishment in the efforts which it makes for its own gratification" (*Europe [1841]* 2:211).

Hence although his work was to achieve a more-than-epic length, Alison's view of the French Revolution remains essentially a morality-tale. The question remained as to whether tory history could do more than merely warn against innovation. One possibility was that once the unwise course of Revolution had been begun, a good leader might redirect the energies of the masses. Thus a consequence of the reconstruction not of history as it was known but of history as it might have been was a renewed British interest in a hitherto-neglected leader of the First French Revolution, the Comte de Mirabeau.

The Reclaiming of Mirabeau

Until the 1830s, the part played by the Comte de Mirabeau in the first French Revolution had been overshadowed by subsequent developments. Mirabeau had died in April 1791 while the revolution was still struggling to formulate a constitutional direction, leaving the field open for the so-called "Terror" of Robespierre and the Jacobins, and ultimately for the dynastic ambitions of Napoleon.[17] With the new emphasis not only in Britain but also in France on the role of documentation in history during the 1830s, however, many more materials on the French Revolution were catalogued and published, including some significant works on Mirabeau. In consequence, fresh thought was given to what had actually been achieved in Mirabeau's political and personal life. British attempts to reclaim Mirabeau as a leading inspiration not just to the French Revolution itself but to subsequent political ideas are evidence of a new attitude towards the events of forty years earlier, and to the possibility raised by Peel, that "settlement" might be an alternative for "revolution."

The numerous discussions of Mirabeau's part in the first French Revolution suggest that in the era of Louis Philippe, commentators were more comfortable with the pragmatic attitude to revolution that they attributed to him in contrast with what was still seen as the

Jacobin extremism of Robespierre or the stern idealism of the Girondists. Essays by Macaulay, Carlyle, and others in response to newly-available biographical materials prompted a reconsideration of his historical role, which in turn raised even larger philosophical questions concerning the function of individuals and freedom of human action within history.

From a nineteenth-century perspective, Mirabeau's life story reflects many of the worst aspects of France under the *Ancien Régime*. Honoré Gabriel Riquetti was born in 1749; his early life was unhappy, his family attempting to keep him from his love Sophie de Monnier even by use of imprisonment. Only when in the later 1780s he was elected to the National Assembly did his personality and talents at last find a function. Through his oratory, he rapidly became one of the most influential leaders of the Revolution, but at the time of his death on April 1 1791, attributed by many to the eighteenth-century cause of debauchery, his long-term goals were still unclear. He was certainly in negotiation with the King, and may also have been representing the interests of the Orléanist faction, possibly in return for money.[18] The first to be buried in the newly-named Panthéon, his remains were ejected during the "Terror"—a significant statement that humans can both make and unmake their gods.

From the perspective of forty years later, Mirabeau's life was a historical curiosity. The troubles of his youth were those of a world that no longer existed: even detractors of the French Revolution conceded the abuses of power during the reign of Louis XV, and the use of *lettres de cachet* as a means of imprisonment without trial that blighted his early years was no longer permissible. Mirabeau's immorality itself seemed to many in the increasingly sober 1830s the failings of an earlier age. Mirabeau, then, seemed to embody two whig principles: first, that sometimes political change was necessary, and second, that history was unrepeatable since society had "progressed" beyond such abuses.

Alternatively, Mirabeau could be seen in a less deterministic light. If human beings have the freedom to influence the course of events, his life might not merely symptomize the state of French society, but present the possibility that he could have reshaped it. Had Mirabeau not died, the course of the Revolution might have been different. Louis XVI might have been spared, Robespierre and the Reign of Terror would have been avoided, and France might then have become a constitutional monarchy. In effect, he would have achieved France's 1830 pattern of government in 1789—or he might even be seen as like Sir

Robert Peel, controlling the damage already done by revolution. In such a reading, Mirabeau is not "the man of his time," but rather the potential creator of an alternative history, one that validates the events of the July Revolution of 1830 (and for British observers their own political situation) as the "correct" historical pattern.

Neither of these readings is threatening from the perspective of the 1830s. Mirabeau was either created by historical circumstances that no longer exist, or represents a hypothetical option cut off by history (or destiny) before it could come to pass, to be satisfactorily reformulated as the *status quo* forty years later. A less comforting option is to identify the "type" of Mirabeau the man and statesman and apply it to the present. For Britons, the effect is doubly disturbing when the prospect of a British Mirabeau is considered. Perhaps, like Peel, he might encourage freedom of thought and aid in the process of constitutional reform; or perhaps, like the Whigs, he might lose control of reform and leave the nation in the hands of the mob. In various degrees, all three of these historical approaches—Mirabeau as symbol of a past age, as historical alternative, and as historical example by providing the type of a great (or misguided) man—inform British readings of his significance during the 1830s.

At a time of new emphasis on authentic sources for history, an important impulse to Mirabeau's reconsideration was more biographical information. Most readily available to British readers were Étienne Dumont's *Souvenirs sur Mirabeau*, of which an English translation appeared in 1832; and *Mémoires biographiques, littéraires, et politiques de Mirabeau*, a massive collection of papers written by or relating to Mirabeau edited by Mirabeau's illegitimate son Gabriel Lucas de Montigny, which appeared in 1834–38. These works attracted the attention of two emerging writers on historical and political subjects, Thomas Carlyle and Thomas Babington Macaulay. Macaulay reviewed Dumont's book for the *Edinburgh Review* in 1832, while Carlyle's essay, composed by mid-1836 before he wrote the last volume of *The French Revolution, A History* and appearing in the *London and Westminster Review* in 1837, focused on Lucas de Montigny (the editor John Stuart Mill added a footnote dissociating himself from Carlyle's belittling of the Benthamite Dumont). The two essays have a claim to interest not only for what they say about Mirabeau in their endeavors to place his achievements in broader historical and philosophical terms, but also for what they do not say.

Macaulay's essay is declaredly time-specific, having been completed and published immediately after the passing of the Reform Bill in

1832. As a leading supporter of the Bill in the House of Commons, he had followed the whig party in citing the nobility's failure to reform and compromise as a cause of the French Revolution. This historical view was disputed by the Tories, the debate begun in Parliament continuing in the reviews. Dumont's book had earlier been critiqued by Archibald Alison, who had maintained that Mirabeau's life demonstrates the impossibility of giving a nation a new constitution, and rejected Macaulay's assertion in the House of Commons that the French nobility should not have resisted change.[19]

Conversely, with reform safely passed, Macaulay is more open in declaring political change to be a positive revolution than he had been in the House of Commons on March 2, 1831, when he had called reform "our best security against a revolution." Macaulay begins his essay by stating his respect for Dumont, also paying tribute to Jeremy Bentham, for whom Dumont had worked in an editorial function. He then discusses both the theory of revolution in general, the condition of France under the *Ancien Régime*, and the state of post-Reform Britain, and only then turns to Mirabeau.[20] Macaulay's seemingly limited focus on Mirabeau in an essay bearing his name places the revolutionary within his historical context: Mirabeau was a product of the *Ancien Régime*, and his life proved the necessity of its overthrow to continue the progress of history.[21]

As a complement to this message, the anglophilia of Dumont's book doubtless attracted Macaulay. Dumont's ostensible reason for working with Mirabeau was that he hoped that the French National Assembly would champion constitutionalism in his native Geneva.[22] While Barbara Luttrell has argued that Mirabeau had a low opinion of the British constitutional system and was very little influenced by it in the changes he endeavoured to introduce in France,[23] Dumont, an admirer of the English constitution and the English character,[24] gives a different impression. Dumont states that unlike most of his peers, who repeatedly asserted that they wanted "nothing English" (*Recollections of Mirabeau*, p. 133), Mirabeau believed that continued friendship with Britain was necessary (p. 208). Dumont's final verdict on Mirabeau, however, is the strongest statement of the British connection: although his character and historical circumstances were such that Mirabeau never had definite longterm plan, he "was desirous of giving to his country, a constitution as nearly resembling that of England as local circumstances would admit" (p. 234). Had he lived long enough to follow the British constitution as a plan, Dumont suggests, the entire revolution might have been different: Mirabeau was "the only man of whom it may be thought, that if providence had spared his life, the destinies of France would have taken another course" (p. 235).[25]

But although this conditional presentation of an alternative history privileges the British constitution, it was incompatible with Macaulay's reading of revolution. In "Mirabeau" he concedes that contemporaries of the first French Revolution might have "regarded it with unmixed aversion and horror," but argues that from the broader historical perspective, "the evil was temporary and the good durable."[26] Even if Mirabeau had been able to control the Jacobins, the historical necessity of the French Revolution is such that this avoidance of bloodshed would have held back human progress.

Mirabeau hence cannot represent for Macaulay the French Revolution that was not. In a continuation of Dumont's depiction of an anglicized hero, however, he can represent a different form of revolutionary: one who combines the ability to judge popular needs and feelings of the charismatic Whig democrat John Wilkes, with a respect for existing institutions of the cautious Tory statesman the Earl of Chatham.

For some Tories, though, this was insufficient praise. Macaulay was criticized, notably in two scurrilous essays in *Fraser's Magazine*, for accepting Dumont's implication that since he himself had written many of Mirabeau's speeches, Mirabeau's greatness is almost a committee product, thereby diminishing a man who, the *Fraser's* essayist's *alter ego* Sir Charles Botherall contends, was greater than the compound of Wilkes and Chatham since he "soared far above the minister, and never sunk to the standard of the Common Councilman." In these two pieces, Dumont is called a "liar and a scoundrel" and a "paltry humbug,"[27] while Macaulay is called, among other less repeatable epithets, a "sucking statesman."[28] The first of the articles concludes with a lengthy comparison between Mirabeau and Byron.[29] Thus while disagreeing with Macaulay, the *Fraser's* essayist simultaneously agrees with him by claiming Mirabeau as more like a Briton than a Frenchman. Certainly, in spite of his eighteenth-century characteristics, Mirabeau has the advantage over figures such as Robespierre in displaying "manliness." The stated purpose of Lucas de Montigny's account of Mirabeau's persistent erection, which was even visible for several hours after his death, for example, is to explain that his sexual appetite was physiologically-based. Yet it simultaneously confirms the dead hero's virility, a "manly" quality that the British believed (or tried to believe) was lacking in many of the French. Mirabeau is not, like the

French Revolution, completely alien to the British way of thinking, but can be understood as a true man.

Even granted that part of the reason for the attack on Macaulay is simply because he is a Whig, the passion expressed in the *Fraser's* articles seems disproportionately intense. It seems reasonable to assume that despite the exaggerated satirical tone, the writer is genuinely indignant at what he perceives as an attack on one of the greatest men of the age, even to the extent of misreading Macaulay. Macaulay's Mirabeau, far from being a Byron, is an 1832 Reformer—and the *Fraser's* writer's jibe that Macaulay cannot criticize Mirabeau's ugliness because he himself, like his associates Brougham, Durham, and others, is an ugly man, misses the point. Macaulay nowhere suggests that Mirabeau's ugliness is to his detriment, but subtly identifies with it when he implies that physically unappealing men with a gift for oratory may change their nations.

In contrast, for Thomas Carlyle, Mirabeau's attraction is that he is "an Original Man."[30] Carlyle rejects the the typology of those who seek to understand Mirabeau by analyzing his similarities to other men, yet retains the emphasis on masculinity. If Macaulay's essay on Mirabeau may be considered an early exploration of the significance of revolution that was to be developed in his *History of England*, the relationship of Carlyle's "Mirabeau" with his *French Revolution, A History*, also published in 1837, is more problematic. As John P. Farrell has observed, Carlyle says relatively little in the longer work about Mirabeau's "bizarre career prior to 1789."[31] This might suggest that Carlyle assumes that the story has already been much told—or that this essay can be seen as a companion piece. It is Carlyle's opportunity to explore a unique human being in more detail, and to wrestle further with the problem of historical determinism as suggested by Mirabeau's life and death.

As a lowland Scot, Carlyle had been born into a Calvinist tradition, and the concept of a predestined universe, in which the deity has predetermined the entire course of history and thus freedom of individual human action is an appearance rather than a reality, was a part of his heritage. Yet to characterize Carlyle, who had rejected orthodox Christianity some years previously, as consistently determinist may be too simple: his writings might instead be interpreted as an exploration of what human beings, and not divinities, can contribute to history. Carlyle's Calvinist background may have attracted him temperamentally towards the Hegelian reading of history as a general progress towards freedom directed by the divine Will; yet a distinction exists between Hegel's sense of the Will and the Calvinist conception of a personal God implicated in the minutiae of human affairs. The French Revolution, which by the 1830s had become monumentalized as the most cataclysmic "event" of modern history, mirrors this distinction by representing a similar dichotomy between the "individual" impacting history and an event of such magnitude that individuals cannot significantly affect its course. In *The French Revolution*, Carlyle frequently portrays the revolutionaries not as individuals, but as a mass that almost takes on a personality of its own. If Hayden White is correct in classing Carlyle among what he terms "Formist" historians for whom "the uniqueness of the different agents, agencies, and acts which make up the 'event' to be explained" is central to the historical inquiry,[32] the nature of the "uniqueness" creates a difference in approach between the two works. In *The French Revolution*, an entire historical event is explored virtually as though this unique phenomenon itself were a personality; in "Mirabeau," Carlyle chooses to focus on a unique individual who is never entirely contained by the narrative of history.

Carlyle thus notes of the French Revolution, "A greater work, it is often said, was never done in history by men so small." Robespierre is cited as a "Formula of a man" who under other historical circumstances would have been insignificant.[33] Rather than concluding from this that the Revolution was an act of destiny, however, Carlyle names three "original men" who stand out in the history of the French Revolution: Napoleon, Danton, and Mirabeau. Napoleon's story has already been exhaustively told; "public opinion" is not yet ready to rehabilitate the fiery democrat Danton; but the time is right to reconsider "the far most interesting, best-gifted of this trio," Mirabeau (*Works* 28:412).

Carlyle's essay is ostensibly a review of Mirabeau's son's edition of family papers. While Carlyle asserts that the eight volumes by the self-styled "Adopted Son" can only be written of "in the disparaging sense" since Lucas de Montigny has "lent himself so resolutely to the washing of his hero white" (*Works* 28:413), the fragmentary nature of this narrative may have appealed to the creator of Teufelsdröckh and the admirer of John Paul. Carlyle is certainly intrigued by the stories of Mirabeau's grandfather, father, and uncle, and his early struggles against his father's authority. Indeed, just as much of Macaulay's essay does not discuss Mirabeau at all, Carlyle devotes only a fleeting two or three pages to Mirabeau's achievements after the summoning of the States-General at the close of 1788. Lucas de Montigny's text, Carlyle's essay, and Mirabeau's life are all alike in seeming to lack the appropriate closure.

If, then, Mirabeau was a great man, what was the nature of his greatness? Carlyle's concluding observations suggest that Mirabeau is both unique and typical in how he used his abilities:

> in these centuries men are not born demi-gods and perfect characters, but imperfect ones, and mere blamable men; men, namely, environed with such shortcomings and confusion of their own, and then with such adscititious scandal and misjudgment (got in the work they did), that they resemble less demi-gods than a sort of god-devils ... (*Works* 28:479)

Mirabeau's imperfections, which unlike the revolutionary tendencies of many other great man have not been given a veneer of respectability by history, are evidence of the mixed nature of humanity. As Carlyle proceeds to state, individuals such as Mirabeau are "made" by the Upper Powers; yet within the portion of life allotted to them, it is left to "blamable men" of this kind to make history.

Carlyle's reading of history can therefore be seen as less determinist than Macaulay's in that as far as humans can detect, history may seem almost an accident. Retelling the story of Mirabeau's grandfather, who was severely wounded in battle but who was preserved from death by being covered by a camp-kettle, Carlyle points out "How nearly, at this moment, it was all over with the Mirabeaus" (*Works* 28:425). Ultimately, Carlyle retreats from what in *The French Revolution* he calls the *"would-have-beens,"*[34] but he himself has raised the idea that history might be different, and that one man can change the course of historical events. Carlyle is already embarked on the direction in which his subsequent writings on heroes were to take him: that even if the "Upper Powers" initially "make" human beings what they are, the greatest of humans leave their mark on history.

Although unquestionably they created the British debate over Mirabeau, the periodicals did not have the final word on his significance. The extent of new interest in his life and actions during the reign of Louis Philippe is demonstrated by his inclusion in two texts by women. Mary Shelley included a life of Mirabeau in her collection of essays on "Eminent Literary and Scientific Men of France" that she wrote anonymously for Dionysius Lardner's *Cabinet Cyclopaedia* in the 1830s.[35] The choice confirms both topical interest in the statesman's life, and also Shelley's personal interest, for although Mirabeau's contribution to literature remains in dispute, the biography is equal in length to that of Rousseau, and only exceeded by that of Voltaire. Whereas other commentators presented Mirabeau as a Byron figure, Mary Shelley's version is perhaps more like her dead husband Percy. The essay suggests that she was one of the few Britons to have read Mirabeau's extremely frank letters to Sophie de Monnier. Possibly influenced by the editor Pierre Manuel's presentation of this sexual freedom as a mirror of political freedom,[36] Shelley asserts that Sophie, described in whig terms as "the hapless victim of a depraved state of society," regarded herself spiritually as Mirabeau's true wife.[37] Shelley's sympathy for the predicament of Sophie de Monnier may suggest some identification with her: as Mary Godwin, she had left her father's house for the already-married Percy Shelley, whose father had taken legal actions against his son; thus the French lovers' story provides a model of the Romantic generation's rebellion against their parents' oppressive moral codes.

Mirabeau's private life also plays a role in a slightly later work, Geraldine Jewsbury's 1845 novel *Zoë, The History of Two Lives*. In this comparatively neglected work, in its time considered daring in its portrayal of sexuality,[38] the heroine has an affair with an ugly but interesting Frenchman—who is none other than Mirabeau. The history is vague, the scene apparently being in the mid-1780s (when Mirabeau did visit Britain), but the intrigue being carried on around a performance of *King Lear* by David Garrick. who died in 1779. Mirabeau explains to Zoë the problems of absolute monarchy, and tells her that real heroes are not gods, but "men, only of larger soul; and they have to do their work like men, with all the impediments of an imperfect will, fiery passions, and the sense of an illimitable task spreading itself out before them ... ."[39] When a "career" opens up for Mirabeau in France, Zoë refuses to accompany him as his soul-mate, stating that her own freedom is limited by regard for her children, and Mirabeau abandons her.

Jewsbury's Mirabeau appears to have been reading Carlyle's version of heroism. In fact, Carlyle's wife had creative input into what originally seems to have been planned as a collaborative project between Jewsbury, Elizabeth Paulet, and Jane Welsh Carlyle.[40] The choice of Mirabeau as the embodiment of late eighteenth-century intellectual and sexual freedom suggests that by the early 1840s, when the novel was conceived, Mirabeau had become a significant symbol for revolution: far from being something to be shuddered at, it was still dangerous, but nevertheless appealing. *Zoë* is a book about revolutionary possibilities, and Mirabeau gives revolution a human aspect through suggesting, in Carlyle's phrase, the impact on history of "an Original Man."

To construct a hypothetical history based on one man, however, was to deemphasize the tory possibility that if the French Revolution was ever replayed, the consequences would again be bloody. In *The French Revolution, A History* Thomas Carlyle posed the potentially radical question of whether if the French Revolution was understood as a human phenomenon, the pattern of events might be interrupted and revised before the final bloodshed. Such a question required more human sympathy than a simple whig dismissal of the sufferings of revolution as part of historical progress; yet while more closely aligned with the tory interpretation of history as moral lesson, the book itself resists categorization in party terms.

Carlyle's *The French Revolution: A History*

Carlyle's title, *The French Revolution, A History*, might in itself seem a rejection of both whig and tory history: if it is *a* history, one of a number of possible histories, it implies neither history as inevitable progress nor history as a repeating pattern of events. Alison's *History of Europe* had shown the limitations of the tory reading of history. John Stuart Mill remarked of it that if a history were to confine itself to the moral sphere,

> surely some less common-place moral result, some more valuable and striking practical lesson, might admit of being drawn from this extraordinary passage of history, than merely this, that men should beware how they begin a political convulsion, because they never can tell how or when it will end … .[41]

Mill was by this time friends with Carlyle, and acknowledging Carlyle's influence, his review of Alison suggests that biographical and moral approaches to history are not incompatible. For all the gory horrors of his account, Alison had diminished the uniqueness of the French Revolution as an event in history by making human nature in its most generalized form the key to cause and effect. Mill was certainly justified in maintaining that if this was the only possibility for tory history, then its scope was severely limited. Yet this did not prove the whig approach, its self-confidence replacing tory fear of anarchy, truly superior. British whigs, following their French liberal counterparts, belittled the national and human tragedy of the period by a quasi-scientific necessitarianism—the French Revolution was an inevitable stage in social progress, and thus firmly located in the past. A place still remained for a work which would recreate the human experience of the French Revolution, and suggest its continued relevance. In *The French Revolution: A History*, Carlyle contributed a new human focus to the French Revolution that broadened its significance for British readers from the merely symbolic. In many aspects of its philosophy of history, Carlyle's book may still be classified as tory; but it is a product of a new age in which simple blanket opposition to "innovation" was no longer politically feasible.

Carlyle had previously used French history as a starting-point for consideration of the British *status quo* in *Sartor Resartus*, which first appeared in *Fraser's Magazine* in 1833–1834. The "Germanness" of this work is immediately apparent, but the musings of Professor Teufelsdröckh begin after the French Revolution of July 1830:

> while the din and frenzy of Catholic Emancipations, and Rotten Boroughs, and Revolts of Paris, deafen every French and every English ear, the German can stand peaceful on his scientific watch-tower … .[42]

The Germans may claim a philosophical superiority, but Carlyle associates revolution with France. The philosophical discussion of clothes that follows coincides with neither a whig nor tory reading of history, both of which would suggest that as much as clothes mark caste, they confirm existing conditions of property-ownership. Through Teufelsdröckh, Carlyle suggests that clothes are not in fact merely the marker of one's pre-existing identity, but rather a masking of one's deep identity, the "Soul." In this way Carlyle presents the radical proposition that identity is not only determined by individual will or lack of it, but is also distinct from matters of property. Teufelsdröckh's observation that "there is something great in the moment when a man first strips himself of adventitious wrappages" prompts the question of whether he is a "Sansculottist"—the word both for a man who wears no breeches and for a Jacobin Revolutionary. Carlyle's alter-ego is thus divided from the dispassionate thought of Germany and associated with the egalitarian passion of the French Revolution (*Works* 1:45). In *Sartor Resartus* Carlyle begins his association between Sansculottism and Transcendentalism: a man, says Teufelsdröckh, might be defined as "an omnivorous Biped that wears Breeches," the garments concealing spirit (*Works* 1:51). The Sansculottists are deprived of the signifier of civilization and are left with nothing to conceal the spiritual: in them, the transcendent spirit of humanity is dangerously exposed. Carlyle was already coming to the realization that the French Revolution revealed human passions in all their nakedness.

Fittingly, then, Carlyle locates Teufelsdröckh's moment of triumph over "the Everlasting No" in Paris. In the appropriately-named "Rue Saint-Thomas de l'Enfer," Teufelsdröckh realizes that he is not just a citizen of Hell, but also a "Child of Freedom," who has the right to assert his opposition to the infernal forces. In Paris, the city of Revolution, Teufelsdröckh "began to be a Man" (*Works* 1:148), and the French Revolution is for Carlyle not a test of political theories of history, but rather a test of the nature of humanity itself.

By the time that *Sartor Resartus* appeared in print, Carlyle was contemplating a more extensive work on the French Revolution that would continue this philosophical exploration. In *The French Revolution: A History*, Carlyle was to take a personal political direction, but one that did not so much abandon the traditional British associations of the French Revolution as use them in a new way.

Carlyle moved to London from Scotland in the summer of 1834, and seems almost immediately to have determined upon the French Revolution as the subject of his next major work. He informed his brother in July, "I mean to make an artistic *Picture* of it."[43] Carlyle's initial impulses towards the French Revolution, indeed, are defined in literary or artistic terms: he saw it as "such a Book! Quite an Epic Poem of the Revolution: an Apotheosis of Sansculottism!"[44] *The French Revolution* has therefore often been categorized according to literary genre. John P. Farrell argues that the book, like Carlyle's other works, is essentially tragic, an utterance of "transcendental despair," and that "Mirabeau's death constitutes the major tragedy of *The French Revolution*."[45] Chris Vanden Bossche has reanalyzed John Stuart Mill's view, which was that the book was "not so much as history as an epic poem."[46] Vanden Bossche sees the epic form as a conscious part of Carlyle's intention, and adds that Carlyle "did not write *The French Revolution* as a factual chronology of political events but as a sequence of symbolic episodes through which the narrator, and the reader, discover the meaning of their own era."[47]

Both the "tragic" and the "epic" components are useful approaches to this text, but Vanden Bossche has additionally detected an aspect of the work that merges literary form with political utterance. Carlyle had already provided social commentary in *Sartor Resartus*; but he may not have yet personally acknowledged that even his history writings were to be, like Burke's writings on France, in the prophetic mode. The phrase that Carlyle was fond of quoting, "History is Philosophy teaching by Experience,"[48] sets up the parallel between past and present, but in the tory tradition, Carlyle implies that this past experience facilitates the prediction of the outcome of future events. Past and future, of course, have a place in the secondary epic, yet probably this was not the central connection made by Mill. The "epic" label, indeed, becomes more suspect in association with Mill. Mill could respond to the aesthetics of his friend's book and describe it as "epic"; he was less comfortable in exploring the philosophical implications of its vision of history and politics. Indeed, Mill's deflection of attention from philosophy of history to literary genre may be in part explained by his realization of the substantial differences between Carlyle's sense of history and his own.

Even before his decision to settle in London, Carlyle had been in communication with John Stuart Mill. Still in his twenties, Mill at this stage did not identify fully with the Utilitarianism of his father James Mill and Jeremy Bentham; his references to "scientific" history in his review of Alison, however, imply that although he was not a Whig since he rejected the fundamental association of property with political rights, like the Utilitarians he was a whig historian in believing in the material and intellectual progress of civilization.[49] Yet as Vanden Bossche notes, that Mill's communication with Carlyle became frequent only after Bentham's death in 1832 may be significant: perhaps Mill was looking for a new radical prophet. Mill's knowledge of France, and especially of French historical sources, proved invaluable to Carlyle. Mill had spent time learning the language in France as a child, and in 1830–1831 had worked as Paris correspondent for the *Examiner*. He supplied Carlyle with books during his composition of *The French Revolution*, and contemplated writing on the subject himself: as late as October 1833, he responded to Carlyle's suggestion that he write on the topic, "it is highly probable I shall do it some time if you do not ..." (*Early Letters* 1:180).

Mill's assumption that if Carlyle wrote on the French Revolution he would be speaking for them both did not last. Carlyle could certainly be described as a radical at this period since he was pointing to a need for deep-rooted change in British government and society. He apparently agreed with Mill, who dismissed the reformed Parliament as "ridiculously like what I expected" (*Early Letters* 1:145), that in essence the 1832 Reform Act had not changed much, although perhaps in noting that it had brought forward men of no talent, he already had a distinct idea of what the role of the individual in society ought to be. The Whigs were in Mill and Carlyle's opinion a party of little men; the Conservatives seemed at first crushed by Reform, then later, as Carlyle expressed it in letters to his brother and Emerson, "false" and "a lie."[50]

Thus far, Mill and Carlyle seemed to agree, and Mill was anxious enough for Carlyle's friendship to stress their similarities. Yet Mill was always sufficiently a Utilitarian to reject Carlyle's quest for a moral structure beyond those created by society. Mill finally acknowledged that his ideas were "more *materially* divergent" from Carlyle's than he had been willing to believe in July 1833 (*Early Letters* 1:161). The emphasis on "materially" is Mill's, and surely reveals a key point in their divergence: although throughout his career Carlyle was to insist on society's obligation to satisfy humans' material wants, as *Sartor Resartus* had already demonstrated, for him humans were not ultimately, as for the Utilitarians, material beings.

Mill nevertheless has a presence in the work, since Carlyle's view of the events in France was shaped by the books that Mill lent him. Additionally, Mill had an influence on the shape of the whole narrative in a manner that was unfortunate for Carlyle, but a final strength to the text. The story that Carlyle lent Mill the manuscript of the first volume of *The French Revolution*, and that through Mill's carelessness the manuscript was burned is well known. Some commentators have chosen to blame Mill's companion Harriet Taylor for the mistake, which overlooks the point that the book was entrusted to Mill. More interesting questions might be why Carlyle had no rough copy of the text (rewriting the first volume took six months), and why, in a month when he had been looking for copying work for Leigh Hunt's penniless son, the thought had not occurred to him to ask him to copy his own book.[51] When the burning of the manuscript caused Carlyle such tribulation, it would be harsh to claim that the struggling author had a subconscious urge to begin again. The fact remains, however, that Carlyle was able to start afresh with an overall sense of his book as a three-volume work, and to exploit that structure, something that he had not envisaged when he began.[52] Carlyle started with a sense of the Revolution as history, with beginning, middle, and end, and his narrative voice reflects this sense in showing awareness of chronology, but an ability to step outside it.

The first volume of the three, *The Bastille*, immediately shows Carlyle's departure from tory historians such as Alison: indeed, Carlyle first appears a whig as he explains the specific social conditions that led from the decadence of the *Ancien Régime to* the storming of the Bastille. Alison's narrative approach was strictly that of history as example. He had argued that no drastic change was necessary in France; Carlyle, in contrast, opens his work by depicting Louis XV's death from smallpox as emblematic of the terminal sickness of the state. Alison had further asserted that forcing political change was against nature, which implies a loose acceptance of the concept of Divine Right: kings are created by God, and therefore no humans have the right to put them aside. Carlyle's conception of history complicates the notion of Divine Right by noting that the passing of kings itself is according to natural order: "Sovereigns die and Sovereignties."[53] Since transcendent Right is not located in human institutions, among which Carlyle numbers the development of monarchy, divine right is only seen in "the Acknowledged Strongest" (*Works* 2:9), a category to which France's last two kings cannot aspire. Kings nevertheless have a symbolic function for Carlyle. Louis XIV had claimed to personify the state; similarly, Louis XV and Louis XVI personify the state of the nation.

Carlyle then examines the problems of the time; this is not, he[54] points out, an Age of Gold, but rather an Age of Paper; or (more ironically) an Age of Hope. A symbol of the time is the Montgolfiers' balloon, fragile paper filled with air, "mounting heavenward so beautifully,—so unguidably!" (*Works* 2:51). The historian-narrator would agree that an age that embraces the philosophy of Rousseau is either decadent or desperate, since Rousseau's ideas combine both hope in human improvement and what is presented as a misguided attempt to limit the possibilities of the universe (*Works* 2:54). Nor does he overlook the condition of the lower classes, who are starving and overtaxed. Once again, Carlyle seems to be reproducing the ideas of works such as Russell's *Causes of the French Revolution*.

Yet this is in part the effect of seeing *The French Revolution* as a self-contained work. Even at this comparatively early stage in his career, Carlyle's narrative presence creates a continuity between his different writings, and two essays published in *Fraser's Magazine* before the longer work, "Count Cagliostro" and "The Diamond Necklace," supply clues as to when choices might have been made. Cagliostro and Countess Lamotte, the woman at the center of the "Necklace" plot, are the embodiments of what Carlyle calls "Gigmany": in their own fields they are geniuses, but they are dependent on the corruption of the age to work their impostures. The Diamond Necklace itself is presented as an artifact shaped from the materials of history itself—"Could these aged stones, the youngest of them Six Thousand years of age and upwards, but have spoken, there were an Experience for Philosophy to teach by!" (*Works* 28:333).[55] But it is a product of a decadent age, created for Louis XV's mistress Madame du Barry, and through its implication of Louis XVI's Queen Marie-Antoinette, spreading the taint to the next generation. A "Dramaturgist" himself, Carlyle can hint at admiration for Lamotte's attempt to shape her own drama, but the elements of the story—corruption, suspicion, imposture, financial ruin—bode "Earthquakes."[56] Carlyle here complicates the whig idea of history as the progress of predetermined forces by suggesting that the symbol that the French monarchy becomes is the product of human action—or, perhaps in the case of the king and queen themselves, human failure to act.

Of even more significance, the narrative style developed in these essays and continued in *The French Revolution* is itself not whig. By using the present tense, Carlyle does not locate these events safely in the past, nor characterize the events he describes as a part of history beyond which human society has now progressed. As Barton Friedman observes, *The French Revolution* has a disquieting immediacy, reinforced by the frequent use of the first person plural.[57] At the storming of the Bastille, Carlyle writes:

> Bursts forth insurrection, at sight of its own blood (for there were deaths by that sputter of fire), into endless rolling explosion of musketry, distraction, execration;—and overhead, from the Fortress, let one great gun, with its grapeshot, go booming, to show what we *could* do. The Bastille is besieged! (*Works* 2:190)

The revolutionaries are here made an abstraction, "Insurrection": they are an ungovernable force. By using "we," however, Carlyle identifies his narrative viewpoint (and that of the reader) with the besieger. Barton Friedman and Elliot L. Gilbert have drawn attention to the sense of "wondrous contiguity" in Carlyle's historical writings, by which narrative moves out of the framework of chronology are used to dramatic effect. Yet this is not merely a narrative technique, but a political manifesto. In scenes like the storming of the Bastille, such a point of view is neither whig nor tory; it is radical, in suggesting through the narrative bridge across time and space an identification with the group that party history has hitherto excluded.

For the storming of the Bastille is an indication of the failure of moderate attempts to reform French government. As we have seen, the Parlement of Paris and the summoning of the States-General were first welcomed by British commentators as the French attempt to imitate British constitutionalism. With the hindsight of forty years, Carlyle is in a position to be skeptical about this. He repeatedly describes the *Parlement* of Paris as a "Body"—seemingly a unified social construct.

Yet the *Parlement* symbolizes more the collapse of the old order, "the breaking-up of a World-Solecism" (*Works* 2:96), and the recognition of France's spiritual and economic bankruptcy, than the founding of a new unity. It is thus a "refractory Body," and "an unloved body" (2:82, 85); above all, it is a body that lacks a head.

This lack of a head for the new France becomes particularly apparent after the convening of the States General for the first time in over 150 years at the end of 1788. Whereas earlier British commentators had seen this as the French equivalent of the Glorious Revolution, coming precisely one hundred years after the ousting of James II, Carlyle's attitude is ominous. Those representatives of the Third Estate assembled in Versailles in May 1789 prompt the historian to note that "the whole Future is there, and Destiny dim-brooding over it" (*Works* 2:134), but also to ask:

> Which of these Six Hundred individuals, in plain white cravat, that have come up to regenerate France, might one guess would become their *king*? For a king or leader they, as all bodies of men, must have: be their work what it may … . (*Works* 2:137)

Carlyle's historical objection to Louis XV and Louis XVI is thus confirmed not to be their kingship, but that their kingship was undeserved. The problem of the French Revolution will in the main part be an attempt to found a government without the strong force of leadership.

Whereas Volume One is named after the fallen symbol of the ancient power, Volume Two is called *The Constitution*, in Carlyle's reading another symbol of failed power. The failed Constitution is itself embodied; it will not "march."[58] Volume Two, though, also displays the failure of other authorities. By the end of this section, the Constitution is "burst in pieces"; Louis XVI's always-tenuous hold on rule is destroyed; and above all, Mirabeau, the man who in Carlyle's vision has the "character, faculty, position" fittest for kingship, is dead.

From the beginning, most of the leaders of the French Revolution are depicted as a part of history, rather than as creating it. These self-styled leaders are not merely the tools of whig historical progress because their strengths and weaknesses are given opportunity by historical forces. When Carlyle poses the question "who will be *king*?" in Volume One, he introduces several characters. Many of these—Marat, Desmoulins, Danton, even the monstrous possibility of a female king in the "Demoiselle" Théroigne—are lined up in the style of an epic catalogue, but as the products of the Third Estate's provision of opportunity, rather than because of their personal greatness. Marat for Carlyle is always a horse-doctor, or even less flatteringly, a "dogleech": only in an age in which merit is forgotten can a dogleech become the "Friend of the People." Théroigne de Mericourt, a former prostitute who poses like "the *Maid* of Orleans" (*Works* 2:255, Carlyle's italics) or to her comrades, like Pallas Athene, can only be a leader at a time when insanity is beginning to rule and women and the poor encroach on the world of politics. She becomes a leader of the Insurrection of Women, the group whom Carlyle chooses to term the "Menads"; eventually, however, she will play the part both of Bacchante and of Orpheus, since the women will turn against her, leaving her "become as a brown-locked Diana (were that possible) attacked by her own dogs, or she-dogs!" (*Works* 4:154). Théroigne, who was able to exploit the madness of the age by posing as a historical type rather than as a violation of history, is herself left permanently mad by its excesses. Even Danton, who Carlyle concedes to be "a Man," is introduced as an "esurient, unprovided Advocate" (*Works* 2:136): at the commencement of the Revolution, Danton is looking to prove himself by advocating a cause. Just as in the tory reading of history, change brings additional scope for human wickedness, so in Carlyle's reading the Revolution provides opportunity for individuals not to transcend the historical moment, but rather to take advantage of it.

As in the "Mirabeau" essay, the close link between history and character is especially shown in the presentation of "the meanest" of the delegates who arrive at Paris at the recall of the Third Estate. Maximilien Robespierre may be, Carlyle suggests interrogatively, a "man unfit for Revolutions?" (*Works* 2:142). Robespierre is introduced as a man who can only exploit the historical moment, rather than direct it. The irony of one of Carlyle's favorite epithets for Robespierre, "incorruptible," is revealed. A man who cannot be corrupted by money may nevertheless be corrupted by historical opportunity, through which Robespierre obtained political power of which in any other age he could only have dreamed (and in Carlyle's rendition of him, Robespierre would scarcely be capable of the vision involved in such dreaming). He finally becomes Priest of the Supreme Being, which Carlyle calls "*conscious* Mumbo-Jumbo" since Robespierre "*knows* that he is machinery" (*Works* 4:267). Robespierre's creation of the cult of the Supreme Being is thus one final and ludicrous attempt to lead in an age that is leading him. Like Théroigne and Marat, both of whom had been associated with images of rabid dogs, Robespierre is a product of what Carlyle terms the "rabidity" of the age.[59] Both human beings and "the Time" are rabid (*Works* 4:222), and Robespierre must finally be brought down with "froth" on his lips.

Since Robespierre is not a true leader, Carlyle investigates whether Mirabeau could have been. In his essay on Mirabeau, Carlyle had suggested that Mirabeau, Danton, and Napoleon were the three great figures of the era, and had focused on the creation of Mirabeau the individual through a combination of cultural and family influences and his own peculiarities of temperament. In contrast, in *The French Revolution: A History*, these figures are conspicuous by their absence: Mirabeau dies while the story is yet unfolding, Danton is overshadowed and destroyed by Robespierre, Napoleon is yet to come.

Thus the Mirabeau of *The French Revolution* is placed within the bounds of history. Admittedly, even though he is initially characterized as "the Type-Frenchman of this epoch" (*Works* 2:137), Mirabeau suggests potential to become more than the creature of the process of history. John P. Farrell calls Mirabeau's death "the major tragedy of *The French Revolution*,"[60] yet Carlyle seems to have regarded Mirabeau's personal story as separate from the main course of events.[61] After writing his first two volumes, Mirabeau's death occurring halfway through the second, he proceeded to write not the third volume, but his essay on Mirabeau. Although he personally did not abandon the heroic potential of Mirabeau, within the structure of *The French Revolution*,

> Mirabeau could not live another year ... these same *would-have-beens* are mostly a vanity; and the World's History could never in the least be what it would, or might, or should, by any manner of potentiality, but simply and altogether what it *is*. (*Works* 3:139)

The fatalism of this conclusion contradicts the emphasis on the causality of social circumstances and of human nature seen elsewhere in *The French Revolution*; for all his assertions of human choice, Carlyle finally retains too much of his Calvinist heritage not to wonder whether it is destiny that finally decides. But at the same time that he is dismissing the possibility of rewriting history, he is emphasizing the accidental nature of events of potentially far-reaching consequence. While Mirabeau's untimely death is to some extent the product of his lifestyle, it is still presented more as historical accident than as tragedy. The actual tragedy may be that of the historian, who cannot make history what it is not, and who through historical accidents like that of

Mirabeau's birth and death, is made to ask the question that of all questions may have been most disturbing to Carlyle: whether any human being may really be in control of history. Without Mirabeau, the pattern of history must finally be a tory one. Mirabeau, the "Original Man," might have provided a way out of history's repetitions—but the only leader left for the final book is the embodied crowd of Paris citizens, well-known to British readers of history as the "mob."

Carlyle avoids this word, yet he cannot avoid the connotations of "mob-rule" in his description of the Reign of Terror—nor, ultimately, would he wish to do so. Appropriately since *The French Revolution* depicts a world where heads are severed from bodies, Volume Three is named *The Guillotine* after this symbol of lack of heads. It nevertheless begins with what appears to be an anti-tory appeal to calm. Carlyle concedes that

> Very frightful it is when a Nation, rending asunder its Constitution and Regulations which were grown dead Cerements for it, becomes *trans*cendental; and must now seek its wild way through the New, Chaotic—where Force is not yet distinguished into Bidden and Forbidden, but Crime and Virtue welter unseparated—in that domain of what is all the Passions. ... (*Works* 4:2)

The Reign of Terror is terrifying because it transcends historical precedent, making passions rather than socially-created structures the governing force. Carlyle makes a connection between this fear of the anti-historical and the hysterical: "It is unfortunate, though very natural, that the history of this Period has so generally been written in hysterics" (*Works* 4:2). That hysteria is a diagnosis almost exclusively applied to women in the nineteenth century suggests that the disruptive power of the French Revolution can affect history itself, making male historians respond like women. Carlyle disarms the threat to history—or possibly implies that real historians should be real men—by using his frequent metaphorical connection between clothing and social convention to emphasize that France's "clothing" (the nation's "Rules and Regulations") consists of "dead Cerements." This counters the tory fear that if this happened to France it could happen to Britain; but does not quite echo the whig complacency that the French Revolution was the product of a specific historical moment, since at this moment, history has been destroyed.

The self-created world with no law, no history, of the France of Volume Three finally shows the connection of Carlyle's vision with tory history. Deprived of the potential manly leadership of Mirabeau, the People are not a source of hope or evidence of the perfectibility of humankind, but descend into an animal, or perhaps worse, a female, frenzy. Ultimately, Carlyle must agree with the tories that popular revolution leads to anarchy. Hence by the time of the death of Louis XVI, the power of revolution has led not to true liberty, but has degenerated into "universal suffrage, unlimited liberty to choose" (*Works* 4:5).

This democratic spirit gives strength to the Girondists. The Girondists had been seen by both British and French commentators of generally republican sympathies to have been the lost hope for France. Initially, Carlyle seems to have been swayed by the presentation of such historians as Thiers, who had portrayed the stoic response of the Girondists to their fall as "sublime," and had called them "noble and courageous citizens, who fell a sacrifice to their generous Utopia."[62] In 1833, writing to Mill, who himself believed Girondism to have been an ideal solution to French government,[63] Carlyle spoke of the emotional effect that reading Thiers's account of Madame Roland and the other Girondists had had upon him,[64] and this admiration for Madame Roland survives in his own version. She, indeed, almost transcends the historical status of her sex: she has true "worth" and "greatness," and is "the creature of Sincerity and Nature, in an age of Artificiality, Pollution, and Cant" (*Works* 3:46). At her death, too, Carlyle honors "Nature" for creating a "Daughter of the Infinite" (*Works* 4:211): one who briefly defies history itself.

Towards the principles of Girondism, however, Carlyle is less sympathetic; and while his definition of "Nature" is different from Alison's—for Carlyle, going against the natural order dictated by history can be heroic, whereas for Alison it is always misguided—the suspicion arises that for Carlyle just as for Alison, the Girondists may be like British Whigs. Bowing to the populist demands for change, the Girondists permit the execution of the monarchs, but cannot themselves consolidate popular leadership: in other words, the Girondists leave the way open for a Robespierre, one with a more astute sense of the historical moment.

One brief flash of transcendence has preceded (and in part precipitated) the fall of the Girondists in the form of Charlotte Corday, assassin of Marat. In a time of a shortage of heroes, Corday is a hero in her personal attempt to control history. Pointedly, Corday states that she was "a Republican before the Revolution, and never wanted energy" (*Works* 4:171); unlike Robespierre, whose identity is shaped by the

Revolution, the "angelic-demonic" Corday has her own moral consistency. Nevertheless, she too is a symptom of her age:

> Alas, how were peace possible or preparable, while, for example, the hearts of lovely Maidens, in their convent-stillness, are dreaming not of love-paradises, and the light of Life; but of Codrus'-sacrifices, and death well earned. That Twenty-five million hearts have got to such temper, this *is* the Anarchy. ... (*Works* 4:172)

The story of Charlotte Corday opens a subsection of Volume Three called "Terror," and the attempt by a "maiden" to shape history is symptomatic of the values of a world in which legitimate political forces have dissolved and "Terror" is becoming "the Order of the Day." Similarly, the drawing of women into political history implied by the judgment against Marie Antoinette shows the collapse of natural order. The Revolutionaries have, in Carlyle's ordering of events,[65] just politicized the image of woman through the giant statue of "Nature," an event, the historian-narrator drily remarks, that "History can notice with satisfaction" (*Works* 4:186). As Burke had suggested, Terror marked by such unnatural events could become the order of other days too. The mood of *The French Revolution* is a dark one to the end, since the terror that it describes, while bearing the stamp of historical specificity, is not necessarily safely in the past, as whig concepts of progress would suggest. For France, some temporary light may be on the way. The text holds out a vague promise of the coming of a "little bronze-complexioned Artillery Officer" (*Works* 4:293); yet the history concludes not with the leadership of Napoleon, but instead with an insistence on the survival of the spirit of Sansculottism in the present-day British Isles. The French Revolution is not as the tories would have it, history's most monstrous warning as "the frightfullest thing ever borne of Time" but "One of the frightfullest" (*Works* 4:311): that is, history could indeed repeat itself, and, Carlyle warns darkly, the conditions are right for such repetition in Ireland.

Carlyle is certainly justified in reminding the complacent mainland British of the appalling situation of the poor in Ireland. Yet a side result is the further distancing of the "mob." Although at points Carlyle's narrative voice has appeared to coincide with the revolutionaries as opposed to the representatives of the *Ancien Régime*, Carlyle's reader, who might be tempted to "shrieks" at the thought of terror, is not likely to identify with the Sansculottes. The "Sanspotatoes" image alienates the mob still further by suggesting not that England's own poor might usurp political authority, but that the ever-untrustworthy Irish might. This characterization of the Irish even by one who recognizes their genuine need is symptomatic of a dehumanizing process that was to recur in British writing, connecting the Irish poor with the frenzied, non-individualized mob of the 1790s.

Even with this uncomfortable form of historical repetition, Carlyle continues to believe that Anarchy is merely a phase through which history must pass; give the people sufficient grievances, and anarchy may possibly follow, but being "hateful as Death" and "abhorrent to the whole nature of man" (*Works* 4:313), it must soon die, a brief Carmagnole danced on the pages of history. Carlyle has set up the pattern of degeneracy and social division, popular revolution, anarchy, and the reestablishment of leadership seemingly as one of historical inevitability. But the concluding pages of *The French Revolution* suggest that a lesson may still be learned from France: practical intervention at an early stage in the process, not in the form of repression, but in an attempt to heal the social divisions, might avert a repetition. This would, however, necessitate beginning before the beginning—Carlyle's work opens with the *Ancien Régime* already terminally sick—and an acknowledgment of the necessity of structured intervention. At this stage in his life, for all his criticism of contemporary leadership, Carlyle may still have had hopes for the Conservative party as the faction that might represent the true interests of Britain and Ireland as a whole—and indeed, the Conservatives under Sir Robert Peel were finally to abolish a major impetus to Sansculottism, the hated Corn Laws. To this extent, then, even if a pessimistic work for France, *The French Revolution* could be an optimistic work for Britain, if Britain chose to recognize the exemplary force.

Notes

1. George Peabody Gooch, *History and Historians in the Nineteenth Century*, 2nd edition (Beacon Press, 1959), pp. 267–268.
2. The epithet "Destructives" for the Whigs is used repeatedly in both Alison's "Fall of the Melbourne Ministry," in *Blackwood's Magazine* 37 (January 1835) p. 48, and Croker's "Sir Robert Peel's Address," *Quarterly Review* 53, (February 1835), pp. 280–285.
3. That both Peel and the press realized that his address to his constituents at Tamworth set important precedents is indicated by the release of the complete text of the "Tamworth Manifesto" to *The Times* on Thursday 18 December at 3.30 am: it was immediately rushed into print.

4. Croker, "Peel's Address," p. 265.
5. Croker, *Croker Papers* 2:275.
6. Sir Walter Scott, *The Life of Napoleon Buonaparte* (1827; Gihon, 1853) 1:132. Following references are cited in the text as *Life of Napoleon*.
7. Ibid. 1:109.
8. In his autobiography, Alison notes how reviewers were cruel, even his friends and allies being unenthusiastic about the first edition—Croker declined to comment on it, for example. But later editions were clearly in demand. Alison, *My Life and Writings* (Blackwood, 1883) 1:313–317.
9. Ibid. 1:253–254.
10. Some confusion, or at least association, between the two Burkes seems to have crept into post-Reform minds. In Thomas De Quincey's "Second Paper on Murder Considered as one of the Fine Arts," published in *Blackwood's* in 1839, praise is given to "the Burke-and-Hare revolution in the art" (interestingly because it returns murder to the artistic level of *before* the French Revolution), and the characters toast "the sublime epoch of Burkism and Harism!"—the sublime, of course, being associated with Edmund Burke. Thomas De Quincey, "Second Paper on Murder," *Blackwood's Magazine* 46 (November 1839), pp. 665–667). Thomas Hood writes in the introduction to his 1840 book *Up the Rhine*, which describes a steamboat trip, "As for the romantic, the Age of Chivalry is Burked by Time, and as difficult of revival in Germany as in Scotland." *Up The Rhine*, in *The Works of Thomas Hood, edited by his Son and Daughter* (Moxon, 1861) 7:4. In Robert Surtees's *Hillingdon Hall* a misunderstanding directly reflects class distinction when a tradesman with social aspirations misinterprets an aristocrat. The Duke of Donkeyton, who is actually a Whig, recalls a comment by Edmund Burke and adds, "Fine speech of Burke's; monstrous fine speech"—a telling choice of adverb in itself. Mr. Jorrocks's response reveals their social difference: "'He was 'ung for all that,' observed Mr. Jorrocks to himself, with a knowing shake of the head ... ." Robert Surtees, *Hillingdon Hall* (1845; Folio Society, 1956), p. 99. Obviously, these three instances are jokes; Sir Archibald Alison would surely have been distressed, however, that in the index to his *Life and Writings*, references to both Edmund and William are grouped indiscriminately under "Burke."
11. Ibid. 1:273–274.
12. Archibald Alison, "On the Late French Revolution," *Blackwood's Magazine* 29 (1831), p. 36. This series continued in *Blackwood's* volumes 29–31 under various titles; subsequent references are cited in the text by volume and page number as *Blackwood's*.
13. Alison's own figure for the mortality of the French Revolution, given in his ninth edition, is one million, but this includes an estimated 900,000 from the war in La Vendée. The figure for those actually guillotined is 18,613. See Alison's *History of Europe*, 9th edition (Blackwood's, 1853) 3:110.

14. Archibald Alison, *History of Europe* (1835; Baudry's European Library, 1841) 1:31. Subsequent references to this reprint of the earliest edition are cited in the text as *Europe (1841)*.
15. This is less clear in the latter part of his history, where his admiration for Napoleon seems at odds with his moral purpose.
16. In later editions, the historian's traditionalism reveals a morbid streak when he observes that "there is something solemn and interesting in opening the tombs of the departed great" and proceeds to describe the state of putrefaction of each corpse. See Alison's *History of Europe*, 9th edition 3:21.
17. Hazlitt and Scott, for example, writing before 1830, both note his potential, but rapidly move on to place other characters at the center of their narratives.
18. From the perspective of the 1830s, even such venality could be interpreted as foresight, since the Duc D'Orléans was the father of Louis Phillipe. The accusation was nevertheless strenuously denied by Gabriel Lucas de Montigny in his *Mémoires biographiques, littéraires, et politques de Mirabeau* (Auffray, 1834–38) 6:330–336.
19. Archibald Alison, "Dumont's Recollections of Mirabeau," *Blackwood's Magazine* 31 (May 1832), p. 756.
20. See Thomas Babington Macaulay, "Mirabeau." In *The Complete Works*, volume 8.
21. As Henry Brougham was to remark in a review of the *Memoirs* three years later, Mirabeau's early life and his dysfunctional family proved "the truly wretched state of society under the old Régime." Henry Brougham, "Biographical Memoirs of Mirabeau," *Edinburgh Review* 61 (April 1835), p. 214.
22. Étienne Dumont, *Recollections of Mirabeau*, English edition (Edward Bull, 1832), p. 3.
23. Barbara Luttrell, *Mirabeau* (Harvester/Wheatsheaf, 1990), pp. 68–70.
24. For example, Dumont recounts somewhat naively how when Sièyes was attempting to formulate new constitutional proposals, he was impatient at Dumont's suggestion that they should follow the English model (*Recollections of Mirabeau*, p. 52). Following references are cited in the text from this translation.
25. The point is echoed by the editor of the English edition: "Had his life been spared, there is no doubt that the French revolution would have taken another direction, and that the horrible excesses of the reign of terror never have blackened the page of French political regeneration. His death was the knell of the French monarchy—the glory of a long line of Kings was buried in the grave of Mirabeau" (*Recollections of Mirabeau*, p. xv).
26. Macaulay, *Complete Works* 8:220.
27. "Speeches delivered in Banquo Reginae," *Fraser's Magazine* 7 (May/June 1833), pp. 505–507. The *Wellesley Index to Victorian Periodicals* suggests

that the writer was Percival Weldon Banks (who almost certainly wrote the notes).
28. *Fraser's* 7:511. The context of the "sucking" reference ("Botherall" argues that through his associates Macaulay has no right to accuse Mirabeau of cowardice) implies both Macaulay's youth (he was thirty-one at the time), and also his sycophantic—and, in these articles, implicitly homosexual—adherence to the older Whigs. Macaulay and his friends, then, lack the masculinity of the man that they are belittling.
29. The suggestion was not unique since Lucas de Montigny had claimed that an earlier biographer, J. Peuchet, had portrayed Mirabeau's relations with women as like those of Lord Ruthven in John Polidori's Byronic tale "The Vampire" (Lucas de Montigny, *Memoirs of Mirabeau*, English edition 4:144–145).
30. Thomas Carlyle, "Mirabeau," in *The Works of Thomas Carlyle* (Chapman and Hall, 1899; reprinted AMC Press, 1980) 28:405.
31. John P. Farrell, *Revolution as Tragedy: The Dilemma of the Moderate from Scott to Arnold* (Cornell University Press, 1980), p. 222.
32. Hayden White, *Metahistory*, pp. 13–14.
33. Carlyle, *Works* 28:407–408. Subsequent references are cited in the text as *Works*.
34. Thomas Carlyle, *The French Revolution, A History*, in *Works* 3:139.
35. Given the list of "men" discussed—which includes three women—it seems possible that the choice of subjects was Shelley's rather than Lardner's.
36. Manuel calls them "the first French people who swore to live free or die," Pierre Manuel, *Lettres Originales de Mirabeau, Écrites du Donjon de Vincennes* (1792) 1:13.
37. Mary Wollstonecraft Shelley, "Mirabeau." In *The Cabinet Cyclopaedia: Lives of Eminent Literary and Scientific Men of France* (Longmans, 1839), 2:222.
38. For example, Jewsbury's conduct in publishing such a frank book under her own name was condemned as "foolish as well as unwomanly," which doubtless helped sales. See "Sea-side Reading," *Fraser's Magazine* 32 (November 1845), p. 566.
39. Geraldine Ensor Jewsbury, *Zoë* (Chapman and Hall, 1845) 3:153.
40. Surviving letters do not indicate that Jane Welsh Carlyle wrote any of the story, although she read it in manuscript. Her input at the planning stage cannot be determined, since her letters to Jewsbury no longer exist. See *The Collected Letters of Thomas and Jane Welsh Carlyle*, edited by Clyde de. L. Ryals et al. (Duke University Press, 1970), especially 15:244–250.
41. John Stuart Mill, *Essays on French History and Historians*, edited by John M. Robson, in *Collected Works* (Toronto University Press, 1985), 20:119.
42. Thomas Carlyle, *Sartor Resartus*, in *Works* 1:3. Following references are cited in the text as *Works*.
43. *Collected Letters of Thomas and Jane Welsh Carlyle* 7:244.
44. Ibid. 7:301.

45. Farrell, *History as Tragedy*, p. 225.
46. John Stuart Mill, *French History*, p. 134.
47. Chris R. Vanden Bossche, *Carlyle and the Search for Authority* (Ohio State University Press, 1991), pp. 62–63.
48. "On History" (1830), in *Works* 27:85. The expression is a variation on Dionysus of Halicarnassus' "History is philosophy teaching from examples," best-known to the British historical tradition through its quotation by Bolingbroke; see Introduction, above.
49. Mill does not choose to define "scientific" in this essay, but appears to contrast the tory moral model with the progressive model given full articulation by Hegel but adopted by whig historians of this period in somewhat cruder form. See also his letter to Carlyle of January 12, 1834, Mill's *Early Letters*, edited by Francis E. Mineka, in *Collected Works* (Toronto University Press, 1963) 12:207. Following references are cited in the text as *Early Letters*.
50. *Collected Letters of Thomas and Jane Welsh Carlyle* 8:36, 8:45.
51. See *Collected Letters* 8:29; 8:43–44. To be fair to Carlyle, John Hunt's copying fee would have been at least five pounds, and perhaps this seemed too expensive for a draft version; but even then, Carlyle's letters suggest that Hunt might have been prepared to take some of his fee in the form of regular meals.
52. In June 1834, Carlyle seems to have contemplated a single volume (*Collected Letters* 7:240). By December, he was planning two volumes (7:353), and on January 28, 1835, he informed his brother Alick, "I have finished my 'First Part,' which may possibly make a First Volume; and am about beginning [the] Second and the Third" (8:18). In other words, Carlyle had virtually or entirely completed the first version of the first volume before he decided on the three-volume structure.
53. Carlyle, *Works* 2:7. Following references to *The French Revolution* are cited in the text as *Works*.
54. Questions of narrative voice are highly complex in Carlyle's writings; by "he" and "Carlyle," I refer to the self-presentation as historian-narrator in *The French Revolution*.
55. The dating of the diamonds by the Biblical standards of the earth's age would suggest that at this time, Carlyle was not an evolutionist like Alison.
56. In *Works* 28:402.
57. On Carlyle's use of the present tense, see Barton Friedman, *Fabricating History*, p. 114 and Elliot L. Gilbert's essay "A Wonndrous Contiguity: Anachronism in Carlyle's Prophecy and Art," *PMLA* 87 (1972), pp. 432–442.
58. From the French *marcher*, meaning both "to march" or walk, and "to work" in the mechanical sense (*Works* 3:257).
59. Sir Walter Scott also describes the French during the Revolution as being "animated not merely with the courage, but with the rabid fury, of unchained wild beasts" (*Life of Napoelon Buonaparte* 1:56).

60. Farrell, *Revolution as Tragedy*, p. 225.
61. Carlyle himself is far more cautious about the label of "tragedy": in "Mirabeau," for example, Carlyle presents the possibility that Danton's life was a tragedy, but adds as though as an afterthought, "as all human histories are" (*Works* 28:412), and that there are many other Dantons.
62. Adolphe Thiers, *The History of the French Revolution*, 3rd American edition (Carey and Hart, 1845) 2:354–355.
63. In an 1826 review of Mignet's history of the French Revolution, Mill had characterized them, like Mignet himself, as "virtuous and unfortunate" (*French History*, p. 12). In 1828, reviewing Scott's *Life of Napoleon*, he devoted several pages to defending the Gironde.
64. Carlyle, *Collected Letters* 6:446–447.
65. The festival of Nature was on August 10, Marie Antoinette's execution on October 16. In Carlyle's account they are separated by two short chapters.

Chapter 3
1848: The Threat to Property

1848 seemed to vindicate the tory belief in the baneful influence of revolution, but hardly in a manner that was comforting to the British middle classes. After the collapse of Louis Philippe's monarchy in February, further revolutions broke out throughout Europe: in the German states, in the Italian peninsula, in Austria-Hungary, in Poland. Even Britain was not unaffected, with constant violence in Ireland, rioting in Scotland, and the last thrust of the Chartist movement. To attribute all these revolutions to the influence of France would be to oversimplify, since France's revolution shared causes with a number of the others, notably the financial slump resulting from a series of bad harvests and overrapid industrialization. In several of the states involved, revolution was inspired by, or inspired, nationalism—for example, many in the German states began to think of a united Germany; in others that had a long-term sense of nationhood, and especially France and Britain, it was influenced more directly by class and the rise of socialism.

The revolution of 1848 was a more thorough attempt to restructure French society than had been the revolution of 1830. Among its leaders was the poet Alphonse de Lamartine, but the name that initially captured British attention was that of the socialist journalist and historian Louis Blanc. France's new provisional government argued that whereas the accession of Louis Philippe had centralized power in the bourgeoisie, a true role in government would now be given to the workers, who would themselves control the means of production. In this sense, the 1848 revolution was socialist, and as such presented a greater threat to the value that both Whigs and Tories traditionally held most dear—the continuity of property—than any earlier revolution.

By enfranchising all males who owned or rented a house above specified values, Britain's Reform Act of 1832 had established the home as the defining political property. 1848 presented a challenge to property, both material and political, and although scattered British voices, among them Arthur Hugh Clough and John Stuart Mill and his associates, welcomed the new possibilities of socialism, a more common response from Britons was to adopt the whig-historical strategy of dissociation and deny that developments in France and the rest of Europe were relevant to their home country. This denial is represented in literature by the restructuring of what was in reality a domestic threat in terms of those alien to the British political establishment—as French, as Irish, as poor, as female. Increasingly, as the Revolution itself became historically distanced and assumed narrative forms, the sense of difference was achieved through characterization. Its participants thus become characters in a plot that is now fixed with a beginning, middle, and end, generally as the story had been structured by Carlyle: the fall of the monarchy, the fall of the Girondists, and the fall of Robespierre. Even at a moment when the whig interpretation of history seems predominant, this plot continues to represent both whig and tory readings of history, as the representation of Robespierre, the protagonist of the last phase of the plot, as simultaneously the most alien of all and a repeatable type demonstrates. For a new challenge was emerging not merely to party politics, but also to party history.

The *Communist Manifesto* of Karl Marx and Friedrich Engels was hurriedly printed during the French Revolution of February 1848.[1] In some significant aspects, its version of history, in which revolution is part of the continuous progress from one historical epoch to another, has similarities with whig history.[2] Yet the *Communist Manifesto* changed the position from which history is perceived. Both whig and tory history viewed events from the position of power—those who already had authority, and who had property to lose. History was not, however, seen as primarily determined by economic struggle. Even though Marx and Engels might themselves have been born into the middle classes, the center of their history is the worker, and the struggle against the bourgeoisie is ostensibly presented from this point of view, claiming the workers' right to control discourse.

Although the first printing of the *Manifesto* was in London, the text was in German, and no official translation appeared until 1882. An unofficial English translation, by Helen Macfarlane, was serialized in Julian Harney's Chartist newspaper *The Red Republican* in November

1850. Macfarlane translated the "immediate aim" of the Communists as "*The organisation of the Proletariat as a class, the destruction of Middle-class supremacy, and the conquest of political power by the Proletarians.*"[3] Given its context, in a Chartist journal headed by a picture of a Cap of Liberty and with the subtitle "Equality, Liberty, Fraternity," British middle-class readers would doubtless have interpreted the *Manifesto* as stating the intention to replay the first French Revolution in an international arena. Most likely few of the middle classes ever read this journal, while the translation's title *Manifesto of the German Communist Party* has some effect of distancing its concerns. All the same, that the tenets of common ownership were available to the thinking working class and not to the middle and upper classes gives some grounds for the 1840s paranoia envisaging a working-class conspiracy against the traditional structures of power and ownership. Many British works of the period of the 1848 Revolutions reflect a corresponding anxiety over identity that is not only based on a sense of nationality, but that also focuses on a sense of class.

Whereas 1848 seemed to prove the tory insistence on the domino effect—revolutions lead to more revolutions, the result being anarchy—socialism's potential threat to property not simply material but also political and historical gave Tories little comfort in their own historical correctness. For many middle-class British males, enfranchisement had, after all, only become their property in 1832, and now the socialists proposed to distribute political property among everyone.[4] In contrast, 1849, when in most nations (France being the major exception) the previous forms of government were reimposed, should have been more of a historical problem to whig historians. If growing self-awareness causes progress in civilization, revolutions should function as the continuation of that progress, and at the end of 1849, it was unclear precisely what had been achieved. (In hindsight, of course, the nationalism of 1848 did contribute to the unification of Italy and Germany, but this would have required more than Burkean vision to have been predicted in 1849.)

While British commentators freely applied the label of revolution to events overseas, they emphasized that the disturbances in their home country—or more accurately, their home countries, since throughout the 1840s Ireland suffered the most in every respect—never approached the scale of a revolution, the term "riot" being applied to unrest in mainland Britain, and "rebellion" to actions in Ireland. In British law, the word "riot" is less problematic than "revolution," since the reading of the 1715 "Riot Act" defines the event: for example, in April 1848, Archibald Alison, by this time Sheriff of Glasgow, was called back from vacation to read the Riot Act during food riots in Glasgow, and witnessed the shooting of four rioters who were threatening Glasgow property.[5] The words "sedition," "treason," "rebellion" and even "rising" were used to describe Irish struggles for national identity during the early months of 1848. Although the British point of view presented the situation in Ireland as like a riot in being a provincial struggle with which public did not sympathize, concern grew when it was learned that the Irish nationalists were in communication with the French socialist revolutionary government.[6]

Once again, French revolution was linked to British concerns, but in 1848, the loudest British response was not, like Burke, to declare the threat, but rather to deny it. A particular interest was hence expressed in how France, whose constitution in 1830 had been hailed as being similar to Britain's, was now different. Hence writings of the 1840s often disguise their anxiety that Britain and France are too much the same—that traveling between the two is almost too easy. This denial again took a variety of forms, including narrative history and the novel. Two novels of the period just prior to the 1848 Revolution that focus on nationality, property, and class, Edward Bulwer-Lytton's *Lucretia* and William Makepeace Thackeray's *Vanity Fair*, explore the scope of this difference, with uncomfortable conclusions.

Poison and Economic History in *Lucretia* and *Vanity Fair*

By the 1840s, many Britons who had welcomed the expulsion of the Bourbons in 1830 as France's attempt to establish a constitutional monarchy similar to their own were less certain that the values of either France or Britain were those of an ideal new age of growing democracy and commerce that would provide opportunities for a broader band of society than ever before. Two novels, Thackeray's *Vanity Fair, a Novel Without a Hero* (serialized 1847–1848) and Bulwer-Lytton's *Lucretia, or The Children of Night* (1846), question the whig model of the progress of civilization by providing a barbed commentary on the middle-class world where a principle concern is speculation, both financial and moral.

Linked to the theme of speculation is the presentation of France and the French. Even though the main action of *Vanity Fair* takes place in the Napoleonic era while *Lucretia* spans forty years between the first and second French Revolutions, the "impatience" to possess that is the driving force of the central characters in each novel can be identified with both the Britain and France of the 1840s.

Superficially, the form of the novel might appear the ideal means of avoiding implicating the reader in a quest for personal relevance. The "events" of a novel are imagined rather than actual, and moreover the past tense of fiction, confirmed usually in the grammar of the text but always by the final closure of the last page, avoids the problem of the meaning of the present. Were readers to approach novels with the detachment of whig historians, the novel might indeed be a form of escape from one's own present, and self-evidently, entering other people's lives and experiences is one of the fundamental attractions of novel-reading. For most readers, however, tory interpretation begins to impinge: the reader no longer believes "This is not I," but "This is a possible I"—or a possible other by whom "I" am threatened. As this inner dialog suggests, the past of the novel is during the process of reading a present: but even more powerfully, often a present which, as Marxist critics have noted, provides a means of discussing the void of one's own historical present in a way that history itself repeatedly fails to do. I would therefore suggest that the reason why the "political unconscious" theorized by Fredric Jameson after the Marxist model of historical dialectic often works most effectively for conservative writers is because it is not quite as "unconscious" as it initially appears.[7] I am certainly not claiming that tory writing demonstrates a clearer historical grasp of the present; but the tory claim that the present is understood by historical analogy recreates "now" as a historical moment.

Lucretia and *Vanity Fair* exemplify this relationship by creating difference, but retaining immediacy. Writing directly after the French Revolution of February 1848, William Makepeace Thackeray replied to George Henry Lewes's criticism that the yet-incomplete *Vanity Fair* implied that character is determined by money or lack of it by humorously connecting his own Becky Sharp and Louis Philippe as representative types in a bourgeois world dominated by money.

> If Becky had had 5000 a year I have no doubt in my mind that she would have been respectable; increased her fortune advanced her family in the world; laid up treasures for herself in the shape of 3 per cents, social position, reputation, &c—like Louis Philippe let us say, or like many a person highly and comfortably placed in the world. ...[8]

The newly-expelled Louis Philippe was a topical subject; nevertheless, Thackeray's association of his fictional character with a real-life French citizen rather than with a British one is a revealing choice. For many Britons, France and the French continued to provide the means of an only partly conscious self-critique presented in historical terms.

Lucretia and *Vanity Fair* draw heavily on the tory truism that "human nature is ever the same"; but although this suggests that morality is ahistorical, in both novels, historical developments in France and England provide the context for historically specific actions, creating an opposition between British and French attitudes which finally proves not to be as polarized as it may initially appear. Were the most criminal forces in each work to be unequivocally French, the effect might not be as disturbing in its relevance to British readers. But the most unscrupulous intellects of each novel are both English and French, either by birth, as in the case of Becky Sharp and Gabriel Varney; or by adoption, as in the case of Lucretia Clavering Dalibard. A reader who could retain a sense of cultural detachment from these figures could see their stories as whig history, the product of a specific historical situation. Yet the effect of the novels is dependent on a nagging tory-historical undertone: that the characters and situations are not entirely removed from the reader's own world by time or nationality.

Lucretia and Becky Sharp are pragmatists in a pragmatic age. To whig historians at least, the appointment of Louis Philippe in 1830 demonstrated that France had abandoned the passionate idealism of the first French Revolution and instead was following Britain's example in creating a system of government based on compromise. But heavy restrictions on the freedom of the press following the student rising in Paris in 1832 and the insurrection in Lyons of 1834–5 suggested that perhaps the new régime did not mark progress towards enlightened freedom as the whigs had hoped. Thackeray had as early as 1833 had described the "King of the French" as a "snob" whose "zeal for the multitude's gone, and of no numbers thinking, except number one!"[9] and concurred with the tory view in noting that all that had been achieved was repression and "humbug":[10] the French represented not a progressive nation, but a corrupt one.

Nevertheless, despite the risk of moral contamination, Britain could not afford to isolate itself from France in an age of commerce, when political developments in Paris affected share-prices in London. At least in economic matters, the commercial classes of France and Britain had common interests and attitudes. If France and Britain alike were becoming commercial nations at least to the extent that "real" power was still located in property-owning classes, yet those classes were no longer restricted to the traditionally Tory domain of landowners but included the generally more Whiggish merchants, financiers, and manufacturers,[11] the effect would be to diminish previously-stressed differences between the two nations. Hence the anxiety continued as to whether the French shared strengths and weaknesses with the British, or whether certain traits—and especially undesirable ones—could still be dismissed as essentially French. For Britons to condemn French literature as corrupt, for example, would have been a convenient self-dissociation, but the 1830s in Britain were the time of the "Newgate novel," in which crime was presented ostensibly with the object of demonstrating how it did not pay, but often in effect with the result that the criminals themselves became the heroes, their exploits paying very well in monetary terms. Indeed, writers in both Britain and France show concern at the role that money was taking in society, suggesting that the "age of commerce" had replaced all other values.

Perhaps the best description of both financial and moral values under Louis Philippe is Louis Blanc's *History of Ten Years, 1830–1840 (L'Histoire de Dix Ans)*, a book that, I would contend, influenced both themes and specific characterizations in *Lucretia* and *Vanity Fair*: even though he rejected its socialism, Thackeray, for example, read Blanc's book in French in 1842.[12] Anticipating the *Communist Manifesto* by several years, Blanc makes a clear definition between the "people" (those dependent on other parts of society for their living) and the "bourgeoisie" (those "possessing the instruments of labour or a capital").[13] While the Bourbon Restoration brought in "the era of material interests" (*Ten Years* 1:25), following the July Revolution the real power was ceded to the bourgeoisie, and financial concerns became paramount. Blanc laments how by the late 1830s, France,

> which had almost invented chivalry, which had made itself for ever illustrious by the elegance of its manners; that nation which it had been customary to cite for its wit, its grace, its disinterestedness, its courtesy so delicate and high-spirited, now suddenly appeared under the sway of a class that laboured under a loathsome fever of industrialism. For that class every thing was become matter of traffic. Struggling crowds filled the approaches to the banks. To take up shares without paying for them, to sell them, pocket the premium, and make fortunes by the rise, such was the universal mania, such was the dream in which many tens of thousands lived with their eyes open. (*Ten Years* 2:563)

In this translation, Blanc's picture of the over-materialist Paris of the July Monarchy uses language similar to that of Carlyle's over-ideologized Paris of the first Revolution.

Although Blanc argues that an obsession with money entered France at this time, this could scarcely be seen as exclusively French; indeed, Blanc hints that the problems grew as France followed Britain's example in industrializing. As early as 1833, when British middle-class males with a proof of property had just been granted a political identity, Bulwer-Lytton himself had noted that "In other countries poverty is a misfortune—with us it is a crime."[14] By the mid-1840s, speculation, especially in the form of the purchase of railway stock with the potential of paying far larger dividends than the modest three per cent of safe stock, was the height of fashion. In *Lucretia*, speculation is associated with being French and with being unscrupulous, and, also significantly, with being a poisoner. Bulwer-Lytton maintained in his Preface that his goal was to expose these vices rather than celebrate them, but the result was a work that the critics found shocking—in the *Athenaeum*'s words, "a bad book of a bad school."[15]

The shock of entering a world almost entirely without values beyond personal gain is seen in the opening chapter of the work, when Bulwer-Lytton makes use of his readers' sense not of the 1830 French Revolution, but of the French Revolution of 1789. Bulwer-Lytton is notorious for the weakness of the openings of his novels, but in what is perhaps his most effective beginning, the scene is "an apartment in Paris, one morning, during the Reign of Terror."[16] An as-yet unnamed man, later identified as Olivier Dalibard, is first presented as sitting at a table in front of "a tall book-case, surmounted with a bust of Robespierre," working on state papers written by Robespierre and his associate Couthon.

Robespierre has, however, a larger part in Dalibard's character than simply looking over his shoulder. Dalibard fulfills a promise to his young son to take him to an execution, which proves to be that of the child's English mother and her aristocratic lover. The Frenchman's warning to his son, "Learn how they perish who betray me!" (*Lucretia*, p. 9, ch.1) suggests that he is a private Robespierre: his concern is not for the state but for himself.

Dalibard's son Honoré Gabriel grows up detached from the revolutionary idealism implied by being named after Mirabeau to be anglicized as Gabriel Varney. The first half of the story, set in the Napoleonic era, concerns love and a desire for wealth in a complex tangle of inheritances and marriages; but even before the end of Part I—significantly, when Dalibard and his new wife the English heiress Lucretia Clavering move to France—a new element is introduced, that of poison. Dalibard unearths the poisoning skills of

Renaissance Italy, and sets up a laboratory in Paris. Here, Jean Bellanger, a millionaire from whom Dalibard had hoped to gain an inheritance, dies, "not suddenly, and yet of some quick disease—nervous exhaustion: his schemes, they said, had worn him out" (*Lucretia*, p. 235; Epilogue to Part I). His disease is certainly caused by desire for financial gain, but not his own: Dalibard has poisoned him for a legacy. Yet the novel's first speculation by poison fails to pay: Bellanger proves to have an heir, and by implication, Dalibard turns to the expedient of slowly poisoning Lucretia to inherit her property interests, only to be murdered by the contrivance of his wife.

In the second Part, Lucretia herself takes on the role of the scheming villain Dalibard; as L. Ciolkowski observes, she has "become infected with the influence of the French,"[17] and her characterization exploits a fear of such influence. She even takes over Dalibard's son and accomplice Gabriel Varney (her stepson and implicitly her lover) before her return to England, where the pair embarks upon a series of frauds and poisonings.

Yet although the bad end badly, the artistic yet unscrupulous Varney being transported while the androgynous, amoral Lucretia becomes, as those women who had trespassed on the male world during the French Revolution had become, a madwoman, the book upset seemingly all of its reviewers. The *Athenaeum* argued that similar "impatience" for gain existed before Varney gave the reading public lessons in "Strichnine [sic] made Easy."[18] Even more prominently, *The Times* insisted that even if, as Bulwer-Lytton claimed in the Preface to the first edition, the narrative is based on fact, "what valid excuse is this for filling the mind with horrible details that can never by any possibility effect the least public good, and may in the hands of the artist produce incalculable evil?"[19]

This would appear to be *The Times*'s justification for departing from its usual policy by devoting two and a half columns to a review of a novel. Novels may, perhaps, not merely reflect cultural preoccupations, but help create them, and *The Times* continues the concern at the impact of corrupt literature on society. Even before the publication of *Lucretia* and *Vanity Fair*, *Punch*, referring to the case of John Tawell, a completely English poisoner, had presented poisoning as a practice known only to Britons from French literature: "Folks are apt to turn from a novel, though wholly composed of French sentiment and French arsenic, to study the living animal charged with poisoning."[20] Poison had become a symbol for France's baneful and potentially anarchical influence on Britain.

In reality, Bulwer-Lytton's inspiration for his male poisoner in *Lucretia* was English, although a man who spent time in France, some of it in jail, during the 1830s. In the character of the artist Varney, who contrives in the poisoning of a young family connection called Helen, and who is eventually convicted only of forgery, readers would have recognized some details of a real case, that of Thomas Griffiths Wainewright (1794–1852).[21] With the notable exception of L. Ciolkowski's discussion of politics and gender in *Lucretia*, however, the identification of Varney as Wainewright has served for most critics as a distraction from the fact that he is Lucretia's assistant rather than the other way round: like *Vanity Fair*, this is "a novel without a hero," and its most powerful intellect is especially monstrous in being a woman who invades the sphere of the propertied male.

Keith Hollingsworth not unreasonably suggests that Bulwer-Lytton may have been anxious to avoid the identification of Lucretia with Wainewright's wife Frances, still living in Britain at this time.[22] But Lucretia's characterization is certainly influenced by the reputation of French poisoners during this period, and when in his *Examiner* review of the novel John Forster identified Wainewright as the original of Varney he added: "The original of Lucretia was, we believe, a Frenchwoman."[23] Forster's characterization of Lucretia's original as French is significant in itself in following *Punch*'s assertion that poisoning was a French habit.

Traditionally, the British did not attribute the development of the use of poison to France but to Italy: the secrets that Dalibard and Lucretia discover are from the Italian Renaissance.[24] Hence the reason why poisoning should be seen as a French trait is linked to a cultural moment. As Bulwer-Lytton had noted in 1833, from the British point of view, poison was a staple of French theatre: indeed, he borrowed Lucretia's catastrophe, the poisoning of her long-lost son, from Victor Hugo's 1833 drama *Lucrèce Borgia*, the ultimate demonstration of how a French version of Italian poisoning could influence British art.[25] Poisoning was also a feature of popular French romances, including Alexandre Dumas's *Three Musketeers* (1844) and *The Count of Monte Cristo* (1845).[26]

With what might reasonably be termed whig-historical curiosity, the fascination that comes of a sense, however self-deceiving, of cultural detachment, considerable British interest was shown in French poisoning cases both contemporary and historical. (*Punch* and the *Athenaeum*'s reviews of *Lucretia*, for example, both mention the seventeenth-century Madame de Brinvilliers.)[27] Most of the French and

British cases reported in publications such as the *Annual Register* were apparently inspired by the murderer's desire to be rid of a spouse, but cases involving property drew especial attention. Probably the most notorious was the trial of Madame Lafarge for the murder of her husband, reported at exhaustive length in *The Times* in September 1840. British publications disagreed over Lafarge's guilt: the *Examiner* implied that she should have received a death-sentence, and that French courts were too lenient: "Interesting poisoners are not uncommon in France. If the husband be old and ugly and the wife young and spiritual the circumstances of poisoning him are 'extenuating.'"[28] The *Examiner* was drawing on a stereotype confirmed by the fictional examples: poisoners are women who usurp male power. Since France is the country of the overthrow of historical political structures, that poisoners should be Frenchwomen is especially symbolic.[29]

The gender-stereotyping was allied with political critique. Marie Capelle Lafarge was distantly connected with Louis Philippe himself, and the oversimplification of Lafarge as a woman who would poison not merely for passion but also for property helped support the claims of both Louis Blanc and other critics of his administration that Louis Philippe was the embodiment of a corrupt society, motivated only by desire for personal gain. Oddly, then, tory history finds an ally in socialism, both proclaiming the corruption of the whig paradise of the July Monarchy.

Additionally, Blanc's *History of Ten Years* contains a story that may have been of interest not just to Bulwer-Lytton but also to Thackeray. According to Blanc, the old Duc de Bourbon was in the power of

> a woman whose origin was obscure, whose family name was uncertain, who had formerly, it was said, figured on the boards of Covent-garden Theatre, who having afterwards formed a connexion with a foreigner of enormous wealth, had lived at Turnham-green on the wages of dishonour, and who, lastly, having become all-powerful over the heart of the Duc de Bourbon, had married the Baron de Feuchères, a frank, honest soldier, whose abused good faith served for some time to conceal the scandal of adulterous amours.[30]

Madame de Feuchères (identified by George Henry Lewes, who retold the entire story in his review of Blanc's book, as an English actor called Sophy Dawes)[31] implicated the Orléans family in a complex plot involving vast sums of money. The Duc de Bourbon was found hanging in his room in mysterious circumstances, and left his substantial wealth to a son of Louis Philippe. Afterwards, Madame de Feuchères's bourgeois character is revealed:

> She had long been gambling at the Stock Exchange to an enormous amount; she followed up her speculations, and in the course of some months found herself the gainer by considerable sums.[32]

The involvement of an Anglo-French actor like Varney's mother and Becky Sharp in this story is intriguing; Blanc's (and Lewes's) point in devoting so much space to it, however, is to show the depths to which Louis Philippe and his cohorts will sink for financial gain. Although poisoning is not mentioned (Louis Philippe, the one who gained most, was still king at the time of writing), Blanc casts dark hints that the Duc de Bourbon did not meet his death by hanging, and that the postmortem examinations were suspiciously unconvincing. Even if this story is a product of Blanc's anti-Orléanism and nothing more, it helps to contribute to the cultural myth of murder for financial gain as an appropriate symbol for a decadent society.

The horror and fascination with poisoning during this time seems related to the tory fear of anarchy. Poisoning comes to represent the abandonment of a structured society, in which everyone knows his or her natural place. The victim is almost invariably a close relative, suggesting that family values count for nothing compared with the speculative motive of personal gain; and if the family is a microcosm of the state, the disloyalty of women, those outside the power-structure of the state. is especially disturbing. The misogyny of many poisoning reports—the *Examiner*'s account of Madame Lafarge's sentence, which proceeds to mention how when the sex-roles were reversed and an Englishman was tried for murdering his overbearing wife, the jury's verdict was that it "served her right" is a case in point—prompts the conclusion that poison was feared because it took control from men. Poisoning was characterized as a woman's crime because unlike crimes requiring physical strength, poison could be administered just as easily by a woman as by a man—in fact, probably more easily, since women controlled what was eaten and drunk in most households. The connection between real life and literature remains difficult to correlate, but an image had clearly been created of a poisoning society, which peaked about the time of the publication of *Lucretia*.[33] For British readers, it would definitely have been more comfortable to see poison as a domestic form of French Revolution, symptomatic of problems of French society rather than their own.

The outrage at the depiction of Lucretia may hence be that she cannot be dismissed as merely French; she is Anglo-French and middle-class. This present-day Lucretia is, in fact, a bourgeoise Borgia, and while she has the subsidiary motivation of revenge, her main goal is the bourgeois object of obtaining property. Readerly self-dissociation on the basis of nationality was only partly possible—Lucretia is English by birth—and certainly not possible on the basis of class.[34]

Keith Hollingsworth argues in his study of the Newgate Novel that after the scandal over *Lucretia* the subgenre faded away through public disapproval of its implications, and that another novel with an Anglo-French female protagonist, *Vanity Fair*, articulates this disapproval. For Hollingsworth, *Vanity Fair*'s connection with the Newgate tradition suggests that the conception of criminal as both hero and moral example could no longer be taken seriously, or that the seriousness must be carefully submerged.[35]

Hollingsworth is probably justified in asserting that Thackeray took on a personal mission to expose the evils of the Newgate Novel.[36] *Vanity Fair* may, however, be not just a lampoon of the Newgate Novel but rather a concession that Newgate Novel values are part of modern life: Thackeray's historical chronicle has reached the present age of commerce. The critique may thus be read not as Hollingsworth suggests, predominantly generically; but rather as a reflection upon the society that the genre represents.

Thackeray's novel was recognized by readers as a comedy, and moreover as a comedy set in the historic past. Were it indeed a historical novel, then its commentary was somewhat less threatening. The title itself, with its reference to Bunyan and hence to a type of novel where characters represent human virtues and failings, suggests a moral universality. Moral universality is, however, a part of tory history, in that given specific circumstances, specific results can be anticipated. But in other respects, the world created by Thackeray echoes the whig notion of the spirit of the age, in which characters are specifically affected by historical context. *Vanity Fair* may hence be closer to *Lucretia* than its original readers cared to concede in focusing on moral and social preoccupations of the period of its composition.

Consequently, rather than distancing topical concerns, *Vanity Fair*'s historical setting highlights them. Becky Sharp is first presented using Napoleon as a means of showing her social defiance. Pointing out to her "friend" Amelia Sedley that their school mistress Miss Pinkerton "doesn't know a word of French, and was too proud to confess it," Becky continues: "I believe it was that which made her part with me;

and so thank heaven for the French. *Vive la France! Vive l'Empereur! Vive Bonaparte!"*[37]

Becky has already complicated the connotations of France. She has implied a sense of social superiority to those who do not know French and can only value the English language of Doctor Johnson: French, she suggests, is evidence of sophistication. This is a ploy on Becky's part to convince Amelia that Becky herself is not to blame in her dismissal from Miss Pinkerton's; yet in fact the course of the novel bears out her claim that a familiarity with French is advantageous, as Jos Sedley later learns to his cost in the French-speaking nation of Belgium. The child of an English artist father and a French actor mother, described as an "opera-girl" (*Vanity Fair*, p. 48), Becky moves easily between the worlds of England and Europe.

But Becky has simultaneously shocked the conventional Amelia by praising England's enemy Napoleon. Becky herself espouses some of the opportunism of a Napoleon: she has nothing, but aspires to be ruler of her own empire. Thackeray underlined the point in his chapter-heading illustration to the sixty-fourth chapter, where Becky, on the rebound after her London disgrace, is portrayed as Napoleon returning from Elba. At many points in *Vanity Fair*, Thackeray recreates British paranoia concerning Napoleon and his ambitions; readers of the 1840s might smile at their parents' fear of French conquest, but perhaps simultaneously, the conquest of moral values perceived as French in the supposedly gentler era of Louis Philippe might be a new cause for alarm.

In her own world, Becky achieves a Napoleonic rise. One reason for her social success is that she represents a kind of excitement that a truly English woman such as Amelia can never capture. Amelia shares her name with the title-character of Henry Fielding's 1752 novel; she also shares a tireless (or even tiresome) devotion to her scarcely-deserving soldier-husband. But if this allusion is significant, Becky's name is surely also significant: she shares the name of Scott's Rebecca the Jewess in *Ivanhoe* (1819). Because of her position as an outsider Scott's Rebecca is excluded from the possibility of being a heroine, but, as Thackeray insisted through his alter-ego Michael Angelo Titmarsh in his "Proposals for a Continuation of *Ivanhoe*," published in *Fraser's* at the same time that he was beginning work on *Vanity Fair*, she is far more exciting a character than Rowena, the titular heroine of *Ivanhoe* who marries the hero. (Rebecca of York, although accused of using sinister medications, is thoroughly virtuous; but as Becky Sharp herself would point out, her father has the medieval equivalent of five thousand a year, and she can afford to be.) That "Proposals for a Continuation of *Ivanhoe*" and the later *Rebecca and Rowena* are parodic works should not cause question of the concept that inspired them: that for most readers, Rebecca is more interesting a character than her English counterpart.[38] Thackeray's own Rebecca is also an outsider—but one of an age where women who will seek to even the balance in a manner not possible for a heroine of an earlier age.

As a woman who is partly French and raised outside "respectable" life by an artist, Becky has the advantage of recognizing but not respecting social conventions. The English characters of the work (admittedly in most cases with potentially more to lose than Becky, who has nothing) are incapable of being as unconventional in their sentiments and actions. The most politically extreme is Miss Crawley, who in addition to having "a balance at her banker's which would have made her beloved anywhere" (*Vanity Fair*, p. 124) had shown her early Radicalism by affecting French ways, having been

> a *bel ésprit*, and a dreadful Radical for those days. She had been in France (where St. Just, they say, inspired her with an unfortunate passion), and loved, ever after, French novels, French cookery, and French wines. (*Vanity Fair*, p. 130)

The French Revolutionist Miss Crawley is in her mature years highly materialist in her emulation of France, firmly committed to an aristocracy of blood, and hence not likely to bring about radical change. Becky herself presents far more of a threat to the establishment by claiming nobility of birth when it suits her (to the Crawleys she poses as of aristocratic *emigré* stock), but being essentially classless: she herself represents liberty and equality.

But liberty and equality here must be qualified as referring to opportunity. The second reason for Becky's success is that she understands money—and here the novel is less clearly historical, but rather reminiscent of both Britain and France in the period of the July Monarchy, already historicized by Blanc and others as the age of commerce. Becky is a social threat because she is moving in a world where traditional aristocracy is becoming secondary to money—where a mixed-race Miss Swartz, with the wealth of West Indian estates, can marry a Scottish nobleman, and where Becky and her husband can live "on nothing a year," provided that they present the appearance of possessing wealth.

Becky and Rawdon can live well "on nothing a year" because they are part of a society that grants credit to those that it believes to be creditworthy, and Becky is quite capable of manipulating her self-presentation to show that she is. Becky is initially presented as a speculator; her first gamble is for Jos Sedley's Indian riches, and this she loses; her investment of self in a marriage with Rawdon Crawley also fails to earn interest as rapidly as she anticipates. Towards the end of the book she is literally a gambler, playing the gaming tables in her true milieu, cosmopolitan Europe.

Becky's earlier speculations, however, may be a means of making her attractive to an age fascinated by the possibility of investment. Obviously, the novel makes an association between gambling and vice. Yet gambling is a form of speculation that also contributes to mobility between classes, and may even have a bearing on international politics. For example, at Gaunt House in the late eighteenth century:

> Egalité Orleans roasted partridges on the night when he and the Marquis of Steyne won a hundred thousand from a great personage at ombre. Half of the money went to the French Revolution, half to purchase Lord Gaunt's Marquisate and Garter. ... (*Vanity Fair*, pp. 545–546)

The narration, weakening the social critique as usual, ascribes this story to gossip; yet as Thackeray was to make clear in his 1855 lecture series *The Four Georges*, the "great personage" is George Prince of Wales, the future Prince Regent.[39] The English prince's money (granted to him from state revenues) is used to underwrite the French Revolution through the father of Louis Philippe. Lord Steyne's partnership with Egalité—the champion of equality—helps him to rise in the aristocracy: he has in fact speculated correctly on the historical future. In contrast, gambling decreases the rank of the Crawleys, yet they hardly prompt much readerly identification with their financial straits, and certainly fail to function as a moral example. A clue that George Osborne may not supply this novel's need for a hero is his youthful involvement in gambling; on the other hand, his father, who regards gambling as an unforgiveable vice, is an even less sympathetic character. Speculation, then, with its potentially revolutionary effect on class, is part of the attraction of danger in the story. Indeed, Becky herself is seen at her least appealing when she is no longer a gambler, but when Rawdon discovers that she has been storing away large sums of money with no intention of sharing them with him.

A more traditional businessperson in the novel is Amelia's stockbroker father John Sedley. Early in the story, John Sedley jokingly tells his servant to fetch his son Jos an elephant from Exeter Exchange, but his following remark, "It's all fair on the Stock Exchange" (*Vanity Fair*, p. 66) suggests that ultimately, the joke is on him. The stock market is linked to European, and particularly French, political developments, and also to states of mind: Mr. Osborne's bad humor, for example, is explained away by Miss Wirt with "I suppose the funds are falling" (p. 162). The affairs of France, and specifically the news of Napoleon's return from Elba, lead to John Sedley's bankruptcy. Thackeray summarizes the connection succinctly:

> in the month of March, Anno Domini 1815, Napoleon landed at Cannes, and Louis XVIII fled, and all Europe was in alarm, and the funds fell, and old John Sedley was ruined. (p. 216)[40]

Here as elsewhere, history intrudes into the world of the novel, making John Sedley into a small victim of international politics, and an increasingly poor speculator. He invests money in dear coal and bad wines (the latter being a mistake that surely shows his lack of French sophistication), and sinks to the level of the "contemptible," as John Forster characterized him in the *Examiner* in July 1848, when the narration reveals that he has sold the annuity that Jos bought the family "for a sum of money wherewith to prosecute his bootless schemes" (*Vanity Fair*, p. 576). The question left unanswered is whether Sedley is contemptible because he is a speculator, or contemptible because he is an unsuccessful one.

Vanity Fair hints most heavily at a connection between speculation and contemporary crime in its concluding chapters. Becky Sharp's original gamble pays off many years later—in fact, in the time of Louis Philippe—when she takes Jos as her partner. At Jos's death three months later, the insurers holding policies on his life swear it is "the blackest case that had ever come before them" (p. 796), and attempt to stop payment.[41] The strong hint is that Becky has poisoned him;[42] but the matter is left unresolved, the money is paid, and Becky goes on to be a success in the society cities of the 1830s, and to contribute largely to charity. Thus her early thought, described appropriately as "speculations" by the narration, "I think I could be a good woman if I had five thousand a year" (p. 495), takes on a reality at least in appearance in the time of Louis Philippe. History has now caught up with Becky: it is the true age of money, and not surprisingly, she ends tarnished but triumphant.

The possibility that Becky becomes not merely a speculator profiting from the gullible but also a poisoner is both linked to the historical moment, an age where personal gain outweighs all other considerations, even within the family; and also to her "Frenchness." The *Quarterly Review*, for example, published an appraisal of Becky revealing in its self-contradiction. The review of both *Vanity Fair* and *Jane Eyre* by Elizabeth Rigby, who about this time became Lady Eastlake, is best remembered for its attack on the immorality of *Jane Eyre*, and for repeating (or possibly inventing) the rumor that the author was Thackeray's children's governess. But it also shows a reponse to Becky by a writer claiming to speak on behalf of the moral standards of her peers. Eastlake simultaneously argues for the universality of Thackeray's moral structure, and for the uniqueness of Becky Sharp, asserting that readers need not be shocked by her behavior because she is still "not one of us, and there is an end to our sympathies and censures. ..."[43] Yet Becky is not simply "other." Eastlake then calls it "an affront to Becky's tactics to believe that she would ever be reduced to so low a resource" as poisoning Jos, "or, that if she were, anybody would find it out" (p. 160). This makes Becky too "different" from those readers who possess some of her characteristics, or detect them in their associates: "The whole *use*, too, of the work—that of generously measuring one another by this standard—is lost, the moment you convict Becky of a capital crime. Who can, with any face, liken a dear friend to a murderess?"

Eastlake hence recommends that her readers "cut out" the picture of Becky as Clytemnestra; nevertheless, Thackeray has "almost disarmed" her criticism of "the possibly assistant circumstances of Joseph Sedley's dissolution"

> by making her mother a Frenchwoman. The construction of this little clever monster is diabolically French. Such a *luses naturae* as a woman without a heart and conscience would, in England, be a mere brutal savage, and poison half a village. France is the land for the real Syren, with the woman's face and the dragon's claws. (pp. 160–161)

Becky has both elements of appeal and discomfort: if she were entirely French—Eastlake cites Lafarge—and entirely "other," she would merely be amusing; but if she is simultaneously an English bourgeoise, a reflection of the reader, there are limits beyond which she should not go.

Eastlake wants to be an unshockable whig in her response to Becky, but betrays the tory feeling of moral involvement. Her discomfort with the implications of Becky Sharp's character suggests a hint of cultural self-recognition that she endeavors rapidly to dismiss: Becky could, indeed, be one of her friends. She does not suggest, however, that *Vanity Fair* is, as Hollingsworth argues, a parodic indictment of the values of novels such as *Lucretia*. That the Newgate Novel faded as a genre after *Vanity Fair* may hence be better explained as a political reaction. The July Monarchy was described in retrospect by John Stuart Mill as functioning "almost exclusively through the meaner and more selfish impulses of mankind."[44] With the fall of Louis Philippe and other governments throughout Europe in 1848, to which in Britain might be added the fall of another people's king, the railway speculator George Hudson in May 1849, the age of pragmatism was to be superseded by a brief period in which idealism was to outweigh the interests of commerce, notably in France's socialist experiment in which Louis Blanc himself was to play a prominent role. In the light of the threat to the property of which whig and tory history claimed to be guardian by genuine working-class movements seeking power, the threat of private enterprise as embodied by bourgeois financial speculators such as Lucretia Dalibard, Gabriel Varney, and Becky Sharp became relatively insignificant.

Optimism and Denial

Lucretia and *Vanity Fair* depict characters who travel between Britain and Continental Europe; in real life, similar touring might be indicative of a willingness to give up traditional British isolation, and to be influenced by the French. According to Thomé de Gamond, since the introduction of steamships and railways, the number of people crossing the Channel each year had risen from 80,000 in the 1820s, when Paris was six days' journey away from London, to 350,000 in the 1840s: most of these were Britons traveling to France.[45]

When Louis Philippe was forced to flee Paris in February 1848, the tory reaction was predictable, tory historians quickly claiming proof of their power to prophesy like Burke. Archibald Alison, for example, reminded his readers that *Blackwood's* had "ventured, amidst the general transports, to arraign the policy and condemn the morality of the change" which had led to "nothing but a long series of calamities to France and to Europe."[46] Croker claimed for himself and the *Quarterly*: "We never had any faith in the duration of the new monarchy."[47] In a sense, this was true, since Alison had repeatedly prophesied anarchy and bloodshed, while Croker had asserted in 1834 that

"France must again pass through a despotism—a republic—or a restoration—and probably all these—before she can settle down into a constitution which shall command the undivided respect and rational obedience of the nation."[48] Yet such claims hardly made them the Burkes of the age, since Louis Philippe had reigned for eighteen years, and his fall did not follow the pattern of either 1789–94 or the end of Napoleon. Indeed, in his undignified expulsion to Britain, Louis Philippe almost established true legitimacy by following the fate of Charles X, he too being accepted into Britain as an exiled foreign monarch.[49]

Croker in the *Quarterly* recognized the implications of government by socialists, including Louis Blanc, as a drastic restructuring, and made his traditional appeal to historical precedent topical by mixing the vocabulary of the age of socialism with words connoting the first French Revolution:

> Our readers will appreciate the prospects of a country which is to have neither king—nor nobles—nor gentry—nor even a *bourgeoisie*. What remains for it but the bonnet-rouge, pike, and plunder of the Sans-Culottes?

Although the revolutionaries of 1848 were not "maniacs" like Marat, their philosophical principles were incompatible "with what the world has hitherto called social order."[50]

If Croker's response was much as might be anticipated, he gained allies in less expected places, including long-time Whigs of the status of Henry, Lord Brougham. Brougham too associated 1848 with property, but in such a way that he appeared to reconciling his position with that of Edmund Burke. Brougham justified his horror at the "dreadful scenes" on the apparently tory basis of dangerous example: "What men admire they are prone to imitate."[51] He still cautiously ascribes to the whig doctrine that the first French Revolution was ultimately a force for good, and that the July Revolution was also potentially in the interests of progress, but argues that the 1848 Revolution is heading towards Terror.

On the other hand, literati such as Arthur Hugh Clough, Ralph Waldo Emerson and Geraldine Jewsbury (Jewsbury combining idealism with the age of commerce by taking the opportunity to do some shopping) visited France to witness history as it happened—which as always involved the imposition of a reading of the past, and especially the first French Revolution, upon the present.[52] Many of them were hoping that the socialist revolutionaries would be new Girondists and establish a true republic. Early in 1848, Clough had been pondering his position as a Fellow at Oriel College Oxford because of his religious doubts, and his letters assert his interest in revolutions as a new direction for hope: "if it were not for all these blessed revolutions," he wrote in March, "I should sink into hopeless lethargy."[53] Four sonnets by Matthew Arnold addressed to Clough and published as a series in *The Strayed Reveller and Other Poems* in 1849 confirm that at first the latter had high hopes for Europe's new idealism, yet reveal in Arnold himself a degree of confusion beneath the apparently serene philosophy. Sonnets are usually a present-tense form of literature; Arnold's "To a Republican Friend, 1848," apparently composed about the point of Clough's greatest optimism in March, is, however, structured in future conditional. Addressing his friend as the representative of republicanism ("you" here suggesting a plural, since "To a Friend" awkwardly uses "thou" to stress the singular), Arnold states that if the qualities of idealism, namely, rejection of hypocrisy ("to despise/ The barren optimistic sophistries/ Of comfortable moles"); "sadness at the long heart-wasting show"; and positive thinking about the poor and destitute constitute being a republican, then he will be one too.

Arnold has suggested that the revolutionary impulse at least makes an attempt to address major problems of the age—bourgeois complacency and working-class poverty—but has made departure from tradition heavily conditional on historical success. A second sonnet, "To a Republican Friend, Continued," undermines even the heavily-qualified assertions of the first:

> Yet, when I muse on what life is, I seem
> Rather to patience prompted, than that proud
> Prospect of hope which France proclaims so loud—
> France, famed in all great arts, in none supreme. ...[54]

Interestingly, Arnold attributes to France (and implicitly to all republicans, including Clough) the fault that Bulwer-Lytton claimed as his initial subject in *Lucretia*, that of impatience. This is not, though, an impatience for personal gain, but rather an impatience for human improvement, a condition that Arnold seemingly doubts to be attainable in life. If France is "famed in all great arts, in none supreme," then France is not what Clough had hoped—the example that the world should follow.

Arnold's first poem is an English sonnet, where twelve lines lead to an uncomfortable concluding couplet:

> If these are yours, if this is what you are,
> Then I am yours, and what you feel, I share.

The imperfection of the rhyme (it may be significant that in British standard pronunciation, the rhyme is closer to perfect if "are" is pronounced "err"), underlines the improbability of the conditions being fulfilled. Superficially, the poet is rejecting France as example. Yet the choice of writing in sonnet-form at all, and particularly in using both the Shakespearean and the Petrarchan forms, simultaneously concedes part of Clough's argument: that Europe has a common heritage. Arnold can only broaden this to a general statement of human universality.

Another two sonnets follow these, "Religious Isolation," which shows its relation to the previous pair by the subtitle "To the Same Friend"; and "To a Friend." Again, the pairing of an English sonnet followed by an Italian emphasizes that individual assertion must succumb to recognition of the sharing of values, yet in this case, Arnold endeavors to present the latter as a positive creed. Traditionally, the third sonnet is said to refer to Clough's religious doubts, and his decision to leave Oriel. Yet within the sequence, the concluding couplet may be less Arnold's confirmation of his friend's right to live by his individual conscience, but a reassertion of the message of the previous two sonnets, where the impossibility of a group conscience and of a human society living by ideals has been raised. Liberal independence of spirit is simultaneously conservatively anti-revolutionary, even *laissez-faire*, in the lines:

> To its own impulse every creature stirs;
> Live by thy light, and earth will live by hers!

If Arnold can hold out no hope in revolution, and seemingly none in faith, Clough might rightly ask the cumbersome question of the final sonnet: "Who prop, thou ask'st, in these bad days, my mind?" The "bad days" may be times of personal doubt, but almost certainly, since the poem has been dated about August 1848, the "bad days" are the collapse of the French revolution of February, civil unrest in Britain and Ireland, and the waning of the other European revolutions. For Arnold, without the prop of whig, tory, or even socialist history, the present is a void. His refuge is in the permanent human values of Greek literature and philosophy—yet to find these permanent values, he is compelled to turn to the past.

That Arnold included these sonnets in *The Strayed Reveller*, even though he did not put his full name to the collection, makes them a public statement rather than only a moment of private sharing with Clough. This is clearly a more complex declaration of difference than the simple whig assertion that Britain was not like France. Stressing the independence of the personal—unlike Clough, he refuses to identify with a group cause—Arnold nevertheless has to maintain this independence through a shared European heritage.

Other self-proclaimed liberal thinkers remained even more firmly at home, and denied the potentiality of influence through the whig mode of stressing the cultural gulf between Britain and Europe. Two historical works of 1848, John Mitchell Kemble's *The Saxons in England* and the first volumes of Thomas Babington Macaulay's *History of England*, both present the length of the process through which the British national, and to some extent party, identity has emerged as narrative.

Kemble's two-volume work might appear a Continental project in seeking to trace the traditions and institutions of the English back to ancient Germanic stock. Yet the Preface, dated December 1848, points out Britain's stability compared with the rest of Europe:

> On every side of us thrones totter, and the deep foundations of society are convulsed. Shot and shell sweep the streets of capitals which have long been pointed out as the chosen abodes of order: cavalry and bayonets cannot control populations whose loyalty has become a proverb here, whose peace has been made a reproach to our own miscalled disquiet. Yet the exalted Lady who wields the sceptre of these realms, sits safe upon her throne, and fearless in the holy circle of her domestic happiness, secure in the affections of a people whose institutions have given to them all the blessings of an equal law.

Discounting civil unrest in England, Kemble argues that the nation's continuous constitutional values have protected it against revolution. The study of England's early history, then, is a patriotic duty:

> We have a share in the past, and the past yet works in use; nor can a patriotic citizen better serve his country than by devoting his energies and time to record that which is great and glorious in her history, for the admiration and instruction of her neighbours.[55]

Kemble has substituted England for France as the country that provides the example that other nations should follow. Significantly, at least one reviewer approved this work because it provided an alternative history to the myth, used by the Chartists, that England had originally been democratic, with no property qualification for voting—and, of equal concern in 1848, had had a socialist approach to property-ownership. For W. B. Donne in the *Edinburgh Review*, Kemble's book scientifically proved by means of the study of Anglo-Saxon (Old English) manuscripts that

> The deeper we explore the history of tenure in land, the further we recede from any traces of equalization of rank or property, and from any grounds from a theory of communism. The political condition of the Teutonic freemen was indeed determined by the amount of his landed property.[56]

Kemble has reclaimed the Anglo-Saxon world for established order, as opposed to revolution. Kemble's Anglo-Saxons, indeed, seem moderate Whigs in their severance of Divine Right from the monarchy in combination with their continued respect for government by the propertied classes.

Macaulay's *History of England* is a more pointedly "modern" work, but similarly presents Britain, not France, as exemplar for modern states. Although Macaulay concurred with whig historical tradition in regarding the French Revolution as a necessary evil, in this work it is seen as scarcely relevant to British constitutional developments, whose forms were, Macaulay argues, established in the seventeenth century, when in England's great revolution of 1688, the English confirmed their long-held right to choose their monarch.

In crude terms, such a principle sounds republican, recalling the 1790 sermon by Richard Price that prompted Burke's *Reflections*; and sometimes Macaulay uses provocatively republican diction. For example, he not merely justifies the rebellion against Charles I, but even appears to sympathize with Parliament's charge of treason; for Macaulay, even though Charles's death was a strategic "error" in creating inappropriate sentiment on behalf of the monarchical tradition, he is executed in accordance with law, rather than in violation of it.[57] Oliver Cromwell is, moreover, called "the greatest prince that ever ruled England" (*Works* 1:125), emphasizing that princely qualities are not restricted to the monarchical line. Macaulay is nevertheless not so republican to deny the royal line altogether; he implies that it is expedient to keep to it unless no suitable candidate can be found. Cromwell was thus a fitting choice "since there was no prince of the royal blood in the parliamentary party" (*Works* 1:91). The appointment of William and Mary conforms to this principle. The right of William of Orange and Mary II to the throne was not because James II's son was spurious, but because the English people had the right to choose a monarch who represented their constitutional interests.

To present such a argument in 1848 might seem revolutionary—and admittedly, the book did not appear until October, by which time the French socialist government had been replaced by a military caretaker government under Cavaignac, and revolution seemed less immediately threatening. Moreover, Macaulay had been working on his history for almost a decade, and its tone is not a specific response to events of 1848: indeed, some of its conclusions, such as "But it would be a great error to infer from the increase of complaint that there has been any increase of misery" (*Works* 1:319), seem grossly insensitive at a time when deaths from starvation in Ireland were common. For readers in 1848, however, this account of revolution paradoxically provided an explanation of why Britain had not succumbed to revolutionary fervor, and, moreover, why it was not likely to do so in the future. Macaulay's guiding principle was not revolution—in effect, in his interpretation, the true revolutionary of 1688 was James II, who sought to change the structure of British government—but the confirmation of what he saw as the British tradition of government for the people. The English historian's definition of "people" is, of course, distinct from that of Louis Blanc, the "people" for and by whom the country is governed being those with an interest in property. These "people" were asking the question in 1848 as to whether their interests were secure. Macaulay maintained that they were, because England was gradually progressing towards a more reasoned and civilized society.

Croker, who had been at war with Macaulay since the reform debates of the early 1830s, reviewed the *History of England* for the *Quarterly* in March 1849. Using a still-topical metaphor, he complained that Macaulay's "historical narrative is poisoned with a rancour more violent than even the passions of the time."[58] Croker responded to Macaulay's characterization of Cromwell by arguing that Cromwell was a tyrant and a usurper—in fact, like Robespierre, he realized that nothing but "the blood of Kings" could confirm a republic ("Mr. Macaulay's History," p. 577). The famous third chapter, Macaulay's paean to the progress of the nation since 1685, Croker would have dismissed as "puerilities," were it not that he detected a dark purpose behind the descriptions: the reduction of whig history to its crudest level through "a wish to exhibit England *prior to the*

Revolution [Croker's italics] as in a mean and even barbarous and despicable condition" ("Mr. Macaulay's History," pp. 585–586).

Croker has a difficulty here since in his Burkean role, he cannot reject the value of the 1688 Revolution as long as it is seen as a reestablishment of rights, rather than as a historical advancement as Macaulay's emphasis on progress ultimately implies. Croker can, however, claim that the narrative force of Macaulay's history is insidiously placing a value on revolution as a means of progress towards higher civilization. The *History of England* is for Croker the historical equivalent of a novel such as *Oliver Twist* or *Vanity Fair*, and will have the same sort of popular readership: Macaulay "abhors whatever is not in itself picturesque, while he clings with the tenacity of a Novelist to the *piquant* and the startling" ("Mr. Macaulay's History," p. 630).

Macaulay's *History* certainly sold as well as or better than a popular novel, and was in a fifth edition by July 1849. Part of this success, critics and Macaulay himself concluded, was because it presented as lively reading as a novel. Perhaps less obvious was that reading it required only the same level of identification as a novel: this was only the reader's story as much as he or she chose to make it so, particularly significant at the political moment in which it appeared. The corruption of Charles II's court, for example, was not proof of the inevitable corruption of human nature, but the product of specific historical forces. While readers might choose to disssociate their own society from that of Charles II, conversely, they could identify themselves with the moderate whig reason shown by their ancestors in the Glorious Revolution if they wished. If novels can be read as history, history can be read as novels.

As revolutions declined in Europe, Macaulay's book presented hope both through progress and through preservation. First, this most consummately whig history suggested that conditions in society were generally improving and looked towards a more stable and prosperous future, rendering revolution unnecessary. But second, Macaulay did not reject entirely the theoretical construct of revolution; it was not always doomed to failure, if it represented the true values of the "people." Should British readers choose to identify with their ancestors, they could congratulate themselves that in the matter of revolution, if disposing of a failed king is indeed a revolution, they had managed it well, and that once again, the French had managed it badly. Arnold's label of "comfortable moles" seems an apt metaphor for historians such as Kemble and Macaulay, digging among the dead to confirm the present state of affairs. But their reading of 1848 as largely irrelevant to a nation rooted in a just political tradition had obvious attractions; perhaps Britain had caught something of the contagion of moral degeneracy from the the French in the 1840s, but the nation had the experience of history to prevent it from following France's political example on a course to self-destruction.

Robespierre Reconsidered

Once again, that so much happened so quickly in 1848 presented problems for interpretation, and inevitably, the 1789 Revolution was used as a touchstone. Mill accused Brougham, for example, of trying to present the 1848 Revolution as an event unparalleled in history, and quoted Brougham's phrases,

> "The like of it was never witnessed among men." It has "no parallel in the history of nations." It is "wholly at variance with every principle, as well as all experience."[59]

Brougham did use these phrases, but he also argued what Mill chooses not to repeat, that the Revolution, having abandoned Girondist idealism, is providing opportunities for the third phase in the Revolutionary plot, a new Robespierre. Louis Blanc (who had by this time fled to England) embodies the principles of "those famous political economists, Robespierre and Saint-Just."[60] Particularly concerned by the attacks on private property, Brougham accuses the international socialists of composing "panegyrics" to their "predecessor" Robespierre.[61]

This association between Robespierre and socialism might at first consideration seem a curious one. In fact, the February 1848 revolutionaries' respect for property was part of the reason for their failure. The revolutionaries advanced the socialist idea of guaranteeing employment; yet they did not fully control the financial structure, so that the system collapsed when no money was available to pay the workers and the leaders were forced to impose a selective system of employment.

The socialism of 1848 was thus doomed from the outset: it could not be implemented without a more drastic revision of the financial system. Yet analogy was probably also another factor contributing to its downfall: for many French citizens, and certainly for many outside observers such as the majority voice in Britain dependent on commentators like Brougham, the revolutionaries did not seem to be new Mirabeaus as in

1830, or idealistic new Girondists as their radical sympathizers proclaimed, but rather in the mould of Robespierre.

This interpretation was advanced in his posthumously-published *Recollections* by Alexis de Tocqueville, who was one of the delegates in the Assembly and who took on ministerial status after the socialist experiment collapsed. Tocqueville attributes much of the Revolution to the literary-historical sense of its leaders, who through histories, such as those of Thiers and Lamartine, and through literary works such as dramas had "rehabilitated the Terror."[62] He habitually calls the socialist party the "Mountain"—that is, the name of Robespierre's Jacobites—and claims that they took to wearing the light blue coat associated with Robespierre. Some may indeed have seen the principles of the first revolution as worth reviving. Certainly, at this time, a renewal of interest in Robespierre can be traced. In keeping with the growing tendency to treat French revolution through narrative, Robespierre becomes redefined as a character in the larger plot. Lamartine's *History of the Girondists* (1847), criticized by Tocqueville as a text that enflamed the Revolution, provides one such example. Lamartine's focus is mainly on the classical republican spirit of the Girondists as represented by the Rolands and others.[63] Lamartine believes in the virtue of the Girondists, but argues that they should not have executed the king and queen, and also that they were "out of touch with popular feeling."[64]

In 1848, however, when Lamartine himself became a revolutionary, British reviewers seized on what they saw as his overly sympathetic portrait of Robespierre. Lamartine initially states that Robespierre "had nothing: neither birth, nor genius, nor exterior which should point him out to men's notice" (*History of the Girondists* 1:31). Even though Lamartine's Robespierre lacks innate talent, this portrait incorporates elements of the Romantic hero, notably in Robespierre's "ambition" that leads him to court the favor of the people at all costs. After describing Robespierre's death, which he meets firmly without attempting suicide as in some versions, Lamartine argues that "his death was the date, and not the cause, of the cessation of terror" (3:542). Robespierre must "ever remain shadowy—undefined," but his fault was ambition not merely on his own behalf but for the people, his goal being:

> the reign of reason, by the medium of democracy. ... He did not desire evil, and yet accepted it. He surrendered to what he believed the pressure of the situation, the heads of the king, the queen, their innocent sister. ... He was intoxicated with the perspective of public felicity. ... (3:543)

Finally, Lamartine presents Robespierre as a Frankenstein: "He put himself in the place of God. He determined to be the exterminative and creative genius of the Revolution." For Lamartine, this is an error, since "He inspired the future with a dread of the people's reign, repugnance to the institution of the republic, a doubt of liberty."

The association of Robespierre with socialist or at least democratic aspirations was further supported by the fact that the first substantial biography of Robespierre written in English was the work of the Chartist Bronterre O'Brien.[65]

The concept of the "Charter," demanding six points necessary for the achievement of universal male suffrage, was strongly influenced by the idea that the historic rights of Englishmen must be reclaimed. Nevertheless, it did not escape comment that some of the leaders asserting those English rights, first O'Brien and by the 1840s Feargus O'Connell, were Irish. Among the more militant Chartists, the concept of natural right as developed by Rousseau was also argued, and in his biography of O'Brien, Alfred Plummer notes that some Chartist groups manufactured pikes in preparation for an armed rising.[66] The summoning of a nationwide gathering of Chartists in 1839 recalled *Magna Carta* and Runnymede, but naming it a "National Convention" recalled the establishment of the French Republic in September 1792 and the rise of Robespierre to supreme power. About the same time O'Brien had published the first volume of a study of "The Life and Character of Maximilian Robespierre, Proving, by Facts and Arguments, that that much-calumniated person was one of the greatest men, and one of the purest and most enlightened reformers, that ever existed in the world. ..."[67] O'Brien presents Robespierre as making a true effort to reform society and to introduce democracy in defiance of the French nobility and their English allies, with the ultimate goal of community of property. The study is hence of interest in presenting neither whig nor tory history, but rather a proto-socialist version: the alliance of the bourgeoisie and the aristocracy prevents true revolution, at least up to this stage in history. Yet the project was never completed and would probably rapidly have been forgotten, had not George Henry Lewes drawn attention to it in his own 1848 life of Robespierre.

As we have seen, Lewes claimed some expertise on French affairs, and although his review of Blanc's *History of Ten Years* was cautious, Blanc, a friend of Lewes, provided him with some materials for the Robespierre study. Lewes's book is declaredly a response to the revolutions of 1848, and is not entirely unsympathetic to Robespierre. For Lewes, Robespierre is not, as for Carlyle, the embodiment of "humbug": he is something far more dangerous, an insignificant creature fanatically committed to grand ideals, and given power by the historical moment. Whereas Mirabeau was the "genius" of the revolution, "without a revolution," Lewes observes, "Robespierre would doubtless have been a mere provincial advocate with a taste for literature."[68] Lewes thus discloses his reasons for his attention to O'Brien's version: Robespierre presents a warning of the fanaticism that can be given a head when the lack of respect for existing social institutions allows small men to take power. While Lewes's reading of Robespierre is whig in its insistence that historical moments are greater than individuals, it is unusually negative in questioning what the Revolution ultimately achieved. Robespierre himself, Lewes claims, "has not left to the legacy of mankind one grand thought, nor the example of one generous and exalted action."[69] At a time when the European revolutions of 1848 were already waning, Lewes seems to wonder whether revolution really is, as whig history traditionally argued, a longterm gain for civilization.

News of a revolution in France, and especially one led by such characters as Albert the Worker (*Ouvrier*), provided a new inspiration for the British Chartists, whose two previous petitions for manhood suffrage had been summarily dismissed; they began to organize the third and largest. Another incentive, of course, was the same economic hardship that had affected all of Europe. From March 7 onwards, riots broke out in Ireland and Glasgow, and the same week that *The Times* had maintained that French revolutions were exclusively a French concern the leader column showed a new note of alarm:

> We beg to assure our neighbours on the banks of the Seine, that they need not attach over much importance to any rumours of an approaching revolution which may happen to reach them from the British metropolis. Of course, they would be only too happy to find we were following their example. The fox that had lost his own tail commended the example to his friends, and a nation that has thrown away Royalty, as we believe for ever, would like to see all other nations equally enfranchised.[70]

In April 1848 the Chartists planned a rally on Kennington Common to coincide with the presentation of a huge petition to Parliament. *The Times* reminded the Government that the Chartist leaders had "expressly announced" that they were "following and studying the example of Paris and other insurgent cities";[71] the Government was sufficiently alarmed as to call in 150,000 special constables to control the rally. The result was what G. D. H. Cole has called the "great fiasco" that effectively finished the Chartist movement.[72]

One of these special constables was a French political exile who called himself Prince Louis Napoleon, and who was to do more than simply assist in vanquishing small English Robespierres. The discontent in France in 1848 prompted not a search for a replacement Robespierre, but for a new Napoleon. As early as his March article, Croker, still committed to his Burkean role, had included a prognostication which at first sight seems reasonably accurate:

> ... the reign of anarchy cannot be long. In a country so rich and so enlightened as France, the spirit of order and the yearnings for tranquillity, after the warnings of the first Revolution, will soon prevail, and there will emerge some Conservative form of government under which the wearied people will gladly take refuge. What will that be—a President with a legislature *à l'Américaine*? A very probable experiment—if Lafayette were still alive we should have said quite certain.[73]

Croker then spoils the long-term impression of his prophetic powers by dismissing Napoleon's nephew "Louis Buonaparte" as a serious candidate. Other Britons too may have underestimated the appeal of the name of Napoleon. After the collapse of the government of February 1848 an interim government that was in effect military called presidential elections; if the Revolution of 1848 had begun with Louis Blanc as a new Robespierre, it ended with Prince Louis Bonaparte as its new Napoleon.

Notes

1. "Preface to the English Edition of 1888," in Karl Marx and Friedrich Engels, *The Communist Manifesto*, edited by Frederic L. Bender (Norton, 1988), p. 46.
2. An important link is a shared indebtedness to eighteenth-century rationalism, in the case of the *Manifesto* through Hegel.
3. Marx and Engels, *The Communist Manifesto*, translated by Helen Macfarlane, in *The Red Republican* (November 1850), p. 181, italics in original. Macfarlane's translation tends to use the more familiarly British "Middle-class" whereas the authorized 1882 translation uses "Bourgeoisie."
4. The concept of the franchise as property was, it must be emphasized, part of the discourse of the period: Macaulay states this explicitly in his speeches in support of Parliamentary reform.
5. Alison, *My Life and Writings* 1:571–577. Although Alison does not mention it, other sources characterize these rioters as principally Irish.
6. See particularly *The Times*, April 1848. On April 1, a letter to *The Times* drew a distinction between "mere riot, and the early stages of revolt" in Ireland.

7. See Frederic Jameson, *The Political Unconscious* (Cornell University Press, 1981). Marxist literary criticism does not entirely deny a conscious observation of class relations by the novelist: Georg Lukács, presenting Scott as the model for historical fiction, suggests that Scott's awareness of class roles in society was partly conscious, and notes, "the extent to which this expression of thought and feeling outstrips the consciousness of the age is no more than is absolutely necessary for elucidating the given historical relationship," Lukács, *The Historical Novel*, translated by Hannah and Stanley Mitchell (Merlin, 1962), p. 63.
8. *The Letters of William Makepeace Thackeray*, edited by Gordon N. Ray (Harvard University Press, 1946) 2:353–354.
9. Thackeray, *Stray Papers*, edited by Lewis Melville (1901; reprinted Kraus, 1971), p. 17.
10. See *The Works of William Makepeace Thackeray* (Smith and Elder, 1901) 16:37.
11. This division was itself something of a political fiction; while the Tories claimed to protext the landowning interests and the Whigs to be the champions of industry, a remarkable proportion of Whig ministers of this period were from the old aristocracy rather than the products of the new age of speculation.
12. *Letters of William Makepeace Thackeray* 2:829. Bulwer-Lytton may also have read part or all of it, since it was reviewed by George Henry Lewes in the *Foreign Quarterly Review*, to which both novelists were occasional contributors; Thackeray's publishers Chapman and Hall published the English translation.
13. Louis Blanc, *The History of Ten Years*, English edition (Chapman and Hall, 1845) 2:648.
14. Edward Bulwer-Lytton (later Lord Lytton), *England and the English* (Bentley, 1833) 1:31.
15. "Lucretia," *The Athenaeum* (December 5, 1846), p. 1240.
16. Edward Bulwer-Lytton, *Lucretia; Or, The Children of Night* (1846; Little, Brown, 1897), p. 3, ch. 1. Because there is no recent edition of this novel, subsequent references are cited in the text by page-number of the Little, Brown edition and chapter number.
17. L. Ciolkowski, "The Woman (In) Question: Gender, Politics, and Edward Bulwer-Lytton's *Lucretia*," *Novel* 26:1 (Fall 1992), p. 83.
18. "Lucretia," *Athenaeum*, p. 1241.
19. Review of *Lucretia*, *The Times* (17 December, 1846), p. 7.
20. "Poisoners Living and Dead—Arsenic Novels," *Punch* 8 (1845), p. 68.
21. That Varney was based on Wainewright was implied in the author's Preface and noted by the earliest readers of *Lucretia*: John Forster in the *Examiner*, for example, did not name Wainewright, who was still alive in Tasmania at the time of the novel's publication, but made the connection explicit by calling Varney's original "a Janus with two faces," a reference to

Wainewright's *London Magazine* pseudonym of Janus Weathercock. See Forster's review, *Examiner* (December 6, 1846), p. 772.

22. Keith Hollingsworth, *The Newgate Novel 1830–1847* (Wayne State University Press, 1963), pp. 187–188.
23. Forster, review of *Lucretia*, p. 733.
24. The British tradition of associating poisoning with Italians dates back to the Renaissance itself, as demonstrated by *Hamlet*. With this, the French concurred, as in the instance of Hugo's Lucrezia Borgia.
25. See his *England and the English*. This play, the basis of Donizetti's opera of that name, was condemned by Croker in the *Quarterly Review* in 1834 as exemplifying the moral corruption of modern France.
26. In the latter, the Count explains at length to Madame de Villefort (who follows his recommendation) how to poison her family; the method and poisons are those believed to have been used by Wainewright.
27. Charles Mackay devoted an entire chapter to "slow poisoners" in his 1844 *Memoirs of Extraordinary Popular Delusions* (1844; reprinted L. C. Page, 1932), pp. 565–592. Madame de Brinvilliers and the rash of poisoning in France that followed are discussed in detail. The episode also featured in Alexandre Dumas's collection of "Celebrated Crimes," of which Chapman and Hall published an English translation in 1843. Dumas also told the history of the Borgias.
28. "Verdict on Madame Laffarge [sic]," *The Examiner* (September 27, 1840).
29. Comparisons of the level of crime between France and Britain are complicated by differing legal practices. French imposition of the death penalty varied considerably among regions; in Britain, where a murder conviction almost certainly received a death-penalty, even though most were respited, juries may indeed have been more reluctant to convict. G. R. Porter, in *The Progress of the Nation,* 2nd edition (John Murray, 1847), pointed out that once hangings became uncommon in Britain, a higher number of convictions were obtained.
30. Blanc, *Ten Years* 1:270.
31. See George Henry Lewes, "Louis Blanc's History of Ten Years," *Foreign Quarterly Review* 32 (1843), pp. 61–75. The story had topical interest since the Baroness had died in 1840, and her English relatives, named Daw or Dawes, had successfully sued to recover her enormous wealth. They had neglected to pay their lawyers, and in a much-publicized case of 1843, the legal firm sued to recover their expenses. The *Annual Register*'s account of the transaction states openly that the Baroness was suspected of murdering the Duc de Bourbon.
32. Blanc, *Ten Years* 2:283.
33. In 1847, for example, several cases of poisoning for gain were reported in the *Annual Register*. Most of these were for burial-club money, a form of artisan funeral insurance. The practice of insuring a family member, usually a child, with several clubs, killing the child with arsenic, and keeping the

money was said to be common as early as 1844, when Thomas James remarked on its frequency in a *Quarterly Review* article on "Funerals and Funeral Expenses" (*Quarterly Review* 73 [March 1844], p. 459), but even at this time of great hardship for the poor, few prosecutions seem to have been brought.

34. Dumas reversed the equation. Whereas poisoners in English works are partly French, his most famous instances are partly English. Milady of *The Three Musketeers*, who poisons at least three people, the last with a Borgia ring, has a number of aliases and it is never determined whether she is English or French by birth, although she speaks English when she knows she is going to die. The Count of Monte Cristo, who supplies the knowledge to enable another to become a poisoner, begins life as the Frenchman Edmond Dantes, but deliberately creates for himself the character of a man without a nation, and disguises himself as an English lord.
35. Hollingsworth, *The Newgate Novel*, pp. 196–98.
36. Thackeray had been lampooning the Newgate Novel, and especially Bulwer-Lytton, for several years, such as in *Catherine*, serialized in *Fraser's Magazine* in 1839. Thackeray's problem, however, is that the Newgate Novel is impossible to parody successfully, because were the characters totally repulsive, the effect would not be funny. Catherine herself gains some sympathy from her readers, and it is hardly clear that the result is morally superior to Bulwer-Lytton's novels.
37. William Makepeace Thackeray, *Vanity Fair* (1847–1848; Penguin, 1973), p. 47. Following references are cited in the text, as *Vanity Fair*.
38. The suggestion is addressed to Dumas. Since *Ivanhoe* is also largely a "novel without a hero," Wilfred of Ivanhoe being a shadowy character even when he is present, Titmarsh's assumption that marriage with him is a reward is at least questionable, but it might equally be argued that marriage is a questionable reward in *Vanity Fair*.
39. The Steyne is a street in the Prince Regent's favorite retreat of Brighton.
40. History was to repeat itself within a few months after this episode appeared in print when, Richard S. Lambert remarks, the Revolution of 1848 was a major contributor to the collapse of George Hudson's railway companies, resulting in losses to countless investors. See Lambert's *The Railway King 1800–1871* (1934; reprinted Allen and Unwin, 1964), p. 224.
41. In July 1832, insurance companies who refused to pay out on the life of a banker named Kinnear were successfully sued by his widow. The companies maintained that he had poisoned himself in 1830, when depressed by "a fall in the French funds." *The Times*, July 1832.
42. Thackeray's illustration, a picture of a sinister Becky spying on Jos with the caption "Becky's second appearance in the character of Clytemnestra," is a clue that she could indeed have murdered Jos, but misleading in suggesting the use of a knife. In her first appearance as Clytemnestra in the charade sequence, Becky bears a knife—she is, after all, "Sharp"—and Jos has fore-

shadowed such an end when he tells his French-speaking barber, "Coupez-moi." But the reference to Jos's "unheard-of illnesses," the obvious consideration that insurance-brokers do not pay out on clients stabbed to death, and, as I am arguing, contemporary interest in poisoning for the purposes of insurance fraud point to poison. I would raise as a cautious possibility that Thackeray at one point contemplated the novel being more "Newgate" than it finally is, and that Becky was intended to stab him; but that as the novel developed, first this seemed out of character (Thackeray had made her too likeable) and second, poison was of more topical interest.

43. Elizabeth, Lady Eastlake, "Vanity Fair and Jane Eyre," *Quarterly Review* 84 (December 1848), p. 157. Following references are cited by page-number in the text.
44. Mill, *French History*, p. 325.
45. Joseph-Aimé Thomé de Gamond, *Étude pour l'Avant-Projet d'un Tunnel Sous-marin entre l'Angleterre et la France* (Victor Dalmont, 1857), pp. 104–105.
46. Alison, "Fall of the Throne of the Barricades," *Blackwood's Magazine* 63 (April 1848), p. 393.
47. Croker, "French Revolution: February 1848," *Quarterly Review* 82 (March 1848), p. 541.
48. Croker, "Louis Philippe et la Contre-Révolution," p. 569.
49. Thackeray had in 1844 jokingly placed the "Next French Revolution" much later, in 1884, when Louis Philippe would have been not, as Thackeray states, "nearly a hundred years old" but about 110 (*Works* 15:182).
50. Croker, "French Revolution: February 1848," p. 582.
51. Brougham, *Letter to the Marquis of Lansdowne ... on the Late Revolution in France*, 4th edition (James Ridgeway, 1848), p. 2.
52. That Jewsbury and her friend and collaborator on Zoë Mrs. Paulet shopped for hats and saw Rachel act in Paris in early May 1848 suggests that not all of Paris commerce was disrupted. See Susanne K. Howe, *Geraldine Jewsbury, Her Life and Errors* (Allen and Unwin, 1933), pp. 97–99.
53. See *The Oxford Authors: Matthew Arnold*, edited by Miriam Allott and Robert H. Super (Oxford University Press, 1986), p. 513.
54. Ibid., pp. 51–53.
55. John Mitchell Kemble, *The Saxons in England* (Longman's, 1848), Dedication.
56. W. B. Donne, "The Saxons in England," *Edinburgh Review* 90 (January 1849), p. 167.
57. Macaulay, *History of England*, *Works* 1:104. Following quotations are cited in the text as *Works*.
58. Croker, "Mr. Macaulay's History of England," *Quarterly Review* 84 (March 1849), p. 550. Following references are cited in the text as "Mr. Macaulay's History."
59. Mill, *French History*, p. 321.

60. Brougham, *Letter to the Marquis of Lansdowne*, p. 57.
61. Ibid., p. 126.
62. Alexis de Tocqueville, *Recollections*, translated by George Lawrence (1893; Doubleday, 1970), p. 74.
63. Croker sneered that it partook "still more of the character of romance than his verses." Croker, "French Revolution: February 1848," p. 576.
64. Alphonse de Lamartine, *History of the Girondists* (Bohn 1847–1848) 3:36–37. The Bohn translation of this work was remarkably prompt: vol. 1 is dated 1849, vol. 2 1847, and vol 3, which has a memoir of Lamartine dated March 13, 1848, while the socialists were still in power, is dated 1848. Following references to *History of the Girondists* are cited in the text.
65. The self-styled James "Bronterre" O'Brien should not be confused with William Smith O'Brien, transported for sedition after his role in the risings of 1848, although seemingly British commentators confounded Chartism with Irish nationalism. Bronterre O'Brien took no active role in the Chartist activities of 1848.
66. Alfred Plummer, *Bronterre: A Political Biography of Bronterre O'Brien* (Allen and Unwin, 1971), pp. 100–101.
67. O'Brien had earlier translated Philippo Buonarroti's *History of Babeuf's Conspiracy for Equality*, and in his Preface expressed sympathy for Robespierre and for Babeuf's 1796 attempt to reimpose Robespierre's Constitution and establish community of property. An indication of how the July Monarchy had failed the best and worst expectations of socialists and champions of property rights alike is that when Robert Southey had reviewed *Babeuf's Conspiracy* for the *Quarterly* in 1831, he had hinted that Louis Philippe represented a similar danger to property as Babeuf and Robespierre.
68. George Henry Lewes, *The Life of Maximilien Robespierre; with Extracts from his Unpublished Correspondence* (Chapman and Hall, 1849), p. 49.
69. Ibid., p. 391.
70. *The Times* (March 8, 1848).
71. *The Times* (April 7, 1848).
72. G. D. H. Cole, *A Short History of the British Working-Class Movement*, revised edition (Allen and Unwin, 1948), pp. 117–118.
73. Croker, "French Revolution: February 1848," pp. 588–589.

Chapter 4
Historical Repetition and *A Tale of Two Cities*

Charles Dickens's 1859 novel *A Tale of Two Cities* forms the primary focus of this chapter for two principle reasons: first, as the most familiar Victorian reading of the French Revolution as cultural referent; and second, as a book that demonstrates how by the mid-century, both whig and tory historical models, while apparently mutually exclusive, had permeated Victorian consciousness to the extent that a novelist might use elements of both.

Because literary studies have paid so little attention to what the specifics of history meant to mid-Victorian culture, the historiography of *A Tale of Two Cities* has proved perplexing to critics, who acknowledge that history is a crucial resonance of this text, but seem uncertain as to the possibilities of historical interpretation. In its treatment of history, Dickens's *Tale* is frequently considered the novelistic repetition of Carlyle. Dickens himself, who claimed to have read *The French Revolution, a History* five hundred times,[1] made the initial connection, concluding the Preface to the *Tale*: "It has been one of my hopes to add something to the popular and picturesque means of understanding that terrible time, though no one can hope to add anything to the philosophy of Mr. Carlyle's wonderful book."[2] This statement has perhaps been read over-literally, as implying that while Dickens himself assumes responsibility for the "popular and picturesque" elements of his novel, any philosophy of history in general and of the French Revolution in particular found in *A Tale of Two Cities* must be a repetition of Carlyle. Sylvère Monod, for example, asserts that "the novelist's thesis, as he has pointed out himself, is wholly contained in Carlyle's book."[3]

Similarly, Michael Goldberg claims that "*A Tale of Two Cities*, in both form and content, owes almost everything" to Carlyle,[4] and quotes K. J. Fielding's assertion that the novel's "doctrine of determinism" was "derived from Carlyle."[5] Even David D. Marcus, who states that "Dickens unsystematically borrowed details but not any conceptual framework" from Carlyle's book, concludes that historical and philosophical similarities between the two can better be seen in other works, and that "the differences between Carlyle and Dickens should not obscure the basic similarity of their outlooks."[6] For these critics, whatever historical coherence the novel possesses derives from a single source. They assume that Dickens correctly perceives Carlyle's philosophy of history, and that he is able to use it thematically and structurally in the novel.

Such a reading of the *Tale* elevates to a thesis-statement Dickens's clearest repetition of Carlyle's themes in the concluding chapter of the novel:

> Crush humanity out of shape once more, under similar hammers, and it will twist itself into the same distorted forms. Sow the same seed of rapacious licence and oppression over again, and it will surely yield the same fruit according to its kind.[7]

Yet this famous passage, "Carlylean" although it may seem, is not merely a repetition of Carlyle, but of the tory doctrine of history's own repetitions. I hope to demonstrate that even overlooking the point that to read a novel for its political lesson is to read it *as* tory history, the tidy tory warning of the dangers of a new French Revolution (in itself an oversimplification of Carlyle) simply does not work as the overall theme of this novel, the product of a period when the whig historical model of progress was so dominant.

This is not, I trust, automatically to coincide with those critics who have failed to find any philosophy of history at all in the *Tale*. Bernard Shaw, for example, calls it "pure sentimental melodrama from beginning to end, and shockingly wanting in any philosophy of history in its view of the French Revolution."[8] Georg Lukács sees the historical setting as merely "a romantic background": "Dickens, by giving preeminence to the purely moral aspects of causes and effects, weakens the connection between the problems of the characters' lives and the events of the French Revolution ... neither the fate of Manette and his daughter, nor of Darnay-Evremonde, and least of all Sidney [sic] Carton, grows organically out of the age and its social events."[9]

Both critical assessments imply a desire to rewrite the *Tale*: in the first instance, as a simplified version of the tory elements in Carlyle's interpretation of history; in the second, as a Marxist-approved distillation of the causes of revolution. In contrast, I would suggest that while on a conscious level Dickens may indeed have been unable to articulate a theory of revolution, *A Tale of Two Cities* has its own philosophy of history, largely expressed as a transaction between narrator and reader and dependent on the assumption that the reader too has a culturally-received sense of the significance of the past influenced by both whig and tory interpretations of history. My goal is not to deny the influence of Carlyle, but to argue that the shaping force of the historical realization is based on Dickens's application of sometimes incompatible elements of whig and tory conceptions of history's significance to his imaginative recreation of the eighteenth century. In consequence, an important theme of the *Tale* has been largely overlooked. When considered on the strength of its own historical realization rather than through the filter of Carlyle's, Dickens's account of the French Revolution proves to focus less on the recurrent historical threat or actuality of revolution than on revolution as contrast to a more advanced state of civilization—suggesting, in effect, how history escapes from, or at least improves upon, repetition. Yet while this might seem to characterize the *Tale* as a book that clearly states that the past is the past, I also wish to discuss the *Tale* as a response to a still-unhistoricized present.

By the 1850s, the problem of historical repetition was physically embodied in France by Emperor Napoleon III. Napoleon I's nephew Prince Louis-Napoleon Bonaparte had been elected President of the French Republic at the end of 1848. In spite of a dubious early history when he twice led almost laughably disastrous uprisings against Louis Philippe, in the presidential elections that followed the collapse of the socialist experiment of 1848, a few months after he had volunteered in England to help restrain the Chartists, he presented himself as the champion of order. Louis-Napoleon's political manifesto, however, scarcely accounts for his huge majority over other not insignificant candidates such as Cavaignac and Lamartine. As he noted in the concluding speech of his campaign, "My name is offered to you as a symbol of order and security,"[10] and among the rural peasants who formed the bulk of the voters, the name of Napoleon seems to have had the appeal of a historical repetition that promised a powerful and unified France.

In December 1851, the President staged a *coup d'état* that gave him supreme legislative power, again justified on the grounds of the maintenance of order. Many of his opponents were exiled or imprisoned. British commentators were skeptical; *The Times*, as ever concerned with the stability of France, observed: "if 'stability' be the motto of the new Government, that is precisely the quality we are least prepared to find in it; and in closing 'the era of revolutions,' LOUIS NAPOLEON has very possibly brought the country once more within the vortex of anarchy."[11] One year later, an even more symbolic attempt at repetition occurred when on the strength of a huge majority vote favoring the action Louis-Napoleon proclaimed himself Emperor Napoleon III. His speech on this occasion promised historical continuity without the bonds of traditionalism: "Not merely do I recognize the governments that preceded me, but I inherit in some form what they did, whether for good or ill." Arguing that while Napoleon I was entitled to be succeeded by his heirs, his claim was based on the popular vote, he continued, "the title of Napoleon III is not one of those outdated dynastic claims which seem an insult to truth and good sense; it is homage paid to a legitimate government, to which we owe the fairest pages of our modern history. My reign does not date from 1815; it dates from this moment when you have just let me know the votes of the nation."[12]

Future years were to suggest that Napoleon III had some ambition to repeat his uncle's victories and expand if not his Empire, then at least his international influence, notably through his military intervention in Italy, which was interpreted by Italian nationalists and their many British supporters as delaying the cause of Italian unification. Yet in one important aspect, the new Napoleon tried to avoid repeating the history of his predecessor: he liked Britain, and sought to strengthen alliances between the two nations. Similarly, most Britons were anxious not to repeat the mistake of the first French Revolution in taking sides against France's chosen government. Many British Liberals, calling themselves Whigs no longer but more than ever ascribing to the whig reading of history, were eager to accept Napoleon's offers of friendship as a sign that the two most advanced nations in the world were no longer to be enemies, but to be partners—as, indeed, at first sight the title *A Tale of Two Cities* suggests.

A strong indicator of this new mood of partnership is that in 1857, the French engineer Joseph-Aimé Thomé de Gamond published a well-worked-out scheme for a Channel Tunnel that was seriously considered by the governments of both Napoleon III and Queen Victoria: the two cities might indeed one day be linked together by rail.[13] I shall therefore read the *Tale* as a work of a period of international cooperation that led to new forms of strain between Britain and France. To demonstrate the contrast between the time of Carlyle and that of Dickens, though, I shall first discuss a novel published a mere five years after Carlyle's history that initially appears to have similarities with Dickens's book, but that reads the contemporary implications of the French Revolution in a different light.

Zanoni

Read against the background of Anglo-French relations in the 1850s, *A Tale of Two Cities* has such different historical resonances from Carlyle's history of twenty years earlier that rather than historical repetition paralelling Dickens's book with Carlyle's, some readers may have more readily detected narrative repetition associating the *Tale* with an earlier novel. The execution of Sydney Carton in the place of Charles Darnay repeats an important plot device of an 1842 novel set the time of the French Revolution, Edward Bulwer-Lytton's *Zanoni, Or, The Mysteries*. The Revolution provides the setting for this story of a man who has gained the secret of immortality. Zanoni's association with the mysteries of the Illuminati and eventual death on the guillotine suggest that his characterization was influenced by the writer Jacques Cazotte, who was claimed to have prophesied the Terror, although Bulwer-Lytton avoids a direct connection by presenting Cazotte himself and his prophecy in the early chapters of the novel. Even with this link between the Illuminati and history, however, the relationship between the mystical idealism of the main story and the historical component seems strained, and its central conflict, human passion as a barrier to moral idealism, does not require a specific historical context. After various experiments with supernatural powers, the central characters arrive in Paris during the Terror, where Zanoni's love Viola di Pisani is sentenced to the guillotine. Anticipating Sydney Carton, Zanoni gives up his immortality by dying in her place, and is the last victim of the Terror before the fall of Robespierre.

Perhaps unwisely, Bulwer-Lytton prefixed to early editions of his romance a line from the eighteenth-century mystical novel *Le Comte de Gabalis*: "I cannot make head nor tail on't."[14] The *Athenaeum* readily stated its agreement, and called the book "one of those supersublime allegories, in which tinselled truisms figure as new discourse, and obscurity of meaning passes for elevation of thought."[15] Nevertheless, some readers did find a meaning in *Zanoni*, including

Harriet Martineau, whose interpretation of the "allegory" was appended to all editions after 1853. Significantly, Martineau's explication does not mention the French Revolution at all; and at first sight, the clumsy melding between a story of the alchemists' powers and the effect of Revolution merely confirms the novelistic weaknesses of the work. Yet the French Revolution, just as much as his love for Viola, draws the ageless, nationless Zanoni into history. Until this point, Zanoni has been outside history; his sacrifice of power to personal involvement makes him vulnerable to historical influence.

Zanoni also anticipates the confusion of historical theory of *A Tale of Two Cities*. As a former Liberal member of Parliament, Bulwer-Lytton might be expected to subscribe to the whig model of historical interpretation. Although Bulwer-Lytton's principle historical source for his descriptions of the French Revolution in *Zanoni* appears to have been the strongly liberal history of Adolphe Thiers, he was criticized for failing to represent the strong philosophical (and whig) principles of revolution. A review in *The Examiner*, very possibly by his friend John Forster, praised *Zanoni*, but observed that:

> The defect of the book to the thinking reader will be found in what is likely to interest the unthinking most deeply. The author's moral and philosophical view of the French Revolution—as far as we can see it through the flashing and gorgeous scenes of the third volume—seems to us both limited and wrong. There was something far more important in that World Wonder, than either the virtue that springs from endurance and death, or the absurdity that is found in all notions of equality. It was an imposture—its idea of all men being equal, in the sense of *sans culottism*—but it resented a much greater and far more serious imposture.[16]

The reviewer points to the problem of using the French Revolution to provide conflict in the plot, but the reference to the "unthinking" reader is also revealing in implying that such a reader will be attracted to the sensational possibilities presented by the Reign of Terror.

Bulwer-Lytton was neither contented to let his account of events only to appeal to the "unthinking" reader, nor to leave the suspicion that he himself was using the French Revolution in an "unthinking" way. In July 1842 he published in the *Foreign Quarterly Review* a review of Georges Duval's *Souvenirs de La Terreur de 1788 à 1793* which presented a remarkably "un-whig" view of history. Whereas whig history generalizes specific incidents as part of a larger progress, Bulwer-Lytton here argues that such "philosophizing excuses and argumentative dogmas" must prompt "irritation and disgust" in someone who had personally witnessed atrocities against individuals. While conceding that "in the vices of the old *régime* we must seek the causes of the revolutionary crimes," he insists that "humanity itself is endangered if we allow the circumstances that conduce to guilt, to steal away our natural horror of the guilt itself."[17] This essay challenges the whig historical position by denying that the first French Revolution was a necessary stage in the progress towards constitutionalism: "we think it might satisfactorily be shown, that whatever benefit France has derived from the Revolution itself is a wretched recompense for the crimes through which she waded to obtain it." Admittedly, improvements have taken place; that improvement, however, is not to be ascribed to the Revolution, *"but to the spirit that preceded the Revolution, and could have sufficed for all beneficial changes, WITHOUT it."*[18] Bulwer-Lytton concludes by questioning current whig views of the July Monarchy when he asserts that even with a good king like Louis-Philippe, France has made no truly constitutional gains.

If this essay is a philosophical validation of *Zanoni*'s attitude towards the French Revolution, Bulwer-Lytton's history is no longer an avoidance of party; indeed, just as Zanoni dies with the Terror, with Robespierre, and with the eighteenth century, so the novel itself might be seen as a lament for the world of the *Ancien Régime*, when romance still had a power. The novel-form allows Bulwer-Lytton to be more "tory" than he had generally chosen to present himself up to this time—indeed, it marks a declared change in thinking that was to lead to Bulwer-Lytton joining the Conservatives—while the framing device of calling the entire work the manuscript memoirs of an eye-witness (apparently Clarence Glyndon) implies that the bloodshed cannot be justified by the "philosophizing excuses and argumentative dogmas" of the whig view of history.

Yet the framing device of an eye-witness marks a difference between 1842 and the late 1850s. A young person could indeed have witnessed the Revolution and have still been alive in 1842. By 1859, people who could remember the Revolution must have been very few: Wordsworth, for example, had died in 1850, and the Duke of Wellington in 1852.[19] Moreover, from the British retrospective of a few years later, 1848 had suggested that revolution—and particularly French Revolution—might be confronted by British common sense, rather than by fear. Characterizations also show a difference. In *Zanoni*, Robespierre is the personification of "Egotism," with a consciously-constructed public image;[20] in many respects, he is the embodiment of a particularly effeminate form of Romantic individualism. As we have seen, by 1848,

Robespierre had changed from Romantic-period narcissist to socialist-period demagogue; in *A Tale of Two Cities*, he is not present at all as the focus moves from revolutionary leaders to the effect of revolution on ordinary people.

Bulwer-Lytton had anticipated this change in focus in his defense of *Zanoni*, where he pointed to the humanitarian problem with the whig historical model, its necessary disregard of individual human suffering. For Dickens, this was clearly also a problem with tory history: the stability of the *Ancien Régime* was bought at the cost of appalling human tragedies, such as those of Doctor Manette and of the impoverished French tenants. The *Tale* might therefore be seen as asking a new historical question regarding the compatibility of two versions of history that had previously been at best complementary, and more frequently contradictory: namely, whether civilization can advance without the loss of order that affects individuals' quality and security of life.

At least one thinker of this period, an Illuminatus for a new age, argued that it could. Auguste Comte asserted that his system of Positive Philosophy could achieve the most thorough "revolution" of society that had yet occurred in history, yet without the loss of order. "No real order can be established," he claims, "and still less can it last, if it is not fully compatible with progress; and no great progress can be accomplished if it does not tend to the consolidation of order. ... The misfortune of our actual state is that these two ideas are set up in radical opposition to each other."[21] Positive Philosophy was based on Comte's theory that all knowledge, including knowledge of human relations, could be systematized scientifically. While Comte's assertion that "the law of progress is conspicuously at work throughout human history"[22] seems solidly whig in historical outlook, his emphasis on the need to direct progress, with the implied lack of faith in the civilized qualities of "the people," seems more tory. In Harriet Martineau's English translation, the word "evolution" is frequently applied to social structures, yet Comte does not envisage this "evolution" continuing without the guidance of Positive Philosophy.

In the 1850s, however, Comte welcomed Napoleon III as the embodiment of the hope that both progress and order were possible in France. Not even those Britons generally sympathetic towards Positivism, such as George Henry Lewes, automatically coincided with him. Dickens himself interacted with Positivists, and even promised Martineau in 1853 that he was looking forward to seeing her condensation of Comte;[23] he had, however, met the future Emperor in England during the 1840s (they shared a mutual friend in Angela

Burdett-Coutts), and strongly disliked him. Comments in his correspondence during visits to France suggest that Dickens never became a believer in Napoleon III as the embodiment of order and progress: indeed, *A Tale of Two Cities* seems to question order combined with progress is a historical possibility in the present-day world.

Those critics seeking a Carlylean historical exemplum in the *Tale* tend to observe that this historical novel on the French Revolution is a tale of two cities—that the tale of English and French "twins" contains some of Dickens's thoughts on the state of British society. To claim the *Tale* as a book about the France of Dickens's own time would be to go to the other extreme. The book was written, though, shortly after France and Britain's attempt to function as "twins" in the Crimean War, a war for which the British public was inclined to blame Napoleon III, had achieved little beyond exposing the weaknesses of the two nations' organizational structures. Significantly, Dickens's use of twins does not remain on the theoretical level, but is seen in individuals: the Marquis and his brother, Darnay and Carton, to some extent Madame Defarge and Miss Pross. And here the self-sacrifice of Sydney Carton disguises the reality that not all twinning is good: in fact, if we are to take the Carlylean message that the oppressed class of the *Ancien Régime* has a twin in the oppressed class of 1850s Britain, twinning itself challenges historical progress. In the modern world, France and Britain cannot be seen as politically independent. Yet for Dickens, the product is not greater stability, but rather a greater vulnerability, and the final assertion of the values of civilization at the end of the novel is only achieved by the party method of shouting down the opposition.

Then and Now: *Household Words*

In the second Book of *A Tale of Two Cities*, Charles Darnay is tried for treason and acquitted. Following the trial, his representatives at the Bar of the Old Bailey retire to the bar of a Fleet Street tavern. The next chapter begins:

> Those were drinking days, and most men drank hard. So very great is the improvement Time has brought about in such habits, that a moderate statement of the quantity of wine and punch which one man would swallow in the course of a night, without any detriment to his reputation as a perfect gentleman, would seem, in these days, a ridiculous exaggeration.[24]

At first sight, these sentences, apparently from a narrator functioning, as Carlyle's narrator had done, as an all-knowing historian, merely provide background by informing the reader about the customs of eighteenth-century England. Yet even this voice provides a different narrative perspective from that of the opening of the book. "It was the best of times, it was the worst of times" (p. 35) suggests ways in which the people of the eighteenth century might have regarded their own age, before adding that it was like the "present period" in requiring definition. The "drinking days" passage, in contrast, roots its perspective firmly in the nineteenth century, and in doing so creates a number of historical problems that most commentators have avoided. William Oddie, for example, who draws attention to the complexity of the question of Carlyle's influence on Dickens, nevertheless sees Dickens's "theory of history (if the phrase isn't too ponderous to describe what is involved here)" of the *Tale* as "simple enough," and proceeds to quote the "Carlylean" passage from the final chapter.[25] But is this "simple enough," when read against the emphasized differences between the England of Dickens's time and the England of 1781? Is the narrator, speaking as historian, suggesting that readers of 1859 should be shocked at the standards of 1781, or rather that they should not be shocked once they realize that standards were different in the time of their great-grandparents? Similarly, having just emphasized the casualness with which Britain used the death-sentence in the 1780s, is this narrative voice serious in claiming that British habits have improved with time, and is such a claim, as Lukács suggests, in conflict with the eternal (and hence non-historical) moral values presented in the novel's conclusion in the form of what most readers remember best, the self-sacrifice of Sydney Carton?

Since the focus here is on what is shocking, a definition of "shock" is required. For the purposes of this chapter, I will use the term as the reader's instant reaction of outrage, prompted by a sense of strictly non-historical morality: that is, the belief that certain values are not determined by situation or culture, but are universal. This is, I should stress, not the same as asserting that I myself believe that specific values are valid to all cultures; I am nevertheless assuming that the failure to perceive the specific values of a culture—particularly, perhaps, ones that that culture might claim to be universal—results in the loss of an interpretative level of a text, and that in this instance, the loss is a significant one. (Some sophisticated readers, for example, may deny shock when encountering the "drinking days" passage by arguing that its force is ironic, yet an ironic reading requires an initial recognition that the passage is too "shocking" to conform with the rhetorical impetus of the text.) As much as the power of shock suggests authorial intentionality, it may be formulated by the author's unconscious but culturally-determined response to a situation—indeed, I shall argue that in this instance it is at odds with Dickens's verbalized intention. The reader's response is also culturally limited, since the response of an "ideal" reader must implicitly be similar to the author's conscious or unconscious presentation. In summary, shock is a transaction between text and reader dependent on a field of meaning within a culture that enables the detection of, and moral reaction to, difference in values without resorting to the whig strategy of deflection through distancing that difference as irrelevant to oneself.[26]

Dickens's ideal reader would presumably have a similar moral reaction to that of Dickens himself. During the 1850s Dickens had been grooming a readership who would react as he did through the pages of *Household Words*. Yet while Dickens's own response to history seems to have developed beyond the ideas set out in early issues of this journal and to have become closer to Carlyle's, the text of the *Tale* mixes the historical assumptions of the progressive idealist and the prophet of cultural decline.

Judged by their journalistic self-representations in 1850, Dickens and Carlyle seem sharply opposed in their reading of history. Carlyle was publishing the essays now known as *Latter-Day Pamphlets*, in which he explored modern issues from a standpoint familiar to tory history: that Europe was in a state not of historical progress towards an enlightened civilization, but rather of a breakdown of the civilized qualities of humane behavior. For Carlyle, "the Present Time" was characterized by days "of endless calamity, disruption, dislocation, confusion worse confounded. ..." 1848 had been "one of the most singular, disastrous, amazing, and, on the whole, humiliating years the European world ever saw."[27] Carlyle, of course, never advocated tory surrender to the force of history, and continued to hint at some form of statewide intervention; the examples cited of state intervention by the government of the time, however, contradict the whig theory that civilization was moving ever upwards.

While Carlyle was publishing his *Latter-Day Pamphlets*, Dickens began a more ambitious exercise in self-distributing in the form of his own journal. He showed his variance from Carlyle, however, in opening the inaugural edition of *Household Words*, a weekly paper that at twopence a week was within the financial reach of the middle classes and even the skilled working class, with a whig statement of faith in progress. Writing in March 1850, shortly after the Europe-wide revolution of 1848–1849 had ended leaving the British ruling establishment relatively unscathed—once again, the effect on individuals was conveniently overlooked—, Dickens pronounced that

> We seek to bring into innumerable homes, from the stirring world around us, the knowledge of many social wonders, good and evil, that are not calculated to render us any less ardently persevering in ourselves, less tolerant of one another, less faithful in in the progress of mankind, less thankful for the privilege of living in this summer-dawn of time.
>
> No mere utilitarian spirit, no iron binding of the mind to grim realities, will give a harsh tone to our Household Words. ....[28]

This "Preliminary Word" suggests that an accurate view of the good and bad points of the world is possible while retaining a spirit of optimisim overall; it is hard, indeed, to think of a less Carlylean phrase than "summer-dawn of time" to describe the present.

Dickens uses the editorial "we" here, but although he employed other writers on *Household Words*, the entire publication is presented as his personal reading of modern Britain and its empire. Dickens literally placed his stamp all over *Household Words*, heading every double-page spread with the phrase "Conducted by Charles Dickens." Thus although Dickens himself did not write all the articles discussing such topics as the state of British overseas territories or how consumer goods had grown cheaper in recent years, the total vision is declaredly his. A few articles are, of course, socially critical. About the same time that Carlyle produced his "Model Prisons" essay that became part of *Latter-Day Pamphlets*, Dickens published his own view of the subject. "Pet Prisoners" (April 27 1850) seems close to Carlyle's interpretation of the subject in arguing that in the new "Model Prison" at Pentonville, criminals fared better than some of the honest working poor, and in claiming that the only solution to crime was "education." The social criticism of this article, however, was diluted by Dickens's editorial decision that it should immediately be followed in by a story that seems to anticipate some of the phrasing of the "drinking days" passage from *A Tale of Two Cities* and that reveals a solidly whig attitude to history.

In Percival Leigh's distinctly Dickensian story "A Tale of the Good Old Times" (103–106), Mr. Blenkinsop, a country alderman who opposes technological advances, dreams that the statue of the fifteenth-century Wynkyn de Vokes in the town square addresses him on the topic of "the good old times." When Mr. Blenkinsop ventures to suggest that these were the reign of George III, the Statue responds,

> "Those the good old times? What! Mr. Blenkinsop, when men were hanged by dozens, almost weekly, for paltry thefts. When a nursing women was dragged to the gallows with her child at her breast, for shop-lifting, to the value of a shilling. When you lost your American colonies, and plunged into war with France, which, to say nothing of the useless bloodshed it cost, has left you saddled with the national debt. ..."[29]

Wynkyn de Vokes is a whig historian who convinces Mr. Blenkinsop that "The best times ... are the oldest. They are the wisest; for the older the world grows the more experience it acquires. It is older now than it ever was. The oldest and best times the world has yet seen are the present. These, so far as we have yet gone, are the genuine good old times." Mr. Blenkinsop is convinced, and the story concludes with the alderman looking "forwards to the grand object that all human eyes should have in view—progressive improvement."[30]

As editor of *Household Words*, Dickens told Leigh that the story should include "the intimation that we must always go on improving the times," but in a phrase that suggests that for the Victorians "old times" were proverbially synonymous with "good times," added that "Your moral that the real old times, are the oldest times, is charming."[31] Later editions of *Household Words* were more socially critical, notably of the conditions in which the poor were obliged to live; but even here the guiding philosophy was not Carlyle's belief in historical repetition—that the shadow of the French Revolution hung over any society that failed to respond to the warning signs—but a belief that society should and must continue to improve. Even in *A Child's History of England*, serialized in *Household Words* in 1851–3, Dickens uses incidents from English history not as might be expected, to point tory morals to the young through shocking examples, but more in the whig mode to encourage understanding of how England arrived at its present state.

Dickens's prefatory note to the *Tale* nevertheless implies that his major historical debt is to Carlyle, and in this a difference between conscious intention and cultural effect may be detected. Dickens had declaredly used Carlyle's history as a source: certain passages and ideas in the narrative clearly have their origin in Carlyle's *French Revolution*. As has been noted by Michael Goldberg, William Oddie, and others, Dickens follows Carlyle especially closely in his account of the fall of the Bastille and the subsequent hanging of Foulon. From Carlyle also he could have learned of Santerre, the brewer of the Saint-Antoine district who became a revolutionary leader, and who seems to have been the partial inspiration for Defarge.[32]

Dickens's variations on ideas taken from Carlyle, though, tend to be more striking than the repetitions. Even Dickens's most apparently Carlylean figure, Madame Defarge, is a part of the lengthened historical perspective on the causes of the French Revolution. Madame Defarge is reminiscent of monstrous women found in the earlier text, although Dickens chooses to emphasize this monstrousness less as an unwomanly involvement in politics than an unwomanly loss of compassion: John Kucich observes:

> in Dickens' world, the supreme disruption of normal expectations about human nature is an absence of tenderness in woman. In the Parisian violence, even La Guillotine is female.[33]

Madame Defarge is, though, a conflation of two types found in Carlyle's book. First, she is a *tricoteuse*, one of the Jacobin women who knit through meetings and trials, the female domestic skill being combined with a thirst for blood. The description of women knitting by the guillotine and counting heads as they fall, thus closely connecting the monstrous woman with feminized monstrous technology, is not derived from Carlyle and appears to be Dickens's own invention, yet one that in British tradition has almost assumed the status of historical fact. Second, she is a "Maenad," in Carlyle's history the frenzied woman of the Paris mob, and at first this personification of vengeance may seem the embodiment of what Carlyle had called the "rabidity" of the time. Dickens, however, develops the obvious symbolism of the human woman as one of the Fates into something rooted in the historical situation. Barton Friedman's stress on Madame Defarge as the embodiment of French savagery and "in the end, the novel's irredeemable villain, the epitome of evil"[34] overlooks the fact that in whig terms she may be analyzed without moral shock as the product of historical forces—although admittedly, such detachment is only possible because she and the threat that she represents no longer exist. Madame Defarge has historically-specific motives for being both *tricoteuse* and Maenad. Her knitting is unproductive—nothing, seemingly, is ever completed—but it is a means of occupation to ward off hunger, "a mechanical substitute for eating and drinking" (*Tale*, p. 215). Second, her leadership of the mob is inspired by personal revenge for her family, destroyed by the Ancien Régime.

The role of Madame Defarge provides an example of how Dickens's determinism—both in the form of humans as agents of destiny and of cause and effect—goes farther than Carlyle's. As I suggested in Chapter Two, in many respects Carlyle's reading of history is a struggle against determinism. The tragedy of the French Revolution is that until the coming of Napoleon, the people have no head, being governed not by leaders who can transcend history, but merely by those who, like Robespierre, try to exploit the historical moment. The *Tale* is, moreover, not dedicated to Carlyle, to whom Dickens had earlier dedicated *Hard Times*, but to Earl Russell.

Dickens was at this time friends with the former Lord John Russell, and even if he did not read Russell's writings on the French Revolution, it would seem improbable that he was totally unaware of Russell's position on the subject when he dedicated the book to him. Other whig determinist approaches were readily available to Dickens, such as Thiers and Mignet. While Bulwer-Lytton's use of Thiers indicates that to use a history as a source is not necessarily to coincide with its historical interpretation, *A Tale of Two Cities* agrees with A. F. Mignet's history in noting France's readiness for revolution: "When reform has become necessary, and the period for its accomplishment has arrived, attempts to stifle it tend only to hasten its progress."[35] Mignet (who, like Dickens, particularly stresses the part of the faubourg Saint-Antoine) argues that the excesses of the French Revolutionary period were caused by the extension of its duration by continued resistance, but that even these excesses were "transient evils" that led to "solid and enduring improvements." Dickens's sense of inevitability seems closer to the whig models of Russell, Mignet and Thiers than to that of Carlyle, who struggles to resist emplotting his version of revolution in such a way that chance[36] becomes fate in direct contrast with Dickens's interconnection of accident and destiny.

Even if Dickens did not use a whig history explicitly describing the French Revolution, the whig view of history was readily accessible to him and his readers in Lord Macaulay's *History of England*, of which two parts had already been published (Macaulay died at the end of 1859, and the last part completed was published posthumously). In the late 1850s, then, not only Dickens himself, but also his readers, could be reasonably expected to have a sense of the whig view of history.

Macaulay's history had demonstrated that although the whig and tory views of history are generally seen as centered on attitudes to progress, they also imply different responses to cultural distancing. As we have seen, for the whig historian, progress dictates that the past, technologically, intellectually, and morally, is inferior to the present;

for the tory, who sees human nature as consistent and rejects perfectibility, technological and social advances merely give more scope for human wickedness. If there is "difference," it is because the humans of the past were closer to a sense of natural order than their descendants. For tories, then, a reaction of shock is a moral duty in that the reader is thereby warned not to repeat the mistakes of the past. For whigs, history's shock must almost immediately be replaced by a sense of relief: history *is* the past, and its mistakes contribute towards a better future. If Oddie is right, the *Tale* claims a tory thesis; yet its overall rhetorical thrust is surely confused by the combination of Dickens's own inclination to whiggism and Carlyle's version of toryism.

The *Ancien Régime*

Although *A Tale of Two Cities* is remembered as a story of the French Revolution, a far larger proportion of the narrative takes place before the events of July 1789 than in Carlyle's text. Only one-sixth of Carlyle's history describes events prior to the storming of the Bastille. In contrast, the Bastille is stormed more than half-way through the substantially shorter *Tale*. Whereas Carlyle's narrative begins at a point when the Revolution seems inevitable, Dickens presents the world that causes revolution.

Writing twenty years after Carlyle, even if Dickens hypothetically believed that "Crush humanity out of shape once more, under similar hammers, and it will twist itself into the same tortured forms" (*Tale*, p. 399), he had no especial reason to fear revolution in Britain. Clearly, the enacters of the First Parliamentary Reform Act had not been new Girondists idealistically leading Britain into anarchy. The "Irish Sans-potatoes" of whom Carlyle had warned had suffered more than even he can have imagined, but without bringing about revolution in Britain. France also had survived a variety of changes of leadership, admittedly not without bloodshed, but with no repetition of the events of the first French Revolution as the Tories had envisaged. Indeed, critics may have projected Carlyle's fear of revolution onto Dickens's depiction of the Paris populace, for Dickens expresses even less fear of the concept of revolution than do many declaredly whig historians, including Russell. In *A Child's History of England*, for example, Dickens suggests that resistance to established law and leadership is occasionally appropriate, his sympathy during the English Civil War and the 1688 overthrow of James II being clearly with the revolutionaries. Dickens's portrait of Charles I, a king who "deliberately set himself to put his Parliament down and to put himself up" and "in pursuit of this wrong idea (enough in itself to have ruined any king) he never took a straight course, but always took a crooked one"[37] is particularly revealing of his stand on justified revolution.

Simultaneously to assert Dickens's sympathy towards revolution and to argue that the *Tale* finally proves not to be about revolution may seem contradictory. Yet Dickens's innovation is not to follow Burke in pitying the plumage but forgetting the dying bird, but instead to focus his shock on the carcase of the bird itself, France under the terminally-diseased *Ancien Régime*. He is shocked less by revolution than by the eighteenth century that rendered it inevitable—through the self-indulgence of individuals, and particularly by its judiciary cruelty that ignores individual character entirely. Thus Darnay is judged not as a man who has personal convictions, but in the first instance as a Frenchman, in the second as an aristocrat, and in the third as an Evrémonde. For Dickens, the eighteenth century itself is a cause of shock.

In *A Child's History of England*, Dickens had refused to discuss the eighteenth century, informing his young readers that events subsequent to the Revolution of 1688 "would neither be easily related nor easily understood in such a book as this." The few hints that follow, though, suggest that for him, the eighteenth century was a time of pro-Stuart "mischief" and Georgian incompetence.[38] By the time of the composition of the *Tale*, many English writers were eager to repudiate the ways of the eighteenth century. In a sketch of Lord Chesterfield, published in *Bentley's Miscellany* in 1853, the archetypal eighteenth-century gentleman is depicted in terms very close to those of Monseigneur in the *Tale*: he is "a fine gentleman, a courtier, a man of fashion, an idle lounger, lying late a-bed, sipping chocolate with an air. ..."[39]

A sense of the corruption of the aristocracy in the eighteenth century is also at the heart of Thackeray's 1857 lecture series *The Four Georges*. The best that Thackeray can say for George II, for example, is that he was "not a worse king than his neighbours. He claimed and took the Royal exemption from doing right which sovereigns assumed."[40] Of the exact time-period of the opening of the *Tale*, Thackeray cites "the awful debauchery and extravagance which prevailed in the great English society of those days. Its dissoluteness was awful ..." (*Works* 23:68). Even of George IV, who died only thirty years earlier, he asks, "how a great society could have tolerated him? In this quarter of a century, what a silent revolution has been working! how it has separated us from old times and manners!" (*Works* 23:103). Even if, as seems possible, Thackeray is to some extent playing up to what his apparently middle-class audience (the only heroes of his eighteenth century are the middle-class intellectuals) would like to hear, that audience can feel a whig sense of progress: their own "silent revolution," achieved without recourse to the mob, has imposed their morals on the British aristocracy.

Margaret Oliphant, writing in *Blackwood's Magazine* a few years after the publication of the *Tale*, further demonstrates the Victorian conception of the eighteenth century in her account of the "Man of the World" of the reign of George III: "The glimpse herein afforded of the corruption of society is appalling. It was a corruption which had even lost all conscience of itself." She adds, "Fortunately, the sentiments of our grand seigneurs, as well as our habits, have changed since that time."[41]

Oliphant's relief at the changing times seems to have been shared by Dickens, although he portrays the excesses of the French aristocracy more explicitly than those of their British twins. For his recreation of the seigneurs and habits of the France of the *Ancien Régime*, he would appear to have used two principle sources. His account of the condition of the countryside takes hints from Arthur Young's description of the state of French agriculture during the years 1787 to 1789. Young emphasizes the discontent caused by oppressive taxation of the poor, mentioned also in the *Tale*;[42] and Dickens's account of the wretched village, featuring "patches of rye where corn should have been" (*Tale*, p. 143) suggests that it is modelled on Young's account of the district of the Sologne, an area of beautiful chateaux but of miserable farming where, Young argues, "rye has no business."[43]

For Paris, the key source is Louis-Sebastien Mercier's *Tableau de Paris*, originally published in 1782, and reiussed in an expanded twelve-volume edition in 1782–1788. Dickens may have been alerted to the existence of this work by Carlyle's references to it, but since so much more of his narrative predates the revolution, his use of it is far more extensive. Although George Woodcock, whose annotations to the *Tale* contain no direct reference to Mercier, merely observes that Dickens "consulted" this work (Dickens, *Tale*, p. 12), Dickens openly acknowledged his debt, describing Mercier's book in a letter to Bulwer-Lytton as a "curious book … written to make out no case whatever, and tiresome enough in its literal dictionary-like minuteness."[44] Yet whether he realized it or not, Mercier's "case" surely influenced

Dickens's portrayal of the *Ancien Régime*. Oddie is correct in observing that Mercier's text does not contain all of the most horrific details of pre-revolutionary France used by Dickens: notably, while there are numerous hints of abusive feudal rights, there is no direct account of the "*droit de seigneur*" that forms a key element of Dr. Manette's condemnation of the Evrémondes.[45] Nevertheless, printed from the safe distance of Amsterdam, Mercier's text, an unsystematic description of Paris life, is strongly critical of the social divisions of France under Louis XV (who died in 1774) and Louis XVI, and by its vast list of the ills of Paris and French life, it too urges moral shock.

Several elements of *A Tale of Two Cities* have their origin in Mercier's description of Paris. Among the most important are Mercier's repeated references to the reckless manner in which the rich drove their carriages, which seems to have inspired the incident in which the carriage of Monseigneur (a word frequently used by Mercier) kills a child.[46] In Mercier too Dickens would have found stories of notorious eighteenth-century abuses, including one a prisoner released after forty-seven years in the Bastille for an unknown offense, who came to the realization that he had no life outside it, a possible inspiration for the story of Dr. Manette (*Tableau* 3:291). Dickens is most clearly indebted to Mercier, however, for his description of the life of the rich.

Dickens, whose prefatory note claims that his description of France is based "on the most trustworthy witnesses," apparently wishes his readers to notice his debt to Mercier. He closely follows Mercier's account of the Farmer-General, or tax-agent, repeating Mercier's figures of twenty-four male domestics, six chamber-women for his wife, and thirty horses (*Tale*, p. 135; *Tableau* 2:208–209): a detail that at first sight might appear exaggerated thus proves to have an "authentic" source.[47] In his account of Samson the public executioner's appearance at public functions, Dickens even translates Mercier directly, marking the quotation (*Tale*, p. 138). Appropriately for Dickens's image of the eighteenth century, the agent of judicial death is one of the few historical figures featured in the novel.

Yet although Dickens's source-based recreation of the distorted world of the *Ancien Régime* implies that the reality of a society in which an executioner was a respected public figure was stranger than anything a novelist might invent, the resulting effect might initially seem to justify those critics who assert that Dickens was unhistorical. For example, the hangers-on around the great Monseigneur in Paris, such as the Convulsionists and those who claim to have found the "Centre of Truth," are discussed by Mercier (*Tableau* 2:300–302). In fact, just as the character of Madame Defarge is a conflation of historical types, the novelist follows Mercier in conflating events from the reigns of the last two Bourbon monarchs.

Dickens himself acknowledged such a telescoping in his letter to Bulwer-Lytton, but this strategy is more radical than he may have realized. From the time of Burke's *Reflections*, tory historians had conceded the corrupt state of France under Louis XV, but had countered by arguing that immediately prior to the Revolution, the state of France had substantially improved, and that gradual change should have been allowed to continue. Following Mercier's lead, and perhaps also influenced by Young's insistence that by the late 1780s revolution was inevitable, Dickens presents a France that has moved beyond the possibility of moderate reform, and where the citizens are ready for revolution.

In one major respect, however, Dickens differs from Mercier, who is declaredly Anglophile, frequently noting how problems are managed better in England. Mercier believes that the English are more intellectually independent, constitutionally freer, and better organized than their French counterparts: they even have sidewalks to alleviate the dangers of reckless carriage-driving. Dickens, in contrast, maintains the sense of shock when depicting England also. This book of twins avoids the hints of complacency shown, for example, by Young, by depicting eighteenth-century Britain as nearly as brutal as its twin France. Here the historical assumptions most clearly depart from the tory model—in fact, the emphasis on the shocking features of eighteenth-century justice is at odds with the Carlylean "moral" of the novel.

Norbert Elias has suggested that whereas Germans distinguish between *Kultur* (which has intellectual connotations, generally individually-acquired) and *Zivilisation* (a society's standard of behavior), in French and English, the word "civilisation" (American "civilization") embraces both intellectual and behavioral achievements—always, implicitly, in contrast to some other less "civilized" state, be it that of another nation, or, as in Elias's own focus, another historical period.[48] In the "drinking days" passage, for instance, Dickens shows the people of the eighteenth century to be less "civilized" in terms of socially-acceptable behavior, and this cannot be dissociated from a more weighty implication: that in its judicial thinking, the eighteenth century was far removed from the higher standards of justice and humanity of the nineteenth century. Michel Foucault cites Damiens's gruesome execution by torture as a principal instance of the change in attitude towards judicial punishment from the eighteenth to the nineteenth century—from public spectacle, "the gloomy festival of punishment," to "the most hidden part of the penal process."[49] Significantly, Dickens puts an account of this execution into the mouths of the Revolutionaries (*Tale*, p. 200) as an indication of the state of civilization from which they hope to escape. The tragedy of the Revolution is in leading such citizens not into escaping judicial cruelty, but into repeating it.

The rhetorical force of such passages might seem to suggest that Dickens follows his sources in ascribing a higher level of social development to England, yet this story is told long after the reader has seen evidence of English judicial cruelty. The historical narration informs the reader that in England "at that time, putting to death was a recipe much in vogue" (*Tale*, p. 84).[50] Death was the punishment for even minor offenses, "not," Dickens adds with a nineteenth-century regard for practicality, "that it did the least good in the way of prevention." The next chapter states that "They hanged at Tyburn, in those days," followed by references to the "wise old" and "dear old" institutions of the pillory and the whipping-post, before the general conclusion:

> Altogether, the Old Bailey, at that date, was a choice illustration of the precept, that 'Whatever is, is right;' an aphorism that would be as final as it is lazy, did it not include the troublesome consequence, that nothing that ever was, was wrong. (*Tale*, pp. 89–90)

The phrases "at that time," "in those days," and "at that date" all emphasize historic difference, but the sarcasm applied to the ways of the past, a history that is certainly not venerable, suggests that for Dickens, the past should remain shocking. Eighteenth-century philosophy as suggested by the Pope aphorism is itself disturbing, since if "nothing that ever was, was wrong," then revolution can never be justified.

By the time that Darnay is tried by the French revolutionary government, Dickens has already shown that similar casual justice is a feature of England too. In researching *Barnaby Rudge*, Dickens appears to have used the accounts of the anti-Catholic Gordon Riots and the subsequent trials of the rioters in the *Annual Register* for 1780. Only a hardened cultural-relativist would not share to some extent in Dickens's shock at reading these accounts of eighteenth-century justice. The *Annual Register* lists over one hundred men and women capitally convicted for crimes other than murder (mainly for the theft of property of theft of relatively little value; of these, perhaps one-half were executed.⁵¹ In the aftermath of the Gordon Riots, 85 were tried, 35 capitally convicted, and 18 hanged. Appropriately, then, Dickens pairs the "justice" Darnay is to receive from the French revolutionary courts with his English trial for spying. Dickens's principal source for the trial was probably the *Annual Register* for 1781, where alongside the accounts of the trial and acquittal of George Gordon, Dickens would have found the report of the treason trial of a Frenchman named Henry Francis de la Motte. In spite of Mercier's assertion that English justice is more compassionate, De la Motte was sentenced with the full punishment for high treason: "To be hanged by the neck, but not till dead; then to be cut down, and his bowels burned before his face, his head to be taken off, his body cut into four quarters, and to be at his majesty's disposal." Dickens may not have been aware that the brutality of this sentence was slightly diminished in its execution, and for him, such trials suggest the rigor of English law of the 1780s.⁵²

Such a fate awaits Charles Darnay, and Dickens's first task is to register the responses of the 1780s. The Manettes and Jarvis Lorry, who represent the timeless moral values of the work, believe that someone who is innocent should not be found guilty, but this sentiment is hardly a revolutionary one, since it does not contradict law. Jerry Cruncher, in contrast, has previously debated "law" with the "ancient clerk" of the court. The clerk informs him that a treason trial is in progress:

> "That's quartering," said Jerry. "Barbarous!"
> "It is the law," remarked the ancient clerk, turning his surprised spectacles upon him. "It is the law."
> "It's hard in the law to spile a man, I think. It's hard enough to kill him, but it's very hard to spile him, sir."
> "Not at all," returned the ancient clerk. "Speak well of the law. Take care of your chest and voice, my good friend, and leave the law to take care of itself. I give you that advice." (*Tale*, p. 90)

Jerry regards quartering as "barbarous" because judicial cruelty is allowed to outweigh economic considerations. In placing pragmatism above public spectacle, he might appear more "modern" in outlook than the other characters. Yet as a Resurrection-man who supplies corpses for anatomists he himself is a historical curiosity, rendered unnecessary to the nineteenth-century world by a progressive society that, now that body-snatching and the guillotine are safely in the past, keeps the bodies of the respectable classes in one piece. The reader of 1859 can be simultaneously shocked by the barbarity of a previous age—perhaps even to the stage of wondering why the French Revolution was not repeated in Britain—and comforted by the fact that British progress in thought assures that this is past.

Within the structure of the novel, the Revolution itself does not bring about the end of this legal barbarism, the mob very soon forsaking lynching for judicial forms. Indeed, Darnay is called back to France because his uncle's estate agent Gabelle, who bears the name of the hated salt-tax described by Young and Mercier, has been arrested: the emblematic reminder of old injustices is now captive to new injustices. Darnay is subsequently arrested and tried twice, and the second time, at least from the Revolutionaries' point of view, is guillotined. It should be noted that Dickens maintains some distinctions in judicial matters: English law acquits Darnay, and even the Revolutionaries have reasons to accuse him, whereas under the *Ancien Régime* Manette is arrested through a *lettre de cachet* and imprisoned for eighteen years for no offense at all. That this story of judicial cruelty under the monarchy is revealed as a consequence of the judicial cruelty of the Revolutionaries surely prompts relief that choices no longer need to be made between the two: the eighteenth century is over.

The philosophy of the *Tale* could, of course, still be seen as Oddie sees it, encapsulated in the Carlylean point explicitly made by Dickens in the final chapter. In suggesting that given similar circumstances and similar grievances, the same course of events will recur, Dickens implies that he would like to be a tory historian, even if he tinges his exemplary narrative with whig determinism. The stories of Dr. Manette, the Defarges, and the Evrémondes certainly help make the eighteenth century seem "the worst of times," but its *Ancien Régime* horrors are too far from the reader to prompt a lasting shock: British readers of 1859 ought to be able to remain reassured by their higher civilization.

Civilization

This prompts a further question: namely, why in 1859, when, as Foucault has remarked, "punitive practices had become more reticent,"[53] the *Tale* should encourage the reader to contemplate the horrors of an earlier era. The need may partly be explained in terms of Stallybrass and White's analysis of "Carnival." The reader is secure in the knowledge that the type of "carnival" captured in the socially-overturning behavior of the Defarges and their associates has been contained by history, and their activities merely prompt "a long, fascinated gaze from the bourgeoisie."[54] The need for such a self-affirming "gaze" at others, though, may further suggest a deeper underlying Victorian anxiety: that although in most respects their judicial system has become more "reticent," at points, both revolutionary and judicial cruelty may burst the fragile bubble of civilization.

Dickens conceived the idea of *A Tale of Two Cities* in 1857, when Britain was just recovering from the Crimean War—a war that symbolized a major change in the way that Britain and France conceived of each other, and of their roles in the world. Until this time, France and Britain, if not actually at war with each other, had generally found it advantageous to support the other's enemies: as we have seen, each was the obvious Other. Yet the philosophical possibility first raised by Burke, that France was also Britain's most obvious twin, took on a new significance when France and Britain allied themselves against Russia. The political motivations behind the war are not important here—in fact, they seem to have remained shadowy to British readers, and also writers of publications such as *Household Words*—but Britain and France together determined to support the survival of Turkey in the Balkans to counterbalance the influence of Russia, the result being an expensive and largely non-productive two-year war. In July 1854, early in the war, an article in *Household Words* titled "Some Amenities of War" attempted to list the advantages to Britain. Some of these advantages, such as an improvement in general British knowledge of the geography of the Crimean region, seem so unconvincing as to cast doubt on the author's sincerity. Yet the article concludes with the apparently heartfelt claim that the greatest advantage is "that the war has brought closer and firmer together the bonds of intelligence and union between the two bravest, wisest, gentlest nations of the world."[55] The result is a rejection of tory memory of the past:

> Then when the steam argosies bear the peacemakers of the world back to their native shores again; standing hand and hand in a better brotherhood, Saxon and Gaul will agree, rather to repudiate every victory gained in ages gone, in contest with each other; rather to cast every tattered standard, every hard-won trophy, every bloodstained glory, into the fathomless sea, and let their memories perish there; than that one fresh bickering, one new jealousy, one angry word should arise between the great twin brothers of civilisation.

France and Britain should be twins, but in civilization, not in anarchy.

Ironically, the heroic actions for which the war is most remembered, the Charge of the Light Brigade and the innovations of Florence

Nightingale, could both be seen as results of the failure of civilization. In *The Times* in October 1854, the British public learned of the loss of hundreds of cavalrymen as the consequence of poor communication: to change this disaster into a triumph in the popular eye took the genius of Tennyson, so that even the adminstrative failure implied by "Someone had blundered"[56] leads to the triumph of civilized behavior.

If the Charge of the Light Brigade becomes a triumph, it is one that the French, who have no presence in the poem, apparently do not share. The state of medical care during the early stages of the Crimean War, however, set up comparisons between Britain and France. British medical care for their troops was brutally primitive; in contrast, the French had a serviceable medical system, with trained nurses in the form of Roman Catholic nuns. The Sisters of Charity, in contradiction to the British view of the Roman Catholic Church as the enemies of progress, were a potential cause of British feelings of inferiority: also in October 1854, *The Times* admitted that in medical care

> the French are greatly our superiors. Their medical arrangements are extremely good, their surgeons more numerous, and they have also the help of the "Sisters of Charity," who have accompanied the expedition in incredible numbers. These devoted women are excellent nurses, and perform for the sick and wounded all the offices which could be rendered in the most complete hospitals. We have nothing.[57]

Florence Nightingale was already organizing an expedition that would take British nurses, some of them nuns, to the Crimea, and finally make British military hospitals equal or superior to their French counterparts.[58] The defender of civilized British progress thus proved to be a woman, and moreover one influenced by the example of the Roman Catholic Church.

The medical debate had prompted comparisons and rivalry between France and Britain, and as the Crimean War continued and its supposed "amenities" for Britain proved less certain, an obvious recourse was to blame France, and especially Napoleon III for his desire to recoup his uncle's glory. But Britain and France did prove twins in losing heavily in lives and money, and gaining virtually nothing in terms of civilizing the world.

French and British relations were further strained in early 1858. In 1857, at least between the two nations' governments, friendship had been sufficient to prompt serious interest in the construction of a Channel Tunnel. The following January, an Italian exile named Orsini traveled across from England and threw a bomb at Napoleon III. The Emperor was uninjured, but the thought seems to have occurred to the French that a Channel Tunnel would make the entry of undesirables from Britain even easier. Nevertheless, the resulting apologies and recriminations led not to war, but to the abandonment of the tunnel project.

While this might appear a sign of the progress of civilized behavior, in 1857 Britain had seen a more serious challenge to the "higher civilization" implicit in British rule in India, and the response had been far from a manifestation of judicial humanity. Both Hindu and Muslim troops in the British service in India had risen against their leaders, and while in British terms this has become known as the "Indian Mutiny," implying that the rebellion was confined to the army, some contemporary commentators questioned whether this was, in fact, an unsuccessful nationalist revolution. As Disraeli asked, "Is it a military mutiny, or is it a national revolt?"[59] Early in 1857, articles on India in *Household Words* were critical of British behavior there and sympathetic towards the grievances of the Indian troops.[60] By October, however, the mood had changed, as revealed by a letter from Dickens to the humanitarian Angela Burdett-Coutts. Dickens initially expresses what appears to be a sympathy towards ordinary Britons and their lack of opportunities for advancement at a time when army commissions were still in effect reserved for the sons of the upper classes. The letter then continues:

> And I wish I were Commander in Chief in India. The first thing I would do to strike that Oriental race with amazement (not in the least regarding them as if they lived in the Strand, London, or at Camden Town), should be to proclaim to them, in their language, that I considered my holding that appointment by the leave of God, to mean that I should do my utmost to exterminate the Race upon whom the stain of the late cruelties rested; and that I begged them to do my the favor to observe that I was there for that purpose and no other, and was now proceeding, with all convenient dispatch and merciful swiftness of execution, to blot it out of mankind and raze it off the face of the Earth.

This letter has often been quoted as evidence of Dickens's racism; seldom remarked upon, however, is its concluding reinstatement of the niceties of civilization: "My love to Mrs. Brown, with these sentiments."[61]

This is a private letter rather than a public declaration, and the anticlimactic postscript to Burdett-Coutts's companion Mrs. Brown (itself part of the veneer of civilization, since Dickens apparently did not like her) may imply that Dickens is himself aware of the uncharacteristic aggression of his sentiments. He is nevertheless advocating a "merciful" genocide. Dickens's reaction to the 1857 rising, similar to that of many of his fellow-Britons, fails to reflect the "reticence" that Foucault argues is a characteristic of mid-nineteenth justice—as do the very public cruelties used in the execution of some of the Indian participants.[62]

Whereas, therefore, Carlyle's vision of the French Revolution shakes the complacency of those who believe that luke-warm reforms can be successfully carried out within an existing social structure, Dickens's version, safely located in the past, provides a form of comfort at a time when the nineteenth century had shown itself to be disturbingly "uncivilized," even if these illustrations of the fragile nature of civilization are distanced from the British home. While the Crimean War and the Indian disturbances suggest that nineteenth-civilization is not entirely, in Dickens's phrase from *Household Words*, in a "summer-dawn of time," readers may at least be reassured that their world is superior to that of the eighteenth century. The shock of the concluding warning that history may repeat itself is undermined by the reader's knowledge that the Revolution is over, and the frenzied Madame Defarges of the world—Defarge, La Vengeance, and indeed most Frenchwomen in the book being the precise opposite of "Sisters of Charity"—have succumbed to their twins the Miss Prosses, initially "wild" yet tamed by a a loyalty to class distinctions. When Carlyle wrote *The French Revolution: a History* in the 1830s, the outcome of the contest was not entirely clear; for Dickens, writing more than twenty years later, the defeat of the demagogue by the preserver of caste may seem an accident in terms of plot, but this reassertion of civilization and order represents a necessity if a whig view of history is to survive.

Dickens's historical "moral" is, moreover, only the beginning of the final chapter, the concluding focus being on Sydney Carton's self-sacrifice in the place of Charles Darnay. Carton represents all that is most shocking about the eighteenth century: he is a hard drinker, a jobbing lawyer, and a cynical world-hater. Appropriately, the story concludes with one of the most eighteenth-century characters of all becoming the victim of eighteenth-century judicial cruelty, yet simultaneously transcending his historical milieu by the assertion of lasting values as Carton abandons his eighteenth-century egotism for the sake of the happiness of others. While Dickens's preface acknowledges a debt to Wilkie Collins's drama *The Frozen Deep*, in which a man sacrifices his life to save the fiancé of the woman he loves, the similarity to *Zanoni* is also apparent. Whereas, however, Zanoni's death in the French Revolution brings a man belonging to no age or race into history, Carton's self-sacrifice enables him to transcend the historical period to which he so clearly belongs. Carton might seem to conform to tory history in asserting eternal values, but even as he moves outside history, he reasserts the whig doctrine of the progress of civilization, prophesying a revision of law in the century to come. Darnay and Lucy's son is destined to be a Sydney for the nineteenth century, a lawyer who will become "foremost of just judges and honored men" (*Tale*, p. 404). He will also, the reader is led to assume, be a true "Sydney" all his life, rather than merely in the ending of it. Carton's first name recalls Algernon Sydney, executed for treason in the reign of Charles II. Sydney was an idealistic republican, in Macaulay's words "beheaded in defiance of law and justice,"[63] and Dickens echoes this in *A Child's History of England* when he notes that Sydney died "a hero" (*Child's History*, p. 453). In the promise of a true Sydney, *A Tale of Two Cities* thus leaves the reader not with the sense of impending historical repetition in the form of revolution, but with the reassurance that revolution is no longer necessary—not with the shocking Carlylean prognostication that history will repeat itself, but with the soothing promise of children who will be better citizens in a better world than that of their parents.

Notes

1. John Forster, *The Life of Charles Dickens*, new edition (1872–74; Dent, 1969) 2:57.
2. Charles Dickens, *A Tale of Two Cities*, edited by George Woodcock (1859; Penguin, 1973), p. 29.
3. Sylvère Monod, *Dickens the Novelist*, English edition (University of Oklahoma Press, 1968), p. 455.
4. Michael Goldberg, *Carlyle and Dickens* (University of Georgia Press, 1973), p. 101.
5. K. J. Fielding, *Charles Dickens, A Critical Introduction* (Longmans, 1965), p. 199.
6. David D. Marcus, "The Carlylean Vision of *A tale of Two Cities*." In *Charles Dickens's A Tale of Two Cities: Modern Critical Interpretations*, edited by Harold Bloom (Chelsea House, 1987), pp. 23–25.
7. Dickens, *Tale of Two Cities*, p. 399.
8. *Shaw on Dickens*, edited by Dan H. Laurence and Martin Quinn (Frederick Ungar, 1985), p. 46.

9. Lukács, *The Historical Novel*, p. 243.
10. Napoleon III, *Discourses et Messages de Louis-Napoléon Bonaparte* (Plon, 1853), p. 1, my translation.
11. *The Times* (December 4, 1851).
12. Napoleon III, *Discourses*, p. 3.
13. For an account of the initially favorable British and French responses to this scheme, see Hunt, *The Story of the Channel Tunnel*, pp. 20–27.
14. The quotation, also used as an epigraph in some editions of Pope's *Rape of the Lock*, survives as the epigraph to Book 2, chapter 6.
15. "Zanoni," *The Athenaeum* (February 26, 1842), p. 181.
16. "Zanoni," *The Examiner* (Feb 26, 1842), p. 133.
17. Bulwer-Lytton, "The Reign of Terror," *Foreign Quarterly Review* 29 (July 1842), p. 276.
18. Ibid., p. 303; italics in original.
19. Brougham was to live until 1868, but he had only been in his teens during the Terror.
20. Bulwer-Lytton, *Zanoni* (1842; Little, Brown, n. d.), p. 622.
21. *The Positive Philosophy of Auguste Comte,* translated and edited by Harriet Martineau (Calvin Blanchard, 1859), p. 401.
22. Ibid., p. 11.
23. *The Letters of Charles Dickens*, edited by Graham Storey (Oxford: Clarendon, 1989–) 7:67.
24. Dickens, *A Tale of Two Cities*, p. 166. Following references are cited in the text.
25. William Oddie, *Dickens and Carlyle, The Question of Influence* (Centenary Press, 1972), p. 63.
26. The only partially successful attempts to claim a distance between the reader and Lucretia and Becky Sharp show a desire to deflect shock.
27. Carlyle, *Works* 20:1–5.
28. Dickens, "A Preliminary Word," *Household Words* (March 30, 1850).
29. Percival Leigh, "A Tale of the Good Old Times," *Household Words* (April 27, 1840), p. 104.
30. Ibid., p. 106.
31. Dickens, *Letters* 6:60–61.
32. I have not found any source that places Santerre at the fall of the Bastille as does Carlyle (2:193), and Defarge's role here increases the probability that Dickens saw a parallel between Defarge and Santerre.
33. John Kucich, *Excess and Restraint in the Novels of Charles Dickens* (University of Georgia Press, 1981), p. 87.
34. Friedman, *Fabricating History*, p. 154.
35. Mignet, *History of the French Revolution*, p. 14.
36. Obviously, the resistance is limited by Carlyle's visualization of key characters of the Revolution as shaping their own and France's destinies when presented with opportunity, which prompts the question of the origin of

opportunity. His historical ideal, however, remains the individual who shapes history independent of opportunity: Napoleon, for example, would still have been a "great man" in other historical circumstances, whereas Robespierre would not.

37. Dickens, *A Child's History of England* (1851–51; Chapman and Hall, 1907), p. 379.
38. Dickens, *Child's History*, pp. 471–472.
39. "Lord Chesterfield," *Bentley's Miscellany* 34 (1853), p. 222. *Bentley's* had serialized *Oliver Twist*, and originally undertook to publish *Barnaby Rudge*, in which the eighteenth-century gentleman Sir John Chester conforms very closely to this sketch.
40. Thackeray, *The Four Georges*, in *Works* 23:38. Following references are cited in the text.
41. Margaret Oliphant, "Historical Sketches of the Reign of George III—The Man of the World," *Blackwood's Magazine* 103 (1868), p. 511, p. 529.
42. Arthur Young, *Travels during the Years, 1787, 1788, and 1789* (1792), pp. 511–532.
43. Young, p. 357. He also describes how in "the miserable province of Sologne," where nevertheless the Marquis de Coix has "a handsome chateau," he talked to a "man employed on the roads" (p. 12) which might perhaps have given Dickens the idea for the "mender of roads"; Young further explains how good roads are themselves a symbol of oppression, being financed by taxation (p. 30). The soil in the Sologne district is said by Young to be chalky, and the man who hangs under the Marquis's carriage is called "whiter than the miller" (*Tale*, p. 146).
44. *Letters of Charles Dickens* 9:259.
45. Oddie, *Dickens and Carlyle*, p. 67. Oddie is here correcting the assertion by E. Davis, Goldberg and others that Dickens "got the hint of the droit de seigneur" from Mercier; see Michael Goldberg, *Carlyle and Dickens* (Georgia University Press, 1973), p. 108. It seems more probable to me that he knew it from some version of Beaumarchais's *Mariage de Figaro*: Carlyle certainly both knew the play and assumed that his readers would too (*Works* 2:59), and given his love of theatre, it seems improbable that Dickens did not know either the play or Mozart's opera version. Dickens, may also, though, have been influenced by an anecdote (ch. 281, "Badly-hanged Servant") in the *Tableau de Paris* that contains several of the key motifs of the *Tale*. Immediately after the story of Damiens, of which the specifics were used by Dickens (*Tale*, p. 200), Mercier tells how a servant-girl rejected the advances of her master; he had her falsely accused of theft, for which she was hanged, and her body given up for dissection. On the surgeon's table, she revived and lived to demonstrate her innocence, an event that Mercier calls a "resurrection." Louis-Sebastien Mercier, *Tabeleau de Paris*, 2nd edition (1782–1788) 3:286.
46. Dickens, *Tale, p.* 141; Mercier, *Tableau* 2:7. See also Mercier 1:54, where he asserts that the "indifference towards these sorts of accidents demon-

47. Andrew Sanders notes this in *The Companion to A Tale of Two Cities* (Unwin Hyman, 1988), p. 81, but assumes that Dickens's precise reference to an "appropriate cane with a golden apple on the top of it" is the novelist's invention in response to Mercier's observation that canes were fashionable. While doubtless the symbolic possibilities of such an item appealed to Dickens, the source is once again Mercier (3:50).
48. Norbert Elias, *The Civilizing Process: The Development of Manners*, translated by Edmund Jephcott (1939; Urizen Books, 1978), pp. 3–9.
49. Michel Foucault, *Discipline and Punish: The Birth of the Prison*, translated by Alan Sheridan (Random House, 1979), pp. 8–9.
50. For another instance of Victorian assumptions concerning eighteenth-century judicial cruelty, see Sheridan LeFanu's 1872 story "Mr. Justice Harbottle" ("The Haunted House in Westminster").
51. *Annual Register* (1780), pp. 196, 291.
52. See the the *Annual Register* (1781), p. 185. When the sentence was carried out at Newgate on July 27, 1781, even the hangman proved squeamish: La Motte was hanged for 57 minutes, clearly to demonstrate to the onlookers that he was dead, before he was cut down and his head and heart removed. The remains of La Motte were not publicly displayed, but "put into a very handsome coffin, and delivered to an Undertaker" (*Gentleman's Magazine* (1781), pp. 341–342).
53. Foucault, *Discipline and Punish*, p. 11.
54. Peter Stallybrass and Allon White, *The Politics and Poetics of Transgression* (Cornell University Press, 1986), p. 139.
55. "Some Amenities of War," *Household Worlds* (July 1854), p. 524.
56. In his original version, Tennyson named the messenger as "Nolan," but the version which took hold in public consciousness only ascribes the blunder to "someone": nobody is given the individuality of a name. I am aware that "The Charge of the Light Brigade" may be read more ambivalently, but my concern here is with the contemporary reading.
57. *The Times* (October 13, 1854), leader.
58. See Martha Vicinus and Bea Nergaard's edition of Nightingale's letters (virago, 1989), pp. 77–83.
59. See *Hansard* (July 27, 1857), p. 442.
60. For example, "The Himalaya Club" describes the dissolute habits of the British (*Household Words* 15 [March 21, 1857]: 265–272. Even an article published in August, "A Mutiny in India," (*Household Words* 16:154–156) suggests that a minor mutiny was caused by British insensitivity to Indian beliefs.
61. *Letters of Charles Dickens* 8:549.
62. An anxiety to privilege British justice is a subtext of "Lutfullah Khan," a character-sketch published in *Household Words* on November 21, 1857,

which contrasts the "inflexible justice" of Europeans with the treachery and inhumanity of "Oriental justice" (pp. 491–493). Interestingly, in this story a Rajah is depicted as using the infamous punishment employed by the British against the mutineers when he has a Thug "blown from a great cannon" (p. 492).

63. Macaulay, *Works* 1:210. Macaulay in fact usually elects to call Sydney not a republican, but a Whig, the implication being that he represented true opposition to the corrupt monarch Charles II.

Chapter 5
Alternative Worlds and the Franco-Prussian War

The failure of historical repetition came to a tragic conclusion in the war between France and Prussia in 1870 to 1871. Ironically, the results of the third Napoleon's attempt to relive the *gloire* of the first—the collapse of his government, the Republic that succeeded it, and the Paris Commune—seemed closer to a historical repetition of the First French Revolution than any intervening series of events. Yet the British response was, I shall argue, different, less because of any perceived change in France and the French, than because Britons were coming to perceive themselves differently, both ethnically and, to some extent, politically. Geographically, France remained Britain's closest neighbor (although 1870–1871 also saw the continuation of Ireland's struggle to be the larger island's neighbor rather than its property); but British writing begins to explore new kinds of kinship, notably with the Anglophone world, through an increased emphasis on the role of language in history.

When France declared war on Prussia in July 1870, the French leaders evidently believed that they could humiliate their German-speaking neighbors. Mutual distrust between France and Prussia had grown in proportion with the rise of nationalism that had caused the German-speaking states, briefly united at the time of the French Revolution of 1848, gradually to come together politically and economically. France, or at least Napoleon III and his advisers, saw a strengthened German state as a threat to France's Rhineland territories; this sense of distrust was increased by Prussia's assertion of military authority over Austria and Denmark in the 1860s. Then in 1870, the possibility arose that a German prince might be elected the new King of Spain, thus (in Napoleon III's judgment) presenting a German threat to France's south-west perimeter.

After repeated French protests, the Prince of Hohenzollern seems to have been willing to withdraw from candidacy for the Spanish throne before France committed to war.[1] The motivation for war was hence supplied less by this specific incident than by a more general sense of suspicion, each nation maintaining that possession of the Rhineland states was necessary for security against the other. This itself was a form of historical repetition: at least as interpreted by the British press, the two nation would replay the Battle of Jena in 1806, where the first Napoleon destroyed the Prussian army. Obviously, the French were hoping to prove that the relative power of the two countries had not changed, and the Prussians that it had. On July 15, France declared war on Prussia, and the French people jubilantly shouted their goal of "To Berlin!" For a brief moment, they had accepted the new Napoleon as the replaying of the old.

Few people, however, suggested that Britain would replay its role in the Napoleonic War. Four days before war was declared, *The Times*'s editorial argued that a war for the left bank of the Rhine would affect Britain "but little," because

> Russia and the United States are the Powers which the next generation will look upon as the most formidable. Moreover, the interests and attentions of England are chiefly concerned with her own growing colonies and with the vast populations of Asia.[2]

The Times conceded that Britain had an interest in preserving peace between the two nations that represented the height of continental civilization, but claimed a change in international priorities.[3]

The Crimean War had lowered Napoleon III's popularity with the British public, and his opposition to the efforts of Giuseppe Garibaldi and the Risorgimento to unite Italy in 1859–1861 (a movement that the British press lauded not as a revolution but as a fight for national freedom) also contributed to their suspicion. By supporting the Pope and using French troops to prevent Garibaldi from entering Rome, Napoleon was both stressing his Roman Catholicism, always a cause of suspicion to Britons; and also hinting at an ambition to be what the first Napoleon had made his son and heir: the King of Rome. Even though he was technically still Britain's ally, once war was declared in

1870, *The Times* asserted that the "dire calamity" was "the act of France—of one man in France."[4]

What followed, however, in the form of repeated successes of the Prussian army leading to the defeat and capture of the Emperor and the Siege of Paris, prompted some reassessment. Britain had hastily declared neutrality, complaining that both France (which reminded Britain of the ties established by the Anglophile Napoleon III), and Prussia (which initially presented itself as the victim of aggression) were urging it to take sides. Yet since 1860, when F. Max Müller had presented language to British audiences as a science, a new element had entered history: the relevance of language in the creation of identity. While this study has repeatedly emphasized the connections between history and language, whig history of the 1860s went further in claiming that language determines the identity of the makers of history, and through them, the course of history itself. Hence in the Franco-Prussian War, Britain's unofficial sympathies were largely not with its closest neighbor France, but shaped by a new sense of relationship based on language: that Germany was its closest European family. For those who accepted this linguistic relation, history became more clearly determined, not by fate but by racial characteristics that shaped the rise and fall of nations. Carlyle and Bulwer-Lytton, for example, who had earlier dissented from the whig view of history, may be seen realigning themselves if not with the political heirs of the whigs then at least with the whig concept of progress—albeit a harsher form of progress achieved at the expense of others.

Philology and Ethnography

Since the 1848 Revolutions, and particularly in the 1860s, new theories of language and ethnography had emerged.[5] In Britain, these ideas were popularized by the German philologist and lecturer F. Max Müller. Müller's study of Sanskrit demonstrated, he claimed, the common Indo-European or Aryan roots of European civilization, and the English language in its grammatical structure showed itself to be entirely Saxon.[6] About the same time, Charles Kingsley had presented his own series of lectures, *The Roman and the Teuton*, which attempted to identify the racial differences between the "Romans"—those who spoke Romance languages and continued to support the Roman Catholic Church—and the "Teutons"—those who spoke

Germanic languages and who were Protestant. Other writers, notably Thomas Carlyle, complicated the racial division further by associating the Ancient Gaul of France with the Gael of Ireland, but the "Roman" connection was still present in religion.

This study of philological evolution was paralleled by an interest in the evolution of the natural world, and especially the concept of natural selection: Charles Darwin's *Descent of Man* was to appear in 1871. Evidence for evolution was based on the geological record, the strata of the earth demonstrating the successive periods in the development of animal life. Philology was claimed to be similarly scientific in its recreation through the "vestiges" of the past in modern languages: in Müller's opinion, geology was the science from which philologists could learn most, and each word should be examined like a geological specimen.[7] Philology and geology can be seen working together in Jules Verne's 1866 *Journey to the Center of the Earth*, where Professor Lidenbrock is both a geologist and a "polyglot." His interest in language enables him to decode the way into the earth, where he finds material evidence of evolution in the form of living creatures known only in fossil forms by the upper world.

Verne's choice of a German scientist as the embodiment of the progress of knowledge may have seemed discomforting to his French readers.[8] Both philology and natural science were to be used in support of the historical concept of "Manifest Destiny," which, by a strange twist of argumentation, presented the theory that the Germanic-speaking races, and notably the English speakers, were destined to rule the world.[9] Müller had public disagreements with the Darwinists, but in a concept apparently related to "the survival of the fittest," he had argued that languages are not mixed; that is, one language may assimilate vocabulary from another, but in net effect, languages replace each other rather than merging; and undergo "modifications ... by continually new combinations of given elements."[10]

Whig history's interest in progress was given a new lease of life by this evolutionary model. Eighteenth-century rationalism had assumed the upward path of civilization; now progressive history emphasized that such a claim was scientific, the science of history being corroborated by analogies with other sciences. Just as the Romans had succeeded the Greeks as the dominant civilization, argued Kingsley and others, notably the historian Edward Augustus Freeman immediately after the Franco-Prussian War, so the Teutons had succeeded the Romans.[11] Such an interpretation prompted the classification of the

Franco-Prussian War, not merely by extremists but even by the organ of normative politics *The Times*, as representing the inevitable continuation of the struggle between Romans and Teutons. On July 21, *The Times* announced,

> Hostilities have commenced. There is now open war between France and Germany. It is no longer a contest between States. It is the old feud of the two nations. On one side the Gaul, with the Teuton facing him, and the Rhine—the cause of strife and the prize of victory—between them. ... National characteristics never stood forth in bolder relief than at the present supreme juncture. ...

"Latin nations" such as France (significantly, this one article labels the French both Gauls and Latins) are said to "live fast" and to be the victims of their own enthusiasm. In contrast,

> the interest the world will feel for the Germans will be, if not deeper, at least wider than that which will be shown for their adversaries. The Germans are a branch of that race which is destined to people and subdue the earth. From their earliest records they have always been spreading, and their emigrants are now among the most active elements of Transatlantic progress.

The Times now describes Prussia and its allies as "Germany," not merely a state but a nationalist concept, and assumes that a German victory is part of the natural progress, or even evolution, of civilization. Certainly, the war showed advances in technology: the Prussian army (as many Britons pointed out) had the superiority of modern weaponry; and the story of the Siege of Paris was told to the rest of the world through dispatches sent out of the city by balloon.

Yet Britain was not simply an observer, for the war prompted some internal reassessment, notably of political divisions. The Liberal party might seem the direct heirs of the whig ideal, yet Liberals were divided over the appropriate response. While the party had cultivated friendship with France, many members saw Prussia as the ideal of whig progress. The Prime Minister Gladstone, under attack from many of his fellow-Liberals for not showing sufficient support for Prussia, was compelled to deny that his government's stance was driven by self-interest, and that if France and Prussia exhausted one another, it could be to Britain's advantage.[12] The denial might have been more convincing if Gladstone had not published in the October 1870 *Edinburgh Review* an article titled "Germany, France, and England" which criticized both the warring nations, but particularly blamed Britain's erstwhile ally Napoleon III. Gladstone concluded by calling England "happy" since

> the wise dispensation of Providence has cut her off, by that streak of silver sea, which passengers so often and justly execrate, though in no way from the duties and the honours, yet partly from the dangers, absolutely from the temptations, which attend upon the local neighbourhood of the Continental nations.[13]

Although Gladstone concluded that a common European policy of "Public Right" would be "the greatest triumph of our time" (p. 593), his article, which emphasized Britain's colonial interests, could also be seen as implying that the Franco-Prussian War was not Britain's problem. Gladstone apparently hoped that he could publish it anonymously, but his authorship was soon known, and seemed to confirm that the British Government regarded this as the end of France's "military primacy" in Europe, "which she had loftily carried for two hundred and fifty years" (p. 555).

Many other Britons, and particularly Gladstone's fellow-Liberals, went further in disclosing their pleasure that their old enemy France had been so humiliated. More historical and ethnographical justification for such a response came when *The Times* published long letters from two of the most significant German apologists of the time, Max Müller and Thomas Carlyle, which reinforced the sense that Britons should indeed take into consideration their common Teutonic ancestry.

Between late August and early November, Müller wrote five letters to *The Times* representing his interpretation of the conflict. In the first, "A German's Plea for Germany," (August 31), Müller responded to Sir Harry Verney's call for aid for France by insisting that France was the aggressor, and that a threat from Germany "never existed, except in the brains of Corsican statesmen." He wrote, he explained, not as a German, but as one who "ardently" wished that Britain and Germany

> should love each other, and should stand together shoulder to shoulder, and hand in hand, as the guardians of peace, the defenders of right, the champions of all that is good and true, lovely and noble on earth.[14]

Müller was an admirer of Gladstone, and his desire to persuade British Liberals that Germany deserved their support seems to have grown in response to the letters of "Scrutator," which urged aid for France. Both Müller, who claimed to know who "Scrutator" was, and "Scrutator," probably the ardent Gladstonian pamphleteer Malcolm McColl, supported their arguments on the basis of Liberal progress. More letters from Müller repeated that France should admit that it was in the wrong and give up "Elsass" to Germany. By mid-November, however, many people in Britain, including the editors of *The Times*, were displaying more sympathy towards the defeated French,[15] and a letter from the seventy-five-year-old Thomas Carlyle sought to characterize this sympathy as "idle, dangerous and misguided" for both racial and historical reasons. Carlyle presented France as the aggressor against Germany for four hundred years. In a sweeping (and dubious) claim for the interconnectedness of history, Carlyle asserted that to Louis XV's schemes to keep Germany fragmented could be attributed

> loss of America, loss of India, disgrace and discomfiture in all quarters of the world—Advent, in fine, of the FRENCH REVOLUTION, embarcations on the shoreless chaos on which ill-fated France still drifts and tumbles.[16]

The French Revolution is here cited as a warning; yet Carlyle also notes its ideals in this letter, notably its public proclamation "that shams should be no more." Rather than going on to claim, as orthodox tory historians had repeatedly done, that the French Revolution had achieved nothing, Carlyle now hints that in the years following the French Revolution, the "whole world" has become engaged in this "Insurrection against Shams," and that France is the country that has been left behind. The approving references to Bismarck—clearly not a sham—suggest that what Carlyle means by a "sham" is a ruler or system of rule which is not shaped by personal merit: hence the scathing allusions here to the "Napoleonic" ideals to which the self-styled third Napoleon could only vainly aspire. The result is that France is left with the anarchy of the First French Revolution—Carlyle applies wording familiar from his 1837 *French Revolution, A History* to the current France when he describes a "France scattered into anarchic ruin, without recognizable head"—yet without its philosophy. For Carlyle, as for many of his fellow-Britons, "The German race, and not the Gaelic, are now to be the protagonists in that immense world-drama"; and he concludes by observing:

> That noble, patient, deep, pious, and solid Germany should at length be welded into a nation and become Queen of the Continent, instead of vapouring, vainglorious, gesticulating, quarrelsome, restless, and oversensitive France, seems to me the hopefullest public fact that has occurred in my time.

Carlyle's comments, reprinted in his collected works as "Latter Stage of the French-German War 1870–1871," are important not merely for demonstrating his personal response to the Franco-Prussian War in the public forum of a national newspaper. They also suggest a continuing breakdown of a two-party analysis of history. As we have seen, *The French Revolution, A History* sat uncomfortably in the tory camp, providing a prophetic instance of a pattern of historical development that Britain should avoid. This letter, in contrast, is more clearly whig in stance: indeed, it was reprinted with those of the generally Liberal Müller in a book sold to raise money for "the Victoria Institute for Providing for the Widows and Orphans of the German Soldiers." Not only does Carlyle rehearse arguments in keeping with those who identified themselves as Liberal, but he assumes a world-progress which requires the defeat of the French and their supplanting by the German stock.

By November 1870, there was another reason for reminding the public of the excesses of the first French Revolution. France was moving towards yet another socialist revolution, and this had prompted sympathy from a new political power in Britain: that of the Trades Union movement, or in net effect, a third political party.

British commentators were more prepared to discount Irish support for France than than they were the pro-French rallies organized by British working-class groups. Carlyle's historical displacement of the "Gaelic race" in his letter refers first to France, but also links France to Ireland. Early in the conflict, Irish support for France had been dismissed by the British media as typical Irish sympathy for England's enemies—which was to overlook the fact that in theory, France was no more Britain's friend or enemy than was Germany. *The Times* ascribed this to racial enmity:

> The Irish Nationalist papers ... will recognize in any triumph of the Teutonic and Protestant nationality of North Germany a victory for the moral and political forces that stand behind the Empire of England.[17]

The Times also articulated the wish that the United States should restrain the "childish affectation" of sympathy for France, again appealing to race:

> [I]t is for the interest of America and of the world that there should be cordial friendship between all the great nations of Teutonic blood. England, Germany, America, united in a determination to secure the peaceful progress of the two Continents, might shape the destiny of the human race.[18]

Yet the interpretation of events by the English working-class movement was of more concern, since it could not be dismissed as racially-motivated. On September 11, at a rally in Hyde Park, George Odger of "The London Democracy" movement called on the working classes to express their solidarity with the French Republic; a further "Demonstration in Favour of France and Peace" occurred a week later. These rallies sought to place the blame for the war on Napoleon III, not on the French people, just as Gladstone had done. The underlying implication here, though, was that the French were still what they had been in 1789: the leaders in the fight for democracy. The working-class movement seems to have identified more readily with the besieged people of Paris than the Prussian invaders.

The active voicing of an independent working-class opinion presents a challenge to traditional hierarchies at the same time as the theory of a hierarchy of language was emerging. Hitherto, whigs and tories might differ on their interpretation of history, but both factions were agreed that a right reading of history was important as a means of preserving the current distribution of property. In the 1870s, the correlation between political power and property became less automatic. Groups that never before had a voice entered the political arena, notably working men and, from 1870, women. The franchise had been extensively broadened in 1867—ironically, not by Liberal believers but by Disraeli's pragmatic Tories—while the beginning of the Trades Union movement gave the working classes real political involvement. And in a cautious but significant innovation, as the Prussians besieged Paris in December 1870, a few British women were being elected to school boards, the first solid recognition that women could play a part in public government. The monsters of revolution—women and the mob—had arrived to disrupt the binary political power of whigs and tories.

Not surprisingly, literature's response to this changing world took extreme forms. In France, one significant literary response was to be realism, or in Emile Zola's word, naturalism. In his Rougon-Macquart series of novels, which he began in 1871, Zola might be said to have proceeded in the scientific mode of geologists and philologists in deducing the history that had France to the "debacle" of the Franco-Prussian War. While writing *The Debacle* (1892) in particular, which describes the actual events of the war, Zola carried out extensive historical research, so that the route of the defeated soldiers, a journey to the center of the earth itself, could be traced on a map.[19] For his criticism of French policy in 1870 and especially for concluding the novel with an image of scientific replacement—that the decaying limb of a tree has to be cut off in order to be replaced by new growth—Zola was accused of lack of patriotism. The Abbé Delmont, for example, considered that Zola had debased the French Army through presenting them as speaking filthy language, and asked, "But in order to tell the truth, must he insult his country?"[20]

Delmont's critique might seem reactionary, but it touches on a significant point: Zola had claimed that to be realistic, his writings must present the ugly truths about France. But there might be means of avoiding those truths. *The Debacle* ends with the promise of a brighter future, but only because the past has been destroyed. In contrast, as in the instance of Jules Verne's works, fantasy, where worlds can be controlled by authors, provided a possible escape from the unpleasantness of historical realism, since histories could be alternatives rather than successors to other systems. Certainly, in Britain, the response to a world turned upside-down, or at least a world that could be viewed sideways, was what might be claimed as the start of a new genre, that of the "alternative world." Obviously, there are previous examples of alternative worlds, such as Plato's Republic or Sir Thomas More's Utopia. Yet critics have pointed out a sudden expansion of the form after 1869,[21] and in 1871–1872 appeared three significant literary uses of alternative worlds that are precursors to science fantasy, Lewis Carroll's *Through the Looking Glass*, Samuel Butler's *Erewhon*, and Lord Lytton's *The Coming Race*. To claim these three works as direct responses to the Franco-Prussian War would be oversimplistic, the first two at least being conceived before France's disasters of 1870. But all three show a preoccupation with the English language that may explain why Britons responded to the Franco-Prussian War as they did. Furthermore, elements of another form of fantasy writing, that of alternative histories that speculate what might have happened if history were different, can be seen in George Tomkyns Chesney's historically-specific *The Battle of Dorking*—and even, as I shall argue, in Matthew Arnold's *Friendship's Garland*. All of these works were completed, and *The Coming Race* and *The Battle of Dorking* in print, before the final bloodshed of the end of the Commune, when Thiers's government, driven out to Versailles, retook Paris in the "*Semaine Sanglante*" (bloody week) in late May 1871. Yet all can be read as time-specific responses to a world turned upside-down, and all, to a lesser or greater extent, follow the pattern of revolution in suggesting that an alternative may simultaneously be a substitute, not merely presenting another option, but erasing the previously-accepted system.

That elements of both whig and tory history should be seen in futuristic or fantastic works is not as surprising as it might initially appear. From the time of Burke onwards, the past had been used to predict patterns of future events, while both past and future placed the present in perspective; the interest shown in Mirabeau during the 1830s, indeed, almost reaches the level of suggesting an alternative history if Mirabeau had not died. From the British point of view, France had always been a symbolic representation of their own nation as it was or might become. What is different in the turn to fantasy is the substitution of declaredly imaginary worlds for the previous imaginary versions of Britain and France.

Alternative Worlds

The concept of a world opposite to the one that we know was not an innovation: numerous earlier instances can be found of eutopias and dystopias, all of which invite readers to reassess the customs and values of their own culture by presenting something markedly different.[22] The strongest feature that these works have in common is a sense of alternative: there might indeed be different modes of life from that of one's own society. By prompting a model of comparison between the "norm" and the "alternative," they function in the same way as historical analogy in providing a perspective by which to view the present. In the later years of the nineteenth century, these other worlds were in many cases a means of articulating a eutopian vision—William Morris's *News from Nowhere* (1891), for example, presents an idealized vision of a world of achieved equality, while even before the first French Revolution, Louis-Sebastien Mercier had written an alternative to his condemnatory *Tableau de Paris* by imagining a man dreaming of the perfect Parisian society of the year 2440.[23] I would suggest that what distinguishes works of the early 1870s is a preoccupation with language—with linguistic relations, and ultimately with the sense that values may be constructed around language.

An example from before the Franco-Prussian war is W. S. Gilbert's poem published in *Fun* magazine in March 1870, "My Dream." The narrator relates a dream of "Topsy-Turveydom":

> Where vice is virtue—virtue, vice:
> Where nice is nasty—nasty, nice:
> Where right is wrong and wrong is right—
> Where white is black and black is white.[24]

In Topsy-Turveydom, babies are born wise, and grow increasingly foolish with age; soldiers are shot for showing bravery; and judges commit all the crimes.

Moreover, in Topsy-Turveydom, girls are boys, and boys girls, but the narrator observes, "if to think it out you try,/It doesn't really signify." If this is simply a reversal of language, (in the language of this world the word "boy" means "girl") the effect might merely be to parody the preoccupation of the 1860s with parallels in language. But when the police arrest those

> Who practise virtue every day—
> Of course, I mean to say, you know,
> What we call virtue here below...

what might seem to be fixed values become a matter of labeling, and a challenge to a sense of absolutes. The "mad informant" of Topsy-Turveydom—whose sex is not identified—thinks that world superior to that of the narrator, who indeed wonders at the end whether he/she might fit better into a world "where greatest fools bear off the bell."

"My Dream" does not suggest erasure of the world "here below," but rather keeps its reality in the reader's consciousness, much as whig and tory history is dependent on a sense of contrast or connection with the one's own circumstances. The poem presents a reversed world which in its customs reminds readers of their own world, while asking them to look closely at assumed values: are judges always pure and wise? What are crimes? Does the British education system (a significant topic of debate during 1870, when education first became compulsory) encourage people to be fools? The reversed world, with perhaps more oblique challenges to the solidity of its "real" counterpart, provided the structure of Lewis Carroll's second "Alice" book, *Through the Looking-Glass, and What Alice Found There*, which goes much further than Gilbert's poem into what words "signify."

Language has always presented a problem in science fiction. An obvious difference between oneself and others—Britain and France provide a paramount example—is that foreigners speak different languages, and that this, in many ways, marks or is taken to mark other differences. In the interest of advancing the plot when depicting alien encounters (notably in television and movie forms of science fiction), months cannot be spent before the two groups are able to communicate with each other. Science fiction has generally either ignored this problem altogether, so that on the first encounter aliens speak passable

English; or has made flimsy attempts to explain how it might be possible to speak in one language and understand in another.[25] While underlying this may be a form of cultural imperialism—aliens should be expected to conform to "us" rather than the other way round—thematically, the concept that has formed a staple of this study is often reenacted: that the "other" is not simply "other."[26] The alien is more disturbing or challenging if he, she or it has characteristics identifiable in oneself, just as French revolutions would be of little concern to Britons if they had no implications for Britain and its culture and politics.

Such is the case when Alice climbs through the Looking-Glass. Obviously, as Gilles Deleuze and others have noted, this text shows a preoccupation with logic, which is often ascribed to Dodgson's mathematical background. Yet the logic and anti-logic displayed in *Through the Looking-Glass* is frequently based on linguistic rather than mathematical relations, and Alice comes from, and moves into, a world of language. In the Garden of Live Flowers, for example, a metaphor provides the literal explanation for an altered reality. Most flowers, the Tiger-Lily explains, do not speak because they are always asleep: their beds are too soft. Perhaps more interesting in terms of language studies are the puns about the tree in the middle of the garden, who, the flowers maintain, must be there to look after them. A skeptical Alice asks:

> "But what could it do, if any danger came?"
> "It could bark," said the Rose.
> "It says, 'Bough-wough!'" cried a Daisy. "That's why its branches are called boughs!"[27]

This is the type of pun that a small child might find amusing, but the Daisy's explanation moves into the subject of language-derivation, and how words come to mean what they do. It may not be coincidental that Max Müller's theory of the origin of language (his science of glottology being concerned with the "tree" of language and linguistic roots) set itself up in opposition to the theory here echoed by the Daisy—that words originate from imitative sounds—and that Müller called this the "Bow-wow" theory.[28] The historical Alice's father, after all, was Henry Liddell, co-editor of the most important British Greek lexicon, and Müller's friend and adviser.

Moreover, Müller's theories of language provide a means of categorizing Looking-Glass language that makes it less "other" than it might initially appear. Grammatically, Looking-Glass language, once reversed by being held to a mirror, is like English, as the poem "Jabberwocky" demonstrates. Vocabulary, though, is strange, and possibly less fixed. Functioning as Alice's lexicon, Humpty Dumpty explains the unfamiliar vocabulary of the first stanza of the poem, but given his attitude to language, it remains unclear whether he would give the same meaning to the words on another occasion.[29] Alice remarks to Humpty Dumpty, "The question is ... whether you *can* make words mean so many different things," but Humpty Dumpty asserts a mastery that allows a word to mean "just what I choose it to mean" (*Alice*, p. 269). Humpty Dumpty adds, though, that words have "a temper, some of them—particularly verbs: they're the proudest." For Müller, language has an almost autonomous form that would not allow Humpty Dumpty to have even partial mastery, but Humpty Dumpty seems to agree with the philologist that it is not items of vocabulary (especially nouns and adjectives) that define a language, but the grammar, and especially verb-forms. Müller, then, would categorize Looking-Glass language as English, or Saxon, erasing its strangeness.[30] As the British had constantly found in their attempts to construct France as an opposite, what is different is simultaneously the same.

This might seem to link the Looking-Glass world with tory historical allegory; yet like the European world, it is governed by whig determinism in the form of language, which makes people what they are. As Linda Dowling has observed, Müller's theories presented language as beyond human control: the extreme conclusion from this is that human society must fulfill the course set out for it by language. Linguistically, Prussia is Germany, and thus the champion of German nationalism. Tweedledum is Tweedledum and not Tweedledee because his collar says so. Although of course a student of the history of language such as Müller might argue that one is merely a variation of the other, at this point, the apparent fluidity of Looking-Glass language ceases. Recorded or remembered language—a form close to history—enables Alice to predetermine certain events. Because, for example, she knows the rhyme "Tweedledum and Tweedledee," she knows that they must have a battle, and what the outcome will be. While as a little girl outside the world of politics she is not a constructor of the conditions of history, Alice can nevertheless reflect what her culture has taught her about it. She can only stand aside and hope, like *The Times* hoped of France and Prussia, "to make them a *little* ashamed of fighting for such a trifle" (*Alice*, p. 243).

For although language establishes the sameness of the Looking-Glass world to Alice's English world, she is simultaneously an English observer abroad.[31] The difference between Alice's way of life and that of Looking-Glass Land is demonstrated by the Red Queen—red being both a chess-color and the color of socialism as seen in the Paris Commune. When after much running Alice finds herself in the same place and remarks that "in *our* country ... you'd generally get to somewhere else—if you ran very fast for a long time as we've been doing," the Red Queen retorts that Alice's is "a slow sort of country!" because here "it takes all the running *you* can do, to keep in the same place. If you want to get somewhere else, you must run at least twice as fast as that" (p. 210).

Alice's point of view resembles the way that many Britons, both whig and tory, thought of France—as a country always hurrying, but never arriving. As Gladstone wrote in October 1870,

> No French constitution lives through the term of a very moderate farm-lease. The series of perpetual change is not progression; it is hardly even rotation, for in rotation we know what part of the wheel will next come round, whereas the French polity of to-day in no degree enables us to judge what will be the French polity of tomorrow.[32]

Moreover, such indeterminacies can be infectious. Looking-Glass Land causes some erasure of Alice's own world from her consciousness: it takes a Fawn, for example, to remind her of what she calls herself (*Alice*, p. 227). The experience of being taken for a chess-piece, a flower, and above all an alien shows Alice that the practices that she has assumed "natural" are not the only ways of living.

This is a more strident theme in another "reflection" of Victorian society, Samuel Butler's *Erewhon* (1872), of which the subtitle, *Over the Range*, marks the process of entry into this "backward" world. *Erewhon* is a "Topsy-Turvey" society entered by chance when Chowbok, the Evangelical narrator's drunken companion of an unnamed indigenous race, abandons him. Although the narrator claims that he will keep its location a secret, it is apparent that Erewhon, almost "nowhere" backwards in a wry allusion to *Utopia*, is in the region of Australia-New Zealand, where, from the European point of view, night is day, summer is winter, and (in global terms) down is up.

In many respects, this is a more systematically reversed world than that of *Through the Looking-Glass*; here, people are treated with sympathy when they commit crimes and are punished for being in bad health; while technologically, the civilization is anti-progressive (and hence anti-whig) in devolving away from a dependence on machinery.

Butler gives little time to the Erewhonian language, although the narrator apparently acquires it well enough to understand their philosophy in the few months he is there. But many of the names—for example Nosnibor and Yram—are reversals of common English names, while the deity Ydgrun suggests Mrs. Grundy, guardian of British propriety. Apparently, however, Butler was unprepared to go to the extreme of reversing the societal roles of the sexes, and Arowhena, the Erewhonian woman who escapes with the narrator and who seems content to play a traditional female role, has a name that is not a direct reversal, even though Arowhena suggests the negation of Rowena, the last British princess and mother of the Saxons.[33] In language as in morality, Butler uses reversal to prompt his reader to ask why the English-speaking world is as it is.

In this story of Anglophone self-contemplation, events in France and Prussia pass without the narrator even knowing about them. The narrator's visit to Erewhon covers the period of the Franco-Prussian War: he enters Erewhon about mid-July, 1870, and escapes with Arowhena by balloon the following spring, so that their first rescuer, an Italian seacaptain, believes that their balloon has drifted from the Siege of Paris, although it is actually over.[34] The crews of the ships that assist him are unable to speak English, and the narrator is able to disguise where he has been because of the failure of language. As *Erewhon* ends, the narrator is planning to "convert" the Erewhonians to a true religion by means of conquest.[35] The final scene depicts Chowbok as presenting himself to a group of Evangelicals as one of the lost ten tribes of Israel:[36] the narrator induces himself to believe that Chowbok is a successful convert to Christianity. It is more apparent to the reader than the self-oblivious narratior that Chowbok's "conversion" is prompted by self-interest, but the fact remains that it has become advantageous to Chowbok to accept the values of the Anglophone world. In global terms, France is erased, while English-speaking world even has influence when its power is invested in self-righteous fools such as Butler's narrator.

The Coming Race

Butler later attributed the initial success of *Erewhon*—the first edition of one thousand, published by Trübner at his own expense, sold in a few weeks—to the public's belief that Edward Bulwer-Lytton, by this time Lord Lytton, had written it. Butler's Preface to the Second Edition claimed that the manuscript was with a publisher by May 1871, and that he never saw *The Coming Race* until after his complete book was with the printer.[37] The obvious generic difference is that *Erewhon* depicts a "topsy-turvey" society by which the reader's own is defamiliarized, while *The Coming Race* presents in many repects an ideal society that the reader's might become. Whereas the kinship of the Erewhonians to the reader's world is shown by reversal, the kinship of the Vril-ya of *The Coming Race* is shown by magnification: they are an improvement on the reader's type, and show the future of the dominant race. While the analogical thrust of the "topsy-turvey" world is closer to tory history, the "more-evolved" world is closer to the whig model.

While *Through the Looking-Glass* and *Erewhon* can only loosely defined as science fiction, *The Coming Race* is solidly within the genre. The world beneath the earth entered by the narrator is not merely inhabited by different species and cultures, but, in the case of the Vril-ya, by a race with a more developed technology that includes mechanical wings that enable the people to fly, flying boats, and automaton servants; unlike in Erewhonian society, though, where the potential tyranny of technology is feared, in this whig future, progress does not represent a threat. The new world is powered and inspired by an alternative source of energy; that this mystical energy is called *vril* demonstrates that here also language is important. The problem of how the narrator, a United States citizen, acquires the language is overcome by placing him in a vril-induced trance of months' duration—although his tutor Zee learns his language better than he does hers. Yet the language itself is not entirely alien. Lytton dedicated the story to Max Müller, "in tribute of respect and admiration"[38] and like the term *vril*, some of the words and grammar bear a superficial resemblance to Sanskrit and the languages that according to Müller's theory are descended from it, the story acknowledging a debt to Müller's 1868 Rede lecture "On the Stratification of Language." The names of the sexes, an for male (plural ana) and gy for female (plural gy-ei with a softened g), resemble Greek, and the narrator realizes that the speech of the Vril-ya is part of the Aryan group that forms the main focus of Müller's work on language.[39] Müller claims that "-ya" was originally crucial to Aryan grammar, and Lytton correspondingly adopts this particle as significant in his underworld language. Indeed, all the discussion of language is heavily indebted to the German philologist, and the mine surveyor-narrator specifically quotes Müller's explanation of "the analogy between the strata of language and the strata of the earth" (*Coming Race*, p. 717).

Language shows the connection between the Vril-ya and Lytton's English-speaking readers, yet the point of view of the text is a little more problematic. In *Erewhon* and *Through the Looking-Glass* the reversed worlds make fun of the reader's culture, often through presenting other ways of behaving or thinking that initially seem absurd, but which might prompt a thoughtful reader to reconsider whether the values that he or she has always accepted without question might not themselves contain elements of absurdity. In contrast, the perspective of *The Coming Race* is clouded slightly by the American narrator. He is not characterized much, but what identity he has is derived from his nationality. As a citizen of the New World, he observes this even newer world from the perspective that his own "coming race" (the most rapidly-progressing Teutonic nation) has significant values. Occasionally this somewhat naive narrator seems to speak out of voice, with a slightly more satirical reflection on the culture of his readers— for example, he mentions two oddities of the Vril-ya religion: "firstly, that they all believe in the creed they profess; secondly, that they all practise the precepts that the creed inculcates" (*Coming Race*, p. 720). At other points, his account might appear to its readers to contain some aspects of the "topsy-turvey" form in the sense of reversing expectations: for example, children work and adults spend their time in education and leisure. Yet largely through negatives (strife, poverty and crime are not found among the Vril-ya) Lytton uses a eutopian mode to attack topical questions of 1871.

In May 1871, when this book was published, the state of France suggested that Prussia had assumed France's place as the most civilized European power, and France was in a state of anarchy: the Commune was to collapse in a week of fighting at the end of the month. The story hence serves as a critique of the present. But British self-interest, prompted by a consciousness of the closeness of civil strife, is also part of *The Coming Race*, and the very title of the work states that these are the people of the future: a true stock of the Aryans, but larger, wiser, and endowed with the power of *vril*, who will some day supplant the people of the surface as "inevitable destroyers." To the end, the narrator hopes that this fate will be postponed as long as possible. Yet if the Vril-ya are a better adapted species than the current dominant race, then resistance of evolution would appear futile. Also, if the Vril-ya represent an evolutionary improvement, then their culture must be superior, and this might initially seem problematic in the light of one or two cultural elements apparently of the "topsy-turvey" kind: the role of women in their society, and the race's apparent idleness.

To a Victorian reader, the most obvious contradictory element of the society under the earth would probably be the role of women—ironically, the element that Butler had not reversed in *Erewhon*. The Gyei are taller, physically and psychically more powerful, and more free to express their sexuality than the Ana. They have more power over *vril*, and, while this word might look like Sanskrit as transliterated by Müller, it also echoes "virility," or manly strength, here contrarily a female attribute. They have true social and political equality, although in a gesture towards domesticity, the women restrict their freedom by leaving off their mechanical wings when they marry; a hint of Victorian essentialism may also be present in the statements that although they are rational beings, women have more intuitive, or perhaps psychic abilities, than men. The women court the men (the reverse would be immodest), and the narrator finds himself the subject of romantic interest of both a Princess and the stately and professorial Zee.[40] The result is that he is both masculinized (even the handsome Vril-ya, it seems, instinctively recognize a "real man") and feminized (he becomes a prize to be won). Zee's love provides him with his means of returning to the upper world when she carries him up on the strength of her wings.

In a truly eutopian text, the culture would unequivocally present an ideal pattern, and to some extent, Lytton may indeed be declaring himself a feminist. Certainly, the Vril-ya have solved the problem of "the two most disturbing and potential influences on upper-ground society—Womankind and Philosophy." These might appear to be separate, or even naturally contradictory, but the narrator adds, "I mean the Rights of Women" (*Coming Race*, p. 759). Phrasing this initially in the hendyadis form of "Womankind and Philosophy" links the claiming of such rights with abstract concepts: in 1871, women were starting to be acknowledged as thinking beings. One of the traditional disruptive groups in revolution began to enter politics and property as British women began not merely to campaign for rights, but to achieve them. In 1870, women became eligible for some local political offices and voting, and an Act was passed that started the process whereby a woman's property was no longer automatically to become her husband's on her marriage.[41] Significantly, British law called the married woman a *feme covert*—the great eighteenth-century legal expert Sir William Blackstone's explanation of the term being that she was covered by her husband's wing. The Vril-ya have wings of their own—except the married woman. Hence, the married woman is still *feme-covert* in the sense of being under her husband's wing rather than her own: the narrator's escape by being carried upwards on the strength of Zee's wings thus changes gender expectations, even though, unlike Arowhena in *Erewhon*, Zee does not accompany her lover further. The ideal of married womanhood remains submissive, yet the very fact that Lytton posits a future which systemizes a substantial degree of achieved equality between the sexes is evidence that by the 1870s women's claims to constitutional rights were compatible with a model of human progress: in other words, the progressive rights of women were according to natural order, rather than against it, as their roles in revolutionary action had formerly been portrayed.

Whereas women (of a particular pedigree, of course) are part of the power-structure of the Vril-ya, the underclass is more firmly excluded. By the 1870s, the concept of the mob had been largely replaced by the more respectable working-men's movements. If work is defining, though, the general indolence of the adult Vril-ya might seem another significant reason why a Victorian reader, raised with a Carlylean sense of work's value, might not see in them a eutopian ideal of hope for the future. In their society, the children work at manufacturing and at killing monstrous reptilian creatures, while the adults spend much of their time in study and relaxation. Yet this book was published during the Paris Commune, and the constant activity of popular movements, which I have already suggested is represented in *Through the Looking-Glass*, presents a contrast with the calm aristocracy of the the Vril-ya, who associate action with a lack of maturity. Of the other species in the world under the Earth, some are Koom-posh, a word explained as meaning hollow (like the Welsh *cwm*) and nonsense (like "bosh"). This means "the government of the many, or the ascendancy of the most ignorant and hollow" (p. 718). Living in a state "of perpetual contest and perpetual change" (p. 735), the Koom-posh fight until their cultures succumb to a state of Glek-nas, "the universal strife-rot."[42] At the time of the Paris Commune, the idea of neighbors who having embraced democracy are on the point of destroying themselves provides a warning to British readers—one that, however, the American narrator is initially unable to perceive. In discussion with a Vril-ya child, the narrator calls his own nation

> "A settlement of emigrants—like those settlements which your own tribe sets forth—but so far unlike your settlements, that it was dependent on the state from which it came. It shook off that yoke, and, crowned with eternal glory, became a Koom-Posh." (p. 738)

On learning that this has lasted a hundred years, the twelve-year-old Taë replies, "In much less than another 100 years your Koom-Posh will be a Glek-Nas." In the underworld as in the world above, history dictates that anarchy succeeds democracy.

As in the case of *Erewhon*, however, the ideal reader, with a British sense of history and the warning of France across the Channel, should be wiser than the narrator, who, although claiming his commitment to democracy, begins to speculate on whether he could carve out an underworld kingdom for himself. He sees himself as having the energy and ambition that the Vril-ya lack; he rapidly abandons the idea of rule, however, when he realizes that his life is threatened. The apparent idleness of the adult Vril-ya is thus exposed as the product of the narrator's way of seeing: in reality, they are a small aristocratic group with automata in place of an underclass and a controlled population (once the community rises above a certain size, some families volunteer to leave and form a new colony). Their task is to think, and to rule—and to advise the less fortunate people of the world above that certain kinds of activity, especially the competition required in a democracy, must lead to the social destruction that, according to the theory of replacement evident in the stratification of the earth and of language, will cause a superior people to assume their place in world power. If *A Tale of Two Cities* suggests that its characters' better future is the reader's present, *The Coming Race* reinforces the whig notion of progress by suggesting a still better age—and race—to come.

Alternative Histories

The coming of the Vril-ya is both a promise and, in the context of 1871, a threat. If the French might be supplanted as a world power, so might Britain. This formed the theme of George Tomkyns Chesney's *The Battle of Dorking*. An early instance of the science fiction subgenre of "future war"—indeed, I. F. Clarke credits it with originating the genre in English (Clarke 38)—[43]this story appeared in *Blackwood's Magazine* in May 1871, and was clearly written after the end of the Siege of Paris, but, like *Erewhon* and *The Coming Race*, before the bloody end of the Commune. Chesney was a career soldier from the Indian Army, and introductory pages recount how the expanding Empire stretched Britain's military resources, and also made Britain dependent on imports from the colonies. The narrator explains from the perspective of fifty years later that Britons foolishly "thought that all this wealth and prosperity were sent us by Providence," and ignored the "plain warning" of the fate of its "neighbours."[44] Comparatively few names are given here, but the neighbors are clearly the French, who had "beaten the Russians and the Austrians, and the Prussians too, in bygone years, and they thought they were invincible." In the 1870s, as Canada is threatened by the United States and troops are deployed in Ireland, the Channel and the Fleet are seen as Britain's insurance against invasion. Then "the Secret Treaty was published, and Holland and Denmark were annexed" (*Dorking*, p. 8), the implication being a Prussian-Russian alliance (a threat mentioned also in *Friendship's Garland*) that prompts Britain to declare war. The British fleet is defeated, and after various rumors, the enemy lands at Worthing.[45]

The narrator, an office-worker from the county of Surrey, is among the volunteers who meet the enemy at Dorking and are defeated. While the title and the invasion on the Sussex coast recall the Battle of Hastings, the last time that England was invaded and defeated, the choice of Dorking, a comfortable neighborhood which through recent advances in technology—the railway line was only opened in 1867—is now within commuting distance of London, indicates that nobody is safe, not even the complacent middle classes. As a further irony, from Dorking, London is reached via Waterloo, the historical significance of the great British victory being submerged in the name of the railway terminus that takes men to their offices in the City.[46] The trials of the troops before and after the battle resemble those of the defeated French army, best described in Zola's much later novel *The Debacle*. In particular, Chesney draws attention to the inefficiency of supplies and the lack of modern rifles, a topic much discussed in *The Times* during the period of the Franco-Prussian War.

Although Britain apparently does not become part of a German Empire, the long-term result is worse than that for France, since France is relatively self-supporting, whereas Britain depends on its colonies for supplies. The concluding comments, addressed to the narrator's grandchildren who are emigrating, present the war as the price to pay for the national arrogance that assumed the protection of Providence; on what now might be called bleeding-heart Liberalism that looks for non-military solutions; on the growing forces of democracy that challenge strong leadership; and on an imbalance between home and colonial concerns (*Dorking*, pp. 63–64). Chesney's vision of the future thus proves to be founded on the tory historical model, constructing a warning from the pattern of example. Although the tone might seem isolationist, Chesney's warning is, contrarily, that Britain has been too self-absorbed, refusing to see developments in Europe as its own concern: "There, across the narrow Straits, was the writing on the wall, but we would not choose to read it" (p. 63). The story also may appear anti-German, yet by implication it depicts Prussian militarism, associated with a strong and technologically-advanced army and a united sense of nationhood, as the model to be followed. France's fate is to be avoided, but Prussia's destiny must be observed closely.

Chesney's story is stronger on military details than on characterization, and the question might be asked as to what are the British values that are worth preserving against challenges to supremacy, be they from the French, Prussians, Americans, or Aryan superbeings. The usual answer seems to have been a freedom of personal action that should not be confused with democracy, but that is dependent on a national spirit of common sense and practicality.[47] For Matthew Arnold, this answer was not good enough. I therefore wish to turn to *Friendship's Garland* as another instance of the creation of an "alternative world"—although one that does not conquer but is conquered.

The letters later reprinted by Arnold under the title *Friendship's Garland* are provocative in a different way from Chesney's work. Published in periodicals, mainly the *Pall Mall Gazette*, during two moments of Prussian self-assertion, the 1866 war against Austria and the 1870–1871 war against France, they feature a Prussian as a man worth listening to—even if he is a man somehow descended from the fictional world of Voltaire's *Candide*.

The narrative voice of *Friendship's Garland*, supposedly a collection of letters to the *Pall Mall Gazette* by Arminius Von Thunderten-Tronckh, Matthew Arnold, and Adolescens Leo, with other characters ventriloquized, is therefore a problem. Leo, the "young lion" who works for the *Daily Telegraph*, represents the nationalism of British Philistinism. The *Telegraph*, whose best-known writer George Augustus Sala makes a late appearance in the work, provides a strong clue to how to respond to Leo. Ironically, the *Telegraph* was initially concerned about the friendship the British Liberal Party had cultivated with France;[48] but even before the news of Sedan reached England, it was noting that "the German causes appears to be the one adopted by Destiny"; and congratulating its British readers that "above all things, we here in England must understand well and appreciate the safety which we enjoy, girdled as we are by the sea and fenced from the dreadful peril by our cliffs." This editorial of September 1 1870 proceeds to ask,

> Have we as a people deserved better of humanity, or made farther progress, or are we more important in the eyes of Destiny, that our little islands should be

like rocks in the middle of the tempest, unshaken, inviolate, undesecrated by the tread of any invader since serious history began; so secure from attack that we strive in vain to understand what it must be like to behold an enemy quartered in our towns and marching upon London, as the Prussians are marching now upon Paris?

British self-satisfaction prompts a "stratification" analogy:

> It is not more true that the cliffs of Britain are made up of innumerable shells and skeletons of extinct molluscs, than that the majesty and authority of Britain are composed of the countless tasks of faithful work, in arms, art, industry, adventure, toil, philosophy, education, and the range of daily labour, done or doing by all her faithful sons for the love of her and of duty.

Passages like these seem to represent what mainstream British Liberals, were thinking. The difficulty comes in determining what kind of thinking might, from Arnold's point of view, be better.

Although its response to the Franco-Prussian War is very different from Carlyle's, the fragmented *Friendship's Garland* is in some respects Arnold's most Carlylean work, the German cultural commentators recalling such books as *Sartor Resartus* and *Chartism*. The result is a similar obfuscation of narrators. Neither Arminius nor "Matthew Arnold" can straightforwardly be said to represent the point of view of authorial intention—that is, what the "actual" Matthew Arnold wants his readers to think. In this case, the other "alternative world" narrations may be of help. Bulwer-Lytton, Butler, and Chesney all tell their tales through unnamed first-person narrators. Of these, Chesney's Waterloo commuter-turned-soldier is constructed as a representative voice, an ordinary man caught up in events with no parallel in British history. Yet the other two characters have their idiosyncracies, Butler's being a naive Evangelical, and Bulwer-Lytton's a naive American republican. Both are affected by what almost amounts to megalomania towards the end of the narratives, the alternative worlds having opened up new ways of seeing that they largely reject as they consider instead new possibilities for rule. In *Friendship's Garland*, in contrast, the words of Arnold's Arminius are sometimes presented in letters by himself, sometimes as reported by others. The negotiation might be seen as between Arminius, representative of an alternative world, and between two narrator-observers, Leo and Matthew Arnold.

Arminius's comments on British society are important, as are those in the other "alternative world" books, in reminding the British public that other ways of life are possible, and that the mainstream Liberal doctrine, drawn from the pattern of whig history, is an orthodoxy rather than immutable fact. *The Battle of Dorking* depicted ordinary people who traveled on the Waterloo line; the first letter of *Friendship's Garland* opens on the train to Reigate, in a similar area of Surrey to Dorking,[49] in 1866. During this journey, Mr. Bottles the manufacturer, reading of the war between Austria and Prussia in *Punch*, exclaims, "what fools they both are!" As interpreted by Arminius and "Matthew Arnold," Bottles's comment implies the pragmatism of financial interest above political ideology. Moreover, in the Britain of 1866, the foolishness of Prussia and Austria deflect Bottles, content with his country as it is, from the conflicts around him: the Conservative party, led by Lord Derby and Benjamin Disraeli, were proposing a major reform of the electorate which would mean giving votes to most householders. This proposal was ironically contested by supposedly progressive Liberals such as Robert Lowe since, he told the House of Commons, "it will not be likely to stop until we get equal electoral districts and a qualification so low that it will keep out nobody."[50]

Taken in the context of the work as later constructed, Bottles's remark also anticipates the Liberal party's reaction to the Franco-Prussian War. As the letters continue, Arminius sets himself against the modified whig historical view of "Philistines" such as Bottles and his parliamentary champion Lowe (it is not, of course, a truly progressive model, since it assumes that the ultimate in progress is already achieved) as proof of the average Briton's lack of *Geist*, and presents his alternative of German liberalism.

A key theme of *Friendship's Garland* is the replacement of one set of values with another. That Matthew Arnold's writings have to a large extent erased mainstream party Liberalism in the literary tradition by being enshrined as "high culture" helps disguise the fact that Arminius's arguments represent a possible rather than an actual world. The disagreement between Müller and Scrutator shows that some division already existed among the Liberal party itself as to which reaction to the Franco-Prussian War was truly Liberal in the sense of representing whig history, some continuing to associate France with progress towards a higher state of civilization, and many seeing Prussia as the means of advancement. Arminius, a self-proclaimed Republican of the kind about which Arnold had expressed reservations in 1848 (a reason for avoiding a direct identification of Arminius and Arnold's views), also calls himself a Liberal, a term that he associates with French progressive politics and German intellectualism.[51] He finds neither of these qualities in the dominant voices in Britain, a country that he insists is in the rule of the "Philistines." Arminius claims to have taught the use of the word "Philistine" to his "poor disciple" Matthew Arnold, and that it is reclaimed by a German recalls its original German meaning of those who are not associated with a university. But it also points to a problem with the constructed world-view of this text. Mr. Bottles is a Philistine, concerned only with the pragmatics of how European war will affect trade. His son young Bottles, on the other hand, is being educated side by side with the sons of the aristocracy at a public school, and will presumably attend university. By a German definition, he would cease to be a Philistine, yet Arminius maintains that he will not learn "ideas," but merely social behavior, from the upper classes.

The initial topic of *Friendship's Garland* is culture and education as nationally constructed, yet in some respects events overtake it: in 1870, when one might expect the focus to be on the question of universal education, or what education might do for young Bottles, the main attention turns to the Franco-Prussian War. Arminius sets off to fight in the war in August 1870, not, he insists, because of loyalty to the Emperor, who has subverted true German nationalism to serve his own purpose; but because he desires to "take part" in "a war of Germany against France" (*Friendship's Garland*, p. 284). At the Siege of Paris, Leo finds Arminius dying ingloriously from a stray shot: the Prussian sends final messages to acquaintances, real and fictional, in Britain. Leo interprets his dying sentences as a wish to be buried at Caterham. This, R. H. Super suggests, recalls the country house of Robert Lowe, whom Arminius claims as a descendant of Dr. Pangloss because of his belief in present-day England as the best of all possible worlds (*Friendship's Garland*, p. 348). Undoubtedly, Lowe is associated with Caterham, but to readers of the time, Caterham might also suggest a battle on English soil—one driven by economics. Caterham is in the area of Surrey in which the discussion started, but unlike Dorking and Reigate, in railway terms, a dead-end. In 1862 it had been the site of an unpleasant altercation between rival railway companies which received substantial attention in *The Times*, prompting letters from outraged commuters signing themselves by such names as "VIATOR VINDEX" and "OLD FOXHUNTER."[52] In real life Surrey, the battles fought are over rights of property and profits for investors. Thus Arminius's dying utterance itself erases lofty nationalist ideals and replaces them with memories of British middle-class petty provincialism. The best that Leo can do for him is to recruit "three English members of Parliament, celebrated for their ardent charity and advanced Liberalism," who, under the neutrality of the Red Cross, are eating a "Strassburg pie"

(*Friendship's Garland*, p. 312). They bury him hurriedly: British Liberalism buries the European Liberal ideal that Arminius embodies. The Franco-Prussian War has thus put an end to the hope of an alternative liberalism, one that values culture and freedom: in net effect, George Augustus Sala, the voice of the Philistine middle class, has won this war.

If the voice of an alternative liberalism is silenced, and the true victors are the Philistines, for whom the most important city of Alsace-Lorraine suggests a consumable item, fear of France (and, from this point of view, fear of the other European powers too) no longer seems necessary. To commentators like Goldwin Smith, cited in *Friendship's Garland*, the Franco-Prussian War is a decisive step in the triumph of the Anglophone world, carving up its traditional enemy France. The Prussian invasion would seem to naturalize the Looking-Glass image of eating the cake first and sharing it out afterwards. For Britain, or at least for Britain's most strident voices, looking towards the construction of an English-speaking union with North America and the Empire, bigger pies were more inviting; perhaps history had finally progressed beyond the kind of rivalry with France that had shaped the rhetoric of Edmund Burke. In the Epilogue to this study, though, I will suggest that even world domination could not entirely banish the phantom of the French Revolution from British cultural consciousness.

Notes

1. Even this point, however, was not beyond dispute. "Scrutator" published a number of letters supporting France published in *The Times*, later collected as "Who is Responsible for the War?" (1871), arguing that although he might appear to have withdrawn, the Prince was willing to withdraw the withdrawal
2. *The Times* (July 11, 1870), leader.
3. Benjamin Disraeli's 1870 novel *Lothair* captures this transitional moment. The rich young English nobleman Lothair is confronted by a bewildering array of possible answers to the meaning of existence, including religion, revolution, and national identity. Irish revolutionaries use French revolutionary watchwords, but Italian nationalist revolutionaries receive most sympathetic treatment.
4. *The Times* (July 16, 1870), leader.
5. These theories were not, of course, new to everybody, since they owed their origin to eighteenth-century students of language such as Sir William Jones; what was new was the application of theories of language to mainstream political and cultural discourse.

6. F. Max Müller, *The Science of Language*, new edition (Macmillan, 1899). See Clare A. Simmons, "'Iron-Worded Proof': Victorian Identity and the Old English Language," *Studies in Medievalism* 4 (1992), pp. 210–211.
7. Müller, *Science of Language* 2:13. The association between philology and geology began as early as Schlegel, but had more impact after the theory of natural selection suggested that higher forms of life replace lower ones.
8. Even in 1866, however, that the German professor has a Danish servant reflects the balance of power after Prussia and Austria had seized the hitherto Danish provinces of Schleswig-Holstein with little resistance from the rest of Europe in 1864.
9. The concept of "Manifest Destiny" preceded the "scientific discoveries" used to justify it. In many respects, it was an American construct, but that it was embraced by British thinkers of this period is in itself suggestive that Britain was turning its attention from Europe to the rest of the English-speaking world. See Reginald Horsman, *Race and Manifest Destiny* (Harvard University Press, 1981).
10. Müller, *Science of Language* 1:79.
11. For example, Freeman applied Müller's theory of language to the growth of political states, and singled out the Greek, Roman, and Teuton as the highest embodiments of the Aryans: "Each in his turn has reached the highest stage alike of power and civilization that was to be had in his own age, and each has handed on his own store to be further enriched by successors who were at once conquerors and disciples." E. A. Freeman, *Comparative Politics* (Macmillan, 1873), p. 39.
12. See *The Times* (August 1, 1870), and following.
13. W. E. Gladstone, "Germany, France, and England," *Edinburgh Review* (October 1870), p. 588. Following references are cited in the text.
14. *The Times* (August 31, 1870). Less auspiciously, Müller prophesied that "in the whole history of modern Europe Germany and England have never been at war; I feel convinced they never will be, never can be. ..."
15. Even *Punch*, which had persistently ridiculed Napoleon III, now saw him as a gallant loser, portraying him, for example, as a defeated duellist on September 2, and allegorically depicting Paris as a threatened virgin.
16. *The Times* (Nov 18, 1870).
17. *The Times* (August 8, 1870), leader.
18. *The Times* (September 23, 1870), leader.
19. Robert A. Jouanny has laid out the itinerary of the French army in his edition of *La Débâcle* (Garnier, 1975), pp. 547–550.
20. Ibid., pp. 564–565.
21. Darby Lewes, for example, in *Dream Revisionaries: Gender and Genre in Women's Utopian Fiction 1870–1920* (University of Alabama Press, 1995) suggests 1869 as a beginning date because of the expansion of the franchise and the changing role of women in British society. Lyman Tower Sargent's huge bibliography of British and American utopian literature lists an average

of twenty a decade for the first seven decades of the nineteenth century, then fifty in the 1870s, a hundred in the 1880s, and over 200 in the 1890s.

22. Paul Alkon's *The Origins of Futuristic Fiction* (University of Georgia Press, 1987) surveys some of the varieties of approach, including alternative versions of history. Ironically, Alkon's work shows how much British futuristic writing was influenced by French sources.

23. Mercier's future is, however, not a republic, but a kingdom. Like Morris's, the ordered society of *L'An 2440* involves restrictions of individual freedoms, but Mercier's own society under Louis XV clearly left most people with no freedom at all.

24. W. S. Gilbert, *The Bab Ballads*, edited by James Ellis (Belnap Press, 1980), p. 288.

25. When after many years of traveling through time and space, it finally occurred to a human in *Dr. Who* to inquire why, for example, Renaissance Italians spoke such good English, the Doctor told Sarah Jane Smith that the TARDIS bestowed a linguistic "gift" on its passengers (*The Masque of Mandragora*, 1976). A similar idea is used in Douglas Adams's *Hitch-Hiker's Guide to the Galaxy*, where a Babel fish inserted in the ear modifies the hearer, not the message. Deep Space Nine in the *Star Trek* series of that name appears to have a translating system so universal that it is even effective for lip-readers.

26. I have generally avoided the language of the current discourse on colonialism in this study until this point, but when from the 1860s the distinctions between France and Britain become conceived in racial terms, the terminology is useful: see, for example, Homi Bhabha's description of the problem of the fixity of stereotype in *The Location of Culture* (Routledge, 1994), pp. 66–82.

27. Lewis Carroll, *The Annotated Alice*, edited by Martin Gardner (Meridien, 1974), p. 202. Cited hereafter in the text as *Alice*.

28. I would not dismiss the possibility of overreading the "Alice" books, but this type of Oxford "in-joke" seems in keeping with the nature of a project that surely involved more members of the Liddell family than simply Alice herself, who, by the time of *Through the Looking-Glass*, was probably too old to appreciate the sort of humor that might appeal to her fictional six-year-old self.

29. This is a problem that many young students experience when presented with multiple possibilities in the Greek Lexicon. Humpty Dumpty's explanation, however, is to some extent "fixed" by Tenniel's illustration, notably of the first stanza of "Jabberwocky."

30. Scarcely coincidentally, the most notable of the few vestiges of *Alice in Wonderland* apparent in *Through the Looking-Glass* are the March Hare and Mad Hatter, who show their "Saxon" forms as Haigha and Hatta, and mark a disguised continuity by suggesting that the "Looking-Glass" world has not entirely replaced the "Under Ground" world.

31. Daniel Bivona's essay "Alice the Child-Imperialist and the Games of Wonderland," *Nineteenth-Century Literature* 41:2 (September 1986) explores what he calls Alice's "semiotic imperialism"—her inability to comprehend systems of rules different from her own—in *Alice in Wonderland*.
32. Gladstone, "Germany, France, and England," p. 577.
33. A sign of a change in Butler's later thinking, or even of women's functions in society, may be indicated in *Erewhon Revisted* (1901), where the narrator explains that his wife's name was not really Arowhena, but Nna Haras.
34. Ibid., p. 253.
35. According to *Erewhon Revisited*, written forty years later, the narrator, now named as John Higgs, was to achieve this by accident, the balloon escape being interpreted by the Erewhonians as identifying Higgs not as a Parisian but as a deity.
36. Whereas early thinkers had assumed that Hebrew was the original human language, Müller "lost" the Tribes of Israel further through his lack of interest in Semitic languages. Chowbok and the Evangelicals are thus philologically unfashionable.
37. Butler, *Erewhon*, p. 29.
38. Bulwer-Lytton, *The Coming Race* (1871; Collier, n.d.), p. 699. Subsequent references are cited in the text.
39. Although Müller generally left others to draw political conclusions from his researches, his focus on the Aryan group of languages with the implication that others were less worthy of attention was a form of erasure that disturbingly foreshadows the racial erasure that became the policy of Germany's ruling Nazi party sixty years later.
40. In American pronunciation, Zee's name, the last letter of the alphabet, suggests ending.
41. For a well-reasoned discussion of women and property-law reform, see Mary Lyndon Shanley's *Feminism, Marriage, and the Law in England* (Princeton University Press, 1989).
42. The word suggests "nasty," but perhaps Bulwer-Lytton was also influenced by "*nak*," Müller's transliteration of the Sanskrit word for "perishing or destruction" in "On the Stratification of Language," in *Chips from a German Workshop* (Macmillan, 1899) 4:94.
43. I. F. Clarke, *Voices Prophesying War 1763–1984* (Oxford University Press, 1966), p. 38.
44. G. T. Chesney, *The Battle of Dorking* (Blackwood, 1871), pp. 4–5, hereafter cited in the text as *Dorking*.
45. The enemy presumably marched to Dorking from Worthing, since Worthing is on the Victoria line and the train service would require at least two changes (at Ford and Horsham, most probably).
46. When H. G. Wells depicted a Martian invasion in *The War of the Worlds* (1898), the aliens arrive at Pyrford near Woking, also in the Surrey commuter region.

47. In his 1878 essay "The Greatness of England," in *Lectures and Essays* (Macmillan, 1881), for example, Goldwin Smith traces back to the Teutonic heritage of the English their vigor, enterprise, self-reliance, and natural inclination for political liberty (pp. 21–23).
48. See, for example, the editorial of July 8, which mentions "the strong friendship which has long existed between this country and France."
49. The destination "Reigate" itself may be an indication of middle-class snobbery. Reigate station is not on a direct route from London, but on a line that crosses Surrey from the less fashionable dormer community of Redhill that grew up around the railway junction two miles from Reigate, through Dorking to Reading. Given that Mr. Bottles would barely have time to open his *Punch* between Redhill and Reigate, the train where the conversation takes place is probably going to Redhill Station, although the passengers prefer to think of their destination as the more refined Reigate.
50. *Hansard* (April 26, 1866), p. 2100.
51. Matthrew Arnold, *Friendship's Garland*, in *Collected Prose Works*, edited by R. H. Super (University of Michigan Press, 1960–1978) 5: 225–226. Following references cited in the text as *Friendship's Garland*.
52. Most of these letters appear in response to *The Times's* editorial of October 4, 1862, which begins "The art of ingeniously tormenting, which in past days was considered exclusively a domestic study, is now cultivated with eminent success by the managing authorities of British Railways."

Epilogue
Dreams of a Channel Tunnel

France's humiliation in 1871 left it no longer the primary military and ideological threat to Britain and Britishness. The new cooperative links forged between the two nations during the 1870s culminating in Britain's alliance with France in the wars of this century, however, do not imply that historical memory has ceased to be relevant in British constructions of their own and their neighbor's identity.

The historical resonances of France as the country of revolution have continued, albeit in a submerged form, in the debates over what the role of the Channel should be in a global society. As Gladstone remarked in 1870, the Channel could be seen as Britain's blessing, but in a world where political isolationism was impracticable, and where France and the rest of Europe had considerable attractions for Britons, the inconvenience of the crossing was also a curse. In the "Nightmare" song from Gilbert and Sullivan's *Iolanthe*, the very foremost of the "horrible dreams" catalogued at astonishing length by the Lord Chancellor is

> For you dream you are crossing the Channel, and tossing about in a steamer from Harwich—
> Which is something between a large bathing machine and a very small second-class carriage. ...[1]

Channel crossing would seem to be a recurrent nightmare for the privileged classes in Britain. Yet the conclusion of the couplet, written in 1882, points to a more directly topical nightmare. The idea conveyed is that the ship is small; yet it is also like a train, a concept reinforced by the additional information that the dreamer is joined by "a party of friends and relations" who "all come aboard at Sloane Square and South Kensington Stations"—underground railway stations in southwest London.

Figure 2. *Hopes and Fears; Or, A Dream of the Channel Tunnel.* By Linley Sambourne. *Punch* (February 25, 1882).

The Lord Chancellor was not alone in dreaming of a train from London to the Continent in 1882—nor was he unique in that the journey was seemingly never completed. On February 25 of that year, *Punch* published a drawing by Linley Sambourne titled "Hopes and Fears; Or, A Dream of the Channel Tunnel." At the top, a railway train is being swallowed by a serpent; in the center are two Britons dressed like moles, one identified as Lord Grosvenor of the London, Chatham and Dover Railway Company, and the other most likely representing Sir Edward Watkin of the South-Eastern Railway Company. Together, they drive a large cork-screw into the ground, while two laughing rabbits each labeled "Director" frolic on its shaft. They are opposed by three other figures: Father Thames points out that his "tunnel did not pay";[2] an admiral with a white feather in his hat brandishes a picture of a bull slain by frogs;[3] and a bemedaled "Timid Hare" represents Sir Garnet Wolsley, a respected general and active opponent of the Channel Tunnel scheme. At the bottom, an army of frogs carrying muskets marches through the Channel Tunnel.

For the Channel Tunnel was not simply a dream of Company Director rabbits, *Punch* cartoonists, and highly susceptible Chancellors. As I have suggested, interest in tunnel schemes was symptomatic of good official relations between France and Britain. After the Orsini Incident had prompted a French fear that Tunnel trains would be filled with bomb-carrying Italians, Thomé de Gamond had been forced to wait until the late 1860s before his ideas again received a favorable hearing. Once more he was unfortunate in his timing; the Franco-Prussian War brought an end to the negotiations.

After the war was over, however, and France no longer seemed a military threat, serious interest in a Channel Tunnel Scheme revived. Although he had made a serious geological survey, the engineering of Thomé de Gamond's scheme had relied on the future development of technology not yet available. The invention of the rotary boring machine now made excavation feasible, and engineers such as William Low found solutions to the problem of ventilation. Of equal importance, the scheme found financial backing in the form of the French Channel Tunnel Company and, from 1880 onward, Sir Edward Watkin's South-Eastern Railway Company, which proved more successful in putting his scheme into operation than his rival Richard Grosvenor's group. During 1882, more than a mile of tunnel was constructed in each direction.

Gladstone's government was confronted with another embarrassment. Britain and France were officially friendly again, and moreover, after the disaster of the Franco-Prussian War, it seemed hardly possible that France would try to invade Britain, currently the most powerful nation in the world. In the 1874–1875 Parliamentary session, the (Tory) Government of Derby and Disraeli had declared that they had "no doubt of the utility of this work,"[4] and now that the tunnel project was underway, the Government could not immediately change its stance. Lord Brabourne summed up the difficulty in the House of Lords on February 21, 1882:

> What position should we occupy in the eyes of France and the Continent if, having entered into an agreement before the practicability of the scheme was proved, we harked back after it had been shown to be practicable, and plainly told the French that we thought they were dangerous neighbours and not to be trusted?[5]

At least from the declared point of view—of both whigs and tories—the history of all that France represented should be overlooked in a new spirit of neighborhood.

Unofficially, however, memories were stronger. *The Battle of Dorking* had initiated the concept of futuristic tales of invasion, and the possibility of a Channel link to the European mainland prompted a number of stories prophesying disaster should the Tunnel be completed. The usual pattern was that by treachery, the French would capture the Dover end of the Channel, and then allow their army to march through.[6] A story published in *Macmillan's Magazine* in April 1882 shows even more clearly its indebtedness to *The Battle of Dorking*, although with a slightly happier ending. "The Story of the Channel Tunnel, Told to Our Grandchildren" is related from the perspective of the twentieth century (by which time a cure for seasickness has been found, making a tunnel unnecessary). When the Tunnel opens in 1885, few people wish to use it, so that "within two months of the opening of the Tunnel it was decided to employ it entirely for goods traffic, with the exception of a couple of trains daily each way."[7] In 1887, "a dastardly outrage" on English residents in Paris causes rumors of warfare between the nations, the consequence being "one of the craftiest pieces of strategy recorded in modern history, and one which reflects little credit on the nation that perpetrated it." In the revolutionary month of July, and on a Sunday when godfearing Britons are not traveling, a group of disguised French soldiers, including some women for the sake of authenticity, seize a Tunnel train. Invasion is only prevented by the courage of George Walsh, the English enginedriver, and afterwards the Tunnel is blown up.

An even more treacherous portrait of the French is created in *How John Bull Lost London; or, The Capture of the Channel Tunnel*, by "Grip," also published in 1882. In 1900, London is occupied by the French army. In the secure belief that the two nations would now "live as twins"[8] the British public had voted in favor of the Channel link. During the Egyptian crisis, "a large number of French holiday-makers" travel through the tunnel and take Dover, then fight their way to London (*John Bull*, p. 33).[9] A major battle is fought against the English regular army and volunteers at Guildford, a clear allusion to *The Battle of Dorking*.[10] Londoners are left to curse "the miserable national blunder which had brought all this suffering upon them" (*John Bull*, p. 100). Far from showing "the admirable conduct of the Germans as they passed through France in 1870," the French army shows its noted "excesses and want of discipline" (pp. 109–110).

The writer of this story is nevertheless not content to leave Britain permanently under French occupation. The beginning of the story, in language that suggests the connection with science fiction, claims that the "triumph of the alien had been complete" (p. 6). Yet by the end of the story, the North has risen to drive the invaders back to France (oddly, Birmingham is the only city "craven" enough to wish to capitulate), and the tunnel is blown up. Even this worse-case scenario cannot accept that France could be permanently victorious over Britain.

Such magazine stories might seem merely the populist expression of middle-class fears, but a number of writers who have achieved canonical status in the twentieth century also expressed criticism of the Channel Tunnel scheme. In Spring 1882, James Knowles, editor of the generally Liberal journal *The Nineteenth Century*, ran a series of articles pointing out the dangers of the project. Lord Dunsany, for example, who is probably the admiral in Sambourne's cartoon, contended that had such a tunnel existed, Frederick the Great and Napoleon would have known no restraint "when they found themselves in a position to capture the greatest and the richest prize that man has ever dreamt of."[11] Moreover, the threat was presented as both strategic and cultural: although the initial impulse behind the opposition was defensive, as the debate continued, another motivating force was simply that Britain should remain separate in all important respects.

About this time, the phrase "The Silver Streak" became current for the Channel. One source of inspiration for this was John of Gaunt's allusion to "This precious stone set in the silver sea" in *Richard II*: indeed, in April, Knowles quoted this speech at length to demonstrate that Shakespeare himself would have opposed the idea,[12] and it did not escape attention that the Tunnel's English end was at Shakespeare Cliff. More directly, however, it recalled Gladstone's notorious "streak of silver sea" in his *Edinburgh Review* article on the Franco-Prussian War. Gladstone was now theoretically in favor of the Tunnel, but his own reference to the advantages of Britain's island status returned to haunt him.

In addition to citing politicians and poets in cultural opposition, Knowles took the virtually unprecedented step of printing petitions opposing the Tunnel. Tennyson, Browning, and William Morris signed, as did many intellectuals generally associated with progressive views, including T. H. Huxley, Herbert Spencer, and even the Positivist Frederic Harrison in a seeming departure from Comtean ideals of scientific progress.

A short story by Thomas Hardy shows an interesting variation on the "Tunnel invasion" motif by connecting the fears of 1882 with those of Napoleonic times. "A Tradition of Eighteen Hundred and Four," published at the end of 1882, begins:

> The widely discussed possibility of an invasion of England through a Channel tunnel has more than once recalled old Solomon Shelby's story to my mind.[13]

Solomon Shelby, who died ten years ago, used to tell how in 1804—about the time of the first print of an invasion through a Channel Tunnel—he had seen, at Lulworth Cove in Dorset, two French generals who had landed secretly to plan an invasion, one of them being Napoleon himself. The old man concludes that if "the Corsican ogre" had invaded, "[w]e coastfolk should have been cut down one and all, and I should not have sat here to tell this tale."[14]

By presenting this anecdote as the tale of an old man over his ale, Hardy might possibly be suggesting that fears of invasion are unfounded. Yet the story draws on a lasting historical consciousness among the lower classes as to what "Boney" represents. The simple countryman is in effect the mouthpiece for a hypothesis: if Napoleon had had a tunnel, he would have invaded Britain, and if a tunnel were to be built now, a new French threat might arise. Whether Hardy intended to make a late contribution to literary scaremongering or not, his story of a landing by Napoleon was later incorporated into British folk-memory as an actual occurrence: when the cultural conditions are right, novelists can make history.[15]

Just as Hardy's story was written in an atmosphere of alarm at French plots, the possibility did not escape critics that the treacherous

French might find allies in the treacherous Irish, who might help them gain control of the Tunnel. Lord Strathnairn, for example, who believed that there were Fenians among the Irish soldiers, cited

> the deep-rooted disaffection of the Irish masses, and the intensity of their hostility to English government, law, and connection, which proved that it would be a misprision of common sense and every principle of the art of war and strategy to give to a foreign enemy the means of a successful invasion of England by the Tunnel—afforded him by traitors in the camp, such as the Fenian soldiers.[16]

Besides the embarrassment of public figures such as Lord Strathnairn implying that France was an enemy power, the Government's quandary was that this was not a national endeavor, but the product of private enterprise. Watkin and his shareholders owned the land on which they were excavating, and were proceeding on the legal theory that the sea belonged to nobody. Ironically, in *Middlemarch*, which with its 1830s setting and 1870s perspective encapsulates the differences between Britain at the start of this study and Britain at its end, George Eliot had written, "The submarine railway may have its difficulties, but the bed of the sea is not divided among various landed proprietors with claims for damages not only measurable but sentimental."[17] 1882, however, proved that a sense of property extended to the sea itself, so that the problem was how to measure the sentimental: that is, how to legislate for a feeling that the Tunnel was a danger for Britain. The bed of the sea provided the solution when the Government ruled that once the diggings passed the low-water mark, they were no longer on private property, but on Crown property, and therefore a matter of national concern.[18]

By August, the Government was reluctant to authorize the project further, and in October a decision was made to "remonstrate" with the French Government over continued excavation from the Sangatte end. Even though a Military Committee (chaired by Sir Archibald Alison, son of the historian) had already reported to the Government its recommendations for the defense of the Tunnel, a Joint Committee was formed to study the problem further. By this time, relations with France were again under strain, principally for the reason given in *How John Bull Lost London* for the French invasion of England, tensions over spheres of influence during the current Egyptian Crisis. In the Egyptian Campaign in September, Sir Garnet Wolsley, characterized by *Punch* in February as a "Timid Hare" and later by "Grip" as the well-intentioned loser of the Battle of Guildford, gained a rapid success, which gave more authority to his opposition of the Tunnel. On the recommendation of the Committee, the project was halted as prejudicial to British security.

The unusual step of a Joint Committee, comprised of both Liberal and Conservative members of both the Lords and Commons and seemingly chosen to include representatives of England, Scotland, and Wales,[19] indicates that this was no longer seen as a party question, where whigs and tories would automatically differ. In fact, the crisis within the Liberal Party as to what their principles were is a marker of the breakdown of the Victorian two-party system that would lead to the eclipse of the Liberals and their replacement by the Socialist-influenced Labour Party as the opposition to Conservatism by the end of the First World War, the war in which France became not a threatening enemy but a friend in need of defense.[20] Moreover, by the time that the war was over, belief that society was progressing towards a higher civilization seemed questionable indeed.

The Channel Tunnel Question suggests, though, that as early as 1882, the view of history that prevailed was the tory one: historically, the French (and other Europeans) were not to be trusted, and equally historically, the Channel had been the defense against invasion and the moral and political corruption that in its final synecdochic conversion, the French Revolution comes to represent. Herbert Butterfield's suggestion that nineteenth-century is epitomized by the "whig view of history" thus requires some reconsideration. Although obviously later instances exist of the whig view of history—the problematic Lord Acton, for example, was writing in the early years of this century, and displays something of an *"Entente Cordiale"* spirit—the debates over the present-day Channel Tunnel continue to show an interesting split between official policy and popular feeling, and possibly even the feelings of the figurehead of Britishness, the monarch.

The opening of the Channel Tunnel was repeatedly delayed. In May 1994, the day after the Conservative party had suffered major losses in local government elections (ironically largely to the closest heirs of the Whigs, the Liberal Democrats), the Queen of Great Britain and the French President traveled through it at what should have been the official inauguration, the Queen in a train and the President in the Queen's car. The President is reported to have said that he liked the Queen's car. The Queen was able to evince even less enthusiasm, her speech stating that the French and British people "complement each other well, better perhaps than we realise."[21] The Queen's point of view was shared by many of her subjects, who continued to voice concern over potential problems created by the Tunnel: it might, for example, be a target for Irish terrorists; or it might allow rabies into Britain.[22] Two of Carlyle's analogies for the French Revolution—terror as personified by the Irish or as signified by rabies—now became part of a more generalized sense of threat of being joined to France.

The question of whether Britain would be invaded by France, or even become infected by France's revolutionary spirit, however, tended to replaced by a more directly cultural form of fear of assimilation into Europe, probably not helped by the pro-Tunnel *Independent*'s praise for the new temporary London terminal—ironically at Waterloo—as "a spiritual successor to the Eiffel Tower."[23] A sign of some change in attitudes, however, might be that when the Channel Tunnel was used in a leg of the archetypally French *Tour de France*—the cyclists raced through the tunnel to Dover to race legs in Kent and Sussex and Hampshire, but oddly enough, took a boat back—the racers received a generally positive reception, even if the crowds were vainly hoping that the two British riders in the race, Chris Boardman and Sean Yates, would win. Nevertheless, while *The Times*, which was offering its readers a chance to "win a Chris Boardman Superbike," reported that the British public was happy, the *Guardian* quoted a conversation in a pub: "'I reckon they [the locals] want to put down tin tacks,' said Sid Harris. 'The way they treat us with the meat and the fish and things like that, I wouldn't give them twopence.'"[24] Sid Harris is still thinking synecdochically: for him, the Tour de France represents France, and France itself represents Europe and European Economic Community policies against British interests.

Sid Harris's association of Frenchness with national rivalry, though, is in theory opposed by the policy of the New Labour government that succeeded the Conservatives. The assumption appears to be that in order for the nation to continue to progress, certain parts of history, including the fear of France (now almost metonymic for the rest of Europe), must be accepted as past and gone—a whig reading. Popular feeling, however, may yet retain a historical memory of what that past was, accompanied by a vague unease that it has a relevance for the future.

The Tunnel's longterm future is still to be determined. Freight services followed soon after the *Tour de France*, but passenger trains did not pass their safety tests until later in the year. Service on "Le Shuttle," the car-carrier's Franglais name itself suggesting unsatisfactory mutual Anglo-French infection that *The Times* jokingly called a "cross-Channel contamination more invisible than rabies" followed,[25] while a scheduled service on Eurostar, the London to Paris train, began on November 14: the two cities at last had their land-link, and moreover one with a connection to Brussels. Since a mere 140 years after Thomé de Gamond had presented a solution to the different railway gauges in the two countries, Britain's high-speed rail line is still under construction, trains will travel for the meanwhile more slowly in England than in France, which continues to hold its place as innovator.

Once the Tunnel was open, the public did not hold back, the first week's service running at capacity. A year later, however, Eurostar, the Tunnel railway company, was resorting to measures of desperation to retain the goodwill of its passengers, and by Spring 1996, it is believed to have expended a million dollars in compensation to travelers whose journeys were delayed. To cite a personal example, in snowy weather on February 20, 1996, a family journey from Brussels to London took seven hours, four hours longer than scheduled, including an hour virtually stationary in the Tunnel, with the result that we arrived in London after the last train. Without any solicitation on the part of the passengers, Eurostar paid for cabs home or hotels, refunded our fares for the the one-way trip, and sent a two-page letter of explanation that assured us that had we been traveling by sea that day, our experience would have been much worse, something that I can well believe. The only hint of panic that we observed during this experience was caused by the realization that the buffet car had run out of all food except chocolate muffins, which suggests that the travelers might be becoming used to the idea of a united Europe, but that American cultural imperialism remains a different matter.

Certainly, the problem of how to pay for the Tunnel shows signs of lasting as long as the debate over its inception. Whether the final establishment of a geographical link between Britain and France will change national attitudes, or whether it is a symbol of attitudes already changing, remains to be seen. Officially, whig history is the true history; unofficially, however, whig history may not be able to erase tory history while the past still has a power.

Notes

1. W. S. Gilbert, *The Savoy Operas* (Wordsworth Editions, 1994), p. 244.
2. The reference is to Mark Brunel's Thames Tunnel, built at considerable cost in 1825–1842, before the rotary boring engine was developed. See David Lampe, *The Tunnel* (Harrap, 1963).

3. The bull in a jacket is, of course, John Bull or England; the frogs are the French, an epithet seemingly used by the British for their neighbors since the eighteenth century.
4. Quoted in *Hansard* (February 10, 1882), p. 383.
5. Ibid., p. 1220.
6. I. F. Clarke, for example, cites C. Forth's *The Surprise of the Channel Tunnel*, in which a variety of French traders settle in Dover: they are really French soldiers and seize control of the Tunnel at night (*Voices Prophesying War*, p. 113).
7. "The Story of the Channel Tunnel, Told to Our Grandchildren," *Macmillan's Magazine* 46 (April 1882), p. 501.
8. "Grip," *How John Bull Lost London; Or, The Capture of the Channel Tunnel* (Sampson Low, 1882), p. 22. Cited hereafter in the text as *John Bull*.
9. Since the Egyptian Crisis is apparently not yet over, this story would appear to place the invasion in the early 1880s—unless, of course, it was a very long crisis!
10. Guildford is close to Dorking in the Surrey commuter belt; this would seem literary homage to Chesney's story because Guildford would not be on the route to London of an army that landed at Dover.
11. In the *Nineteenth Century*'s series "The Channel Tunnel Debate," edited by James Knowles (February–May, 1882), p. 297.
12. Ibid., p. 498.
13. Thomas Hardy, "A Tradition of Eighteen Hundred and Four," In *Wessex Tales and A Group of Noble Dames* (Macmillan, 1977), p. 33.
14. Ibid., p. 38.
15. According to Hardy's wife, when after the story's publication, people referred to his use of "that well-known tradition of Napoleon's landing," Hardy initially assumed that such a story had existed without his knowledge; later investigation, however, proved this not to be the case. See Florence Hardy's *Life of Thomas Hardy* (1962; Archon Books, 1970), pp. 391–392.
16. *Hansard*, 3rd Series (March 31, 1882), p. 458. Joe Poynter's 1979 novel *Tunnel War* (Atheneum, 1979) imagines a tunnel being constructed on the eve of the First World War, and sabotaged by a conspiracy between Germany and the Irish Republican Army.
17. George Eliot, *Middlemarch*, edited by Rosemary Ashton (1871–2; Penguin, 1994), p. 553.
18. See *Hansard* (February 27, 1882), pp. 1698–99.
19. The members were Lansdowne, Camperdown, Devon, Aberdare, and Shute from the House of Lords, and William E. M. Baxter, William G. V. Harcourt, Sir Massey Lopes, Arthur Wellesley Peel and Henry Hussey Vivian from the Commons.
20. Evidently, some talk of a Channel Tunnel was revived under the Edwardian *Entente Cordiale*, since in 1907 Ellis Ashmead-Bartlett published *The Immortals and the Channel Tunnel: A Discussion in Valhalla* (Blackwood, 1907), in which the illustrious English dead speak against the project in what

appears to be an exclusively Teutonic heaven. Shakespeare, for example, comments: "Can we maintain in all its pride/The great tradition of our island home/If we unite our shores by darksome tubes/To Europe?" (p. 57).

21. Reported in the *Daily Express* (May 7, 1994), which also claimed that the Queen had expressed personal reservations at the idea of a Tunnel: "'I will smile,' she allegedly said, 'But only one smile'" (p. 3).
22. Both cited as popular fears in the pro-Tunnel *Independent* (May 6, 1994), p. 13.
23. *The Independent* (May 6, 1994), p. 15. This report also printed side by side the 1803 invasion print and a photograph of the Eurostar train (p. 13). The *Guardian*'s "Notes and Queries" column prompted debate over how the French might seek revenge by a "symmetrically tactless name" for their terminal: inevitably, one correspondent suggested the "*Gare de l'Hastings*" (reprinted in *Guardian Weekly*, [November 20, 1994]).
24. *The Guardian* (July 5, 1994), p. 24.
25. *The Times* (May 5, 1994).

References

Alison, Archibald. "Dumont's Recollections of Mirabeau." *Blackwood's Magazine* 31 (May 1832): 753–771.
———. "Fall of the Melbourne Ministry." *Blackwood's Magazine* 37 (January 1835): 30–48.
———. "Fall of the Throne of the Barricades." *Blackwood's Magazine* 63 (April 1848): 393–418.
———. *History of Europe from the Commencement of the French Revolution in MDCCLXXXIX to the Restoration of the Bourbons in MDCCCXV.* 10 vols. Paris: Baudry's European Library 1841; rpt of 1835 British ed.
———. *The History of Europe from the Commencement of the French Revolution to the Restoration of the Bourbons.* New issue of 7th ed. 12 vols. Edinburgh: Blackwood's, 1849.
———. *History of Europe.* 9th ed. 12 vols. Edinburgh: Blackwood's, 1853.
———. *My Life and Writings.* 2 vols. Edinburgh: Blackwood, 1883.
———. "On the Late French Revolution." Series of articles in *Blackwood's Magazine* 29–31 (1831–1833); titles vary.
Alkon, Paul. *The Origins of Futuristic Fiction.* Athens: U. Georgia Press, 1987.
Alter, Robert. "The Demons of History in Dickens's *Tale.*" In *Charles Dickens's A Tale of Two Cities: Modern Critical Interpretations.* Edited by Harold Bloom. New York: Chelsea House, 1987, pp. 13–22.
Armstrong, Nancy, and Leonard Tennenhouse. "History, Poststructuralism, and the Question of Narrative." *Narrative* 1 (January 1993): 45–58.
Arnold, Matthew. *Complete Prose Works.* Ed. R. H. Super. 11 vols. Ann Arbor: Michigan U. Press, 1960–78.
———. *The Oxford Authors: Matthew Arnold.* Ed. Miriam Allott and Robert H. Super. Oxford: Oxford U. Press, 1986.
Ashmead-Bartlett, Ellis. *The Immortals and the Channel Tunnel: A Discussion in Valhalla.* Edinburgh: Blackwood, 1907.
Auerbach, Erich. "Figura." 1944. Trans. Ralph Manheim. In *Scenes from the Drama of European Literature.* Gloucester, Mass.: Peter Smith, 1973.
Ayling, Stanley. *Edmund Burke, His Life and Opinions.* London: John Murray, 1988.

Bahti, Timothy. *Allegories of History: Literary Historigraphy after Hegel.* Baltimore: Johns Hopkins U. Press, 1992.

Barzun, Jacques, ed. *Burke and Hare: The Resurrection Men.* Metuchen, N.J.: Scarecrow Press, 1974.

Bhabha, Homi K. *The Location of Culture.* London: Routledge, 1994.

Bivona, Daniel. "Alice the Child-Imperialist and the Games of Wonderland." *Nineteenth-Century Literature* 41: 2 (September 1986): 143–171.

Black, Jeremy. *Natural and Necessary Enemies: Anglo-French Relations in the Eighteenth Century.* London: Duckworth, 1986.

Blackstone, Sir William. *Commentaries Upon the Laws of England.* 4 vols. 1765–69; reprinted Chicago: University of Chicago Press, 1979.

Blanc, Louis. *The History of Ten Years.* English edition. 2 vols. London: Chapman and Hall, 1845.

Bolingbroke, Henry St. John, Lord. *The Works of Lord Bolingbroke.* 4 vols. Philadelphia: Carey and Hart, 1841.

Bork, Robert H. *The Tempting of America: The Political Seduction of the Law.* New York: Free Press, 1990.

Brannan, Robert Louis, ed. *Under the Management of Mr. Charles Dickens: His Production of "The Frozen Deep."* Ithaca: Cornell U. Press, 1966.

Brantlinger, Patrick. *The Spirit of Reform: British Literature and Politics, 1832–1867.* Cambridge: Harvard University Press, 1977.

Brougham, Henry. "The Late Revolution in France." *Edinburgh Review* 52 (October 1830): 1–25.

———. "Biographical Memoirs of Mirabeau." *Edinburgh Review* 61 (April 1835): 186–214.

———. *Letter to the Marquis of Lansdowne ... on the Late Revolution in France.* 4th ed. London: James Ridgeway, 1848.

Broughton, Baron (John Cam Hobhouse). *Recollections of a Long Life.* Ed. Lady Dorchester. 6 vols. London: John Murray, 1909–1911.

Bulwer-Lytton, Sir Edward. *England and the English.* 2 vols. London: Bentley, 1833.

———. *The Coming Race.* 1871. New York: Collier, n. d.

———. *Lucretia; Or, The Children of Night.* 1846. Boston: Little, Brown and Co., 1897.

———. "The Reign of Terror." *Foreign Quarterly Review* 29 (July 1842): 274–308.

———. *Zanoni.* 1842. New York: Collier, n. d.

Buonarroti, Philippo. *The History of Babeuf's Conspiracy for Equality.* Trans. Bronterre [O'Brien]. London: H. Hetherington, 1836.

Burke, Edmund. *The Works of the Right Honorable Edmund Burke.* 12 vols. Boston: Little, Brown, 1866.

———. *The Writings and Speeches of Edmund Burke.* Ed. Paul Langford. Oxford: Clarendon Press, 1981–.

Burrow, J. W. *Evolution and Society.* Cambridge: Cambridge U. Press, 1966.

———. *A Liberal Descent: Victorian Historians and the English Past.* Cambridge: Cambridge University Press, 1981, rpt. 1983.

Butler, Samuel. *Erewhon*. 1872. Ed. Peter Mudford. Harmondsworth: Penguin, 1970, rpt. 1985.
Butterfield, Herbert. *The Whig Interpretation of History*. 1931; New York: Norton, 1965.
Carlyle, Thomas. *The Collected Letters of Thomas and Jane Welsh Carlyle*, ed. Clyde de. L. Ryals et al. Durham, N.C.: Duke U. Press, 1970–.
———. *The Works of Thomas Carlyle*. 30 vols. London: Chapman and Hall, 1899; rpt. New York: AMC Press, 1980.
Chandler, James K. *Wordsworth's Second Nature: A Study of the Poetry and the Politics*. Chicago: U. Chicago Press, 1984.
Chesney, George Tomkyns. *The Battle of Dorking*. Edinburgh: Blackwood, 1871.
Ciolkowski, L. "The Woman (In) Question: Gender, Politics, and Edward Bulwer-Lytton's *Lucretia*." *Novel* 26: 1 (Fall 1992): 80–95.
Clarke, I. F. *Voices Prophesying War 1763–1984*. London: Oxford University Press, 1966.
Clive, John. *Not By Fact Alone: Essays on the Writing and Reading of History*. New York: Alfred A. Knopf, 1989.
Cobban, Alfred, ed. *The Debate on the French Revolution 1789–1800*. London: Nicholas Kaye, 1950.
Cole, G. D. H. *A Short History of the British Working-Class Movement*. Revised edition. London: Allen and Unwin, 1948.
Coleridge, Samuel Taylor. *Biographia Literaria*. 1817. Ed. James Engell and W. Jackson Bate. Princeton: Bollingen, 1983.
———. *On the Constitution of Church and State*. Ed. John Colmer. Princeton: Princeton U. Press, 1976.
Colley, Linda. *Britons: Forging the Nation 1707–1837*. New Haven: Yale U. Press, 1992.
Cone, Carl B. *Burke and the Nature of Politics: The Age of the French Revolution*. Kentucky: U. Kentucky Press, 1964.
Croker, John Wilson. *The Croker Papers*. Ed. Louis J. Jennings. 2nd ed. 3 vols. London: John Murray, 1885.
———. "French Novels." *Quarterly Review* 56 (April 1836): 65–131.
———. "French Revolution: February 1848." *Quarterly Review* 82 (March 1848): 541–595.
———. "Louis Philippe et la Contre-Revolution de 1830." *Quarterly Review* 52 (November 1834): 519–572.
———. "Mr. Macaulay's History of England." *Quarterly Review* 84 (March 1849): 549–630.
———. "Poems of Alfred Tennyson." *Quarterly Review* 49 (April 1833): 81–96.
———. "Present State of France." *Quarterly Review* 52 (August 1834): 262–291.
———. "Robespierre." *Quarterly Review* 54 (September 1835): 517–580.
———. "The Revolutions of 1640 and 1830." *Quarterly Review* 47 (March 1832): 261–300.
———. "Sir Robert Peel's Address to the Electors of the Borough of Tamworth." *Quarterly Review* 53 (Feb. 1835): 261–287.

———. "Stages of the Revolution." *Quarterly Review* 47 (July 1832): 559–589.
———. "State of the French Drama." *Quarterly Review* 51 (March 1834): 177–212.
Croly, George. "Mirabeau." *Blackwood's Magazine* 35 (May 1834): 622–631.
Crosby, Christina. *The Ends of History: Victorians and the "Woman Question."* New York: Routledge, 1991.
Culler, A. Dwight. *The Victorian Mirror of History.* New Haven: Yale U. Press, 1985.
Deane, Seamus. *The French Revolution and Enlightenment in England 1789–1832.* Cambridge: Harvard U. Press, 1988
De Certeau, Michel. *The Writing of History.* Trans. Tom Conley. New York: Columbia U. Press, 1988.
De Quincy, Thomas. "Second Paper on Murder Considered as One of the Fine Arts." *Blackwood's Magazine* 46 (November 1839): 661–668.
Dickens, Charles. *Barnaby Rudge.* 1841. Ed. Gordon Spence. London: Penguin, 1973.
———. *A Child's History of England.* 1851–54. London: Chapman and Hall, 1907.
———, ed. *Household Words.* 1850–59.
———. *The Letters of Charles Dickens.* Ed. Graham Storey et al. Oxford: Clarendon, 1989–.
———. *A Tale of Two Cities.* Ed. George Woodcock. 1859; London: Penguin, 1985.
Disraeli, Benjamin. *Lothair.* 1870.
———. *The Revolutionary Epick.* New Edition. London: Longman, 1864.
Dodgson, Charles. *Alice's Adventures in Wonderland* and *Through the Looking-Glass.* In *The Annotated Alice.* Ed. Martin Gardner. 1960. New York: Meridien, 1974.
Donne, W. B. "The Saxons in England." *Edinburgh Review* 90 (January 1849): 154–184.
Dowling, Linda. "Victorian Oxford and the Science of Language." *PMLA* 97 (March 1982): 160–178.
Dumont, Étienne. *Recollections of Mirabeau.* English ed. London: Edward Bull, 1832.
Elias, Norbert. *The Civilizing Process: The Development of Manners.* 1939. Trans. Edmund Jephcott. New York: Urizen Books, 1978.
Eliot, George. *Middlemarch.* 1871–2. Ed. Rosemary Ashton. Harmondsworth: Penguin, 1994.
Fairbairn, Patrick. *The Typology of Scripture.* 2nd ed. 2 vols. Edinburgh: T. and T. Clark, 1854.
Farrell, John P. *Revolution as Tragedy: The Dilemma of the Moderate from Scott to Arnold.* Ithaca: Cornell U. Press, 1980.
Ferris, David. *Theory and the Evasion of History.* Baltimore: Johns Hopkins U. Press, 1993.
Fielding, K. J. *Charles Dickens, A Critical Introduction.* London: Longmans, 1965.
Forster, John. *The Life of Charles Dickens.* 1872–74. New ed., 2 vols. London: Dent, 1969.

———. "*Lucretia.*" *Examiner* (Dec. 6, 1846): 772.
———. "*Vanity Fair.*" *Examiner* (July 22, 1848): 468–470.
———(?). "*Zanoni.*" *Examiner* (Feb. 26, 1842): 132–133.
Foucault, Michel. *The Archaeology of Knowledge.* Trans. A. M. Sheridan Smith. New York: Pantheon, 1972.
———. *Discipline and Punish: The Birth of the Prison.* Trans. Alan Sheridan. New York: Random House, 1979.
———. *The Order of Things.* New York: Vintage Books, 1973.
Freeman, Edward Augustus. *Comparative Politics.* London: Macmillan, 1873.
Friedman, Barton. *Fabricating History: English Writers on the French Revolution.* Princeton: Princeton U. Press, 1988.
Fullarton, John. "Parliamentary Reform." *Quarterly Review* 44 (February 1831): 554–598.
———. "The Progress of Misgovernment." *Quarterly Review* 46 (January 1832): 544–622.
Furet, François. *Interpreting the French Revolution.* Trans. Elborg Forster. Cambridge: Cambridge U. Press, 1981.
Gladstone, W. E. "Germany, France, and England." *Edinburgh Review* 132 (October 1870): 554–593.
Gilbert, Elliot L. "A Wondrous Contiguity": Anachronism in Carlyle's Prophecy and Art." *PMLA* 87 (1972): 432–442.
Gilbert, W. S. *The Bab Ballads.* Ed. James Ellis. Cambridge: Belknap Press, 1980.
———. *The Savoy Operas.* Ware: Wordsworth Editions, 1994.
Goldberg, Michael. *Carlyle and Dickens.* Athens: U. Georgia Press, 1973.
Gooch, George Peabody. *History and Historians in the Nineteenth Century.* 1913. 2nd ed. London: Beacon Press, 1959.
"Grip." *How John Bull Lost London; Or, The Capture of the Channel Tunnel.* London: Sampson Low, 1882.
Habermas, Jürgen. *The Structural Transformation of the Public Sphere.* Trans. Thomas Burger with Frederick Lawrence. Cambridge: MIT Press, 1989, rpt. 1993.
Halévy, Eli. *The Growth of Philosophic Radicalism.* English version. 1928; New York: Kelley and Millman, n.d.
Hall, Stuart, ed. *Representation: Cultural Representations and Signifying Practices.* London: Sage, 1997.
———, and Paul du Gay, ed. *Questions of Cultural Identity.* London: Sage, 1996.
Hardy, Florence Emily. *The Life of Thomas Hardy 1840–1928.* 1962. Rpt. Hamden, Conn.: Archon Books, 1970.
Hardy, Thomas. "A Tradition of Eighteen Hundred and Four." In *Wessex Tales and A Group of Noble Dames,* ed. F. B. Pinion. London: Macmillan, 1977.
Hazlitt, William. *Life of Napoleon Buonaparte.* In *Works* 13. London: Dent, 1933–35.
Hazlitt, W. Carew, ed. *Thomas Griffiths Wainewright, Essays and Criticisms.* London: Reeves and Turner, 1880.

Hegel, G. W. F. *The Philosophy of History.* Trans J. Sibree. New York: Dover Books, 1956.

Hickson, W. E. "The French Revolution of February 1848." *Westminster Review* 49 (April 1848): 137–198.

Hood, Thomas. *The Works of Thomas Hood, edited by his Son and Daughter.* 8 vols. London: Moxon, 1861.

Hollingsworth, Keith. *The Newgate Novel 1830–1847.* Detroit: Wayne State Univ. Press, 1963

Horsman, Reginald. *Race and Manifest Destiny: The Origins of American Racial Anglo-Saxonism.* Cambridge: Harvard U. Press, 1981.

Houghton, Walter E., et al, eds. *The Wellesley Index to Victorian Periodicals.* 5 vols. Toronto: U. Toronto Press, 1966–1989.

Howe, Susanne K. *Geraldine Jewsbury, Her Life and Errors.* London: Allen and Unwin, 1935.

Hugo, Victor. *Lucrèce Borgia.* In *Oeuvres Complètes: Drame III.* Paris: Hetzel et Quantin, 1880.

———. "Sur Mirabeau." In *Oeuvres Complètes: Philosophy I.* Paris: Hetzel et Quantin, n.d.

Hume, David. *History of England.* 1754–1762. With continuations. 16 vols. London: Washbourne, 1844.

———. *The Philosophical Works of David Hume.* 4 vols. Edinburgh: Black and Tait, 1826.

Hunt, Donald. *The Tunnel: The Story of the Channel Tunnel 1802–1994.* Upton-upon-Severn: Image Publishing, 1994.

Hunt, Lynn. *Politics, Culture, and Class in the French Revolution.* Berkeley: University of California Press, 1984.

James, Thomas. "Funerals and Funeral Expenses." *Quarterly Review* 73 (March 1844): 438–477.

Jameson, Fredric. *The Political Unconscious: Narrative as a Socially Symbolic Act.* Ithaca: Cornell U. Press, 1981.

Jewsbury, Geraldine Ensor. *Zoë.* 3 vols. London: Chapman and Hall, 1845.

Johnston, Edgar, ed. *The Heart of Charles Dickens, as Revealed in his Letters to Angela Burdett-Coutts.* New York: Duell, Sloan and Pearce, 1952.

Kemble, John Mitchell. *The Saxons in England.* 2 vols. London: Longmans, 1848.

Knowles, James, ed. "The Channel Tunnel Debate." *Nineteenth Century,* February–May 1882.

Kucich, John. *Excess and Restraint in the Novels of Charles Dickens.* Athens: University of Georgia Press, 1981.

Lamartine, Alphonse de. *History of the Girondists.* 3 vols. London: Bohn, 1847–49.

Lambert, Richard S. *The Railway King 1800–1871: A Study of George Hudson and the Business Morals of his Time.* 1934; rpt. London: Allen and Unwin, 1964.

Lampe, David. *The Tunnel: The Story of the World's First Tunnel under a Navigable River.* London: Harrap, 1963.

Landow, George P. *Victorian Types, Victorian Shadows: Biblical Typology in Victorian Literature, Art, and Thought.* Boston: Routledge and Kegan Paul, 1980.

Laurence, Dan H., and Martin Quinn, eds. *Shaw on Dickens.* New York: Frederick Ungar, 1985.

Leigh, Percival. "A Tale of the Good Old Times." *Household Words* (April 27, 1850): 1, 103.

Lewes, Darby. *Dream Revisionaries: Gender and Genre in Women's Utopian Fiction 1870–1920.* Tuscaloosa: University of Alabama Press, 1995.

Lewes, George Henry. "Louis Blanc's History of Ten Years." *Foreign Quarterly Review* 32 (1843): 61–75.

——. *The Life of Maximilien Robespierre; With Extracts from His Unpublished Correspondence.* London: Chapman and Hall, 1849.

Liu, Alan. *Wordsworth, The Sense of History.* Stanford: Stanford U. Press, 1989.

"Lord Chesterfield." *Bentley's Miscellany* 34 (1853): 222–224.

"*Lucretia.*" *Athenaeum* (Dec. 5, 1846): 1240–1242.

Lukács, Georg. *The Historical Novel.* Trans. Hannah and Stanley Mitchell. London: Merlin, 1962.

Luttrell, Barbara. *Mirabeau.* London: Harvester/Wheatsheaf, 1990.

Macaulay, Catherine Sawbridge. *The History of England from the Accession of James I to that of the Brunswick Line.* 8 vols. London: Nourse, 1763–1783.

——. "Observations on the Reflections of the Right. Hon. Edmund Burke." Boston, 1791.

Macaulay, Thomas Babington, Lord. *The Complete Works of Lord Macaulay.* 12 vols. London: Longmans, 1898.

——. *The Letters of T. B. Macaulay*, ed. Thomas Pinney, 6 vols. Cambridge: Cambridge U. Press, 1974–81.

Mackay, Charles. *Memoirs of Extraordinary Popular Delusions.* 1844, rpt. Boston: L.C.Page, 1932.

"Mackay's Extraordinary Popular Delusions." *Edinburgh Review* 80 (July 1844): 203–250.

Mahon, Lord (Earl Stanhope). "Russell's Causes of the French Revolution." *Quarterly Review* 49 (April 1833): 152–174.

Mackintosh, Sir James. *Vindiciae Gallicae.* 3rd ed. London, 1791.

Marcus, David D. "The Carlylean Vision of *A Tale of Two Cities.*" In Bloom, *Charles Dickens's A Tale of Two Cities*, pp. 23–35.

Mannheim, Karl. *Essays on Sociology and Social Psychology.* Ed. Paul Kecskmeti. London: Routledge and Kegan Paul, 1953, rpt. 1969.

Manuel, Pierre, ed. *Lettres Originales de Mirabeau, écrites du Donjon de Vincennes.* 4 vols. Paris, 1792.

Martineau, Harriet, trans. and ed. *The Positive Philosophy of Auguste Comte.* 1853. New York: Calvin Blanchard, 1858.

Marx, Karl, and Friedrich Engels. *The Communist Manifesto*. Trans. Helen Macfarlane. In *The Red Republican* 21–24, Nov. 1850.

———. "Preface to the English Edition of 1888." In *The Communist Manifesto*, ed. Frederic L. Bender. New York: Norton, 1988.

———. *The German Ideology*. Ed. C. Rymzanshaya. 2 vols. Moscow, Progress Publishers, 1965.

Mercier, Louis-Sebastien. *L'An 2440*. 3 vols. New edition. 1786.

———. *Tableau de Paris*. 2nd ed. 12 vols. Amsterdam, 1782–1788.

Mignet, F. A. *History of the French Revolution from 1789 to 1814*. New York: Carvill, 1827.

Mill, John Stuart. *The Collected Works of John Stuart Mill*. Ed. John M. Robson. 25 vols. Toronto: Toronto U. Press, 1963–.

Mink, Louis O. *Historical Understanding*. Ed. Brian Fay et al. Ithaca: Cornell U. Press, 1987.

Monod, Sylvère. *Dickens the Novelist*. English edition. Norman: U. Oklahoma Press, 1968.

Montigny, Gabriel Lucas de, ed. *Mémoires biographiques, littéraires, et politiques de Mirabeau*. 8 vols in 3. Paris: Auffray, 1834–1835.

———, ed. *Memoirs of Mirabeau*. English edition. 4 vols. London: Edward Churton, 1835.

Müller, F. Max. *Chips from a German Workshop*. 4 vols. London: Longmans, 1867–1875.

———, ed. *Letters on the War between Germany and France by T. Mommsen, D. F. Strauss, F. Max Müller, and Thomas Carlyle*. London: Trübner, 1871.

———. *Lectures on the Science of Language*. New edition. 2 vols. London: Macmillan, 1899.

Müller, Georgina Max, ed. *The Life and Times of the Right Honourable Friedrich Max Müller*. 2 vols. London: Longmans, 1902.

Napoleon III (Louis-Napoleon Bonaparte). *Discourses et Messages de Louis-Napoléon Bonaparte*. Paris: Plon, 1853.

Newman, Gerald. *The Rise of English Nationalism: A Cultural History 1740–1830*. New York: St. Martin's, 1987.

O'Brien, James Bronterre. *The Life and Character of Maximilian Robespierre* ... vol. 1. London: J. Watson, 1839.

Oddie, William. *Dickens and Carlyle, the Question of Influence*. London: Centenary Press, 1972.

Oliphant, Margaret. "Historical Sketches of the Reign of George III—The Man of the World." *Blackwood's Magazine* 103 (1868): 511–533.

Outram, Dorinda. *The Body and the French Revolution: Sex, Class, and Political Culture*. New Haven: Yale University Press, 1989.

Paine, Thomas. *The Rights of Man*. 6th ed. London, 1791.

"Poisoners Living and Dead—Arsenic Novels." *Punch* 8 (1845): 68.

"Political Conditions and Prospects of France." *Quarterly Review* 43 (May 1830): 215–242.

"Political and Vested Rights." *Edinburgh Review* 53 (June 1831): 502–544.
Porter, G. R. *The Progress of the Nation*. New ed. London: John Murray, 1847.
Price, Richard. "A Discourse on the Love of our Country." London, 1790.
Plummer, Alfred. *Bronterre: A Political Biography of Bronterre O'Brien, 1804–1864*. London: Allen and Unwin, 1971.
Poyer, Joe. *Tunnel War*. New York: Atheneum, 1979.
Rigby, Elizabeth (Lady Eastlake). "Vanity Fair and Jane Eyre," *Quarterly Review* 84 (Dec 1848): 153–185.
Roebuck, John Arthur. *History of the Whig Ministry of 1830*. 2 vols. London: Parker, 1852.
———. "The Trial of Madame Lafarge: French Criminal Jurisprudence." *Edinburgh Review* 75 (July 1842): 359–396.
Ross, Charles. "Political History of France since the Revolution." *Quarterly Review* 43 (October 1830): 564–596.
Russell, John, (Earl). *The Causes of the French Revolution*. London: Longmans, 1832.
Sanders, Andrew. *The Companion to A Tale of Two Cities*. London: Unwin Hyman, 1988.
Sargent, Lyman Tower. *British and American Utopian Literature, An Annotated, Chronological Bibliography, 1516–1985*. New York: Garland, 1988.
Schama, Simon. *Citizens: A History of the French Revolution*. New York: Knopf, 1989.
Scott, Sir Walter. *The Life of Napoleon Buonaparte*. 1827. 2 vols. Philadelphia: Gihon, 1853.
"Scrutator." *Who Is Responsible for the War?* London, 1871.
"Sea-side Reading." *Fraser's Magazine* 32 (November 1845): 559–572.
Shanley, Mary Lyndon. *Feminism, Marriage, and the Law in England, 1850–1895*. Princeton: Princeton U. Press, 1989.
Shelley, Mary Wollstonecraft. "Mirabeau." In *The Cabinet Cyclopaedia: Lives of Eminent Literary and Scientific Men of France*. 2 vols. London: Longmans, 1839.
Shires, Linda M. "Of Maenads, Mothers, and Feminized Males: Victorian Readings of the French Revolution." In *Rewriting the Victorians*, ed. Linda M. Shires. London: Routledge, 1992: 147–165.
Simmons, Clare A. "Caterham as Terminus in *Friendship's Garland*." *ANQ* 11 (Winter 1998): 20–23.
———. *Reversing the Conquest: History and Myth in Nineteenth-Century British Literature*. New Brunswick: Rutgers U. Press, 1990.
———. "'Iron-Worded Proof': Victorian Identity and the Old English Language." *Studies in Medievalism* 4 (1992): 202–218.
Smith, Goldwin. *Lectures and Essays*. New York: Macmillan, 1881.
Southey, Robert. "French Revolution: Conspiracy de Babeuf." *Quarterly Review* 45 (April 1831): 167–209.
———. *Sir Thomas More: Or, Colloquies on the Progress and Prospects of Society*. 2nd ed. 2 vols. London: John Murray, 1831.

"Speeches delivered in Banquo Reginae." *Fraser's Magazine* 7 (May and June 1833): 507–526, 682–705.

Stallybrass, Peter, and Allon White. *The Politics and Poetics of Transgression.* Ithaca: Cornell U. Press, 1986.

"The Story of the Channel Tunnel, Told to Our Grandchildren." *Macmillan's Magazine* 46 (April 1882): 499–504.

Stephens, W. R. W. *The Life and Letters of Edward A. Freeman.* 2 vols. London: Macmillan, 1895.

Strauss, Leo. *Natural Right and History.* Chicago: U. Chicago Press, 1953.

Surtees, R. S. *Hillingdon Hall, or the Cockney Squire.* 1845. London; Folio Society, 1956.

Thackeray, William Makepeace. *Catherine*, Part 1. *Fraser's Magazine* 19 (May 1839): 604–617.

——. *The Letters of William Makepeace Thackeray,* ed. Gordon N. Ray. 4 vols. Cambridge: Mass: Harvard UP 1946.

——. "Proposals for a Continuation of *Ivanhoe*." *Fraser's* 36 (Aug/Sept 1846): 237–245; 359–367.

——. *Stray Papers.* Ed. Lewis Melville. 1901; rpt. New York: Kraus, 1971.

——. *Vanity Fair, A Novel Without a Hero.* 1847–8. Ed. J. I. M. Stewart. Harmondsworth: Penguin, 1973.

——. *The Works of William Makepeace Thackeray.* 26 vols. London: Smith and Elder, 1901.

Thatcher, Margaret. *The Downing Street Years.* New York: HarperCollins, c. 1993.

Thesing, William B., ed. *Executions and the British Experience from the 17th to the 20th Century.* Jefferson, NC: McFarland, 1990.

Thierry, Augustin. *History of the Conquest of England by the Normans.* Trans. William Hazlitt the Younger. 2 vols. London: Bohn, 1856.

Thiers, Adolphe. *The History of the French Revolution.* Trans. Frederick Shoberl. 3rd American ed. 4 vols. Philadelphia: Carey and Hart, 1845.

Thomé de Gamond, Joseph-Aimé. *Étude Pour L'Avant-Projet d'un Tunnel Sous-marin entre L'Angleterre et la France.* Paris: Victor Dalmont, 1857.

Tocqueville, Alexis de. *The Old Regime and the French Revolution.* 1856. Trans. Stuart Gilbert. New York: Doubleday, 1955.

——. *Recollections.* 1893. Trans. George Lawrence. Ed. J. P. Mayer and A. P. Kerr. New York: Doubleday, 1970.

Trevelyan, George Otto. *The Life and Letters of Lord Macaulay.* New impression. London: Longmans, 1900.

Vanden Bossche, Chris R. *Carlyle and the Search for Authority.* Columbus: Ohio State U. Press, 1991.

"Verdict on Madame Laffarge." *Examiner* (September 27, 1840): 611.

Vicinus, Martha, and Bea Nergaard, eds. *Ever Yours, Florence Nightingale: Selected Letters.* London: Virago, 1989.

White, Hayden. *Metahistory: The Historical Imagination in Nineteenth-Century Europe.* Baltimore: Johns Hopkins U. Press, 1973.

——. *Tropics of Discourse: Essays in Cultural Criticism.* Baltimore: Johns Hopkins U. Press, 1978.
Wilkins, B. T. *The Problem of Burke's Political Philosophy.* Oxford: Clarendon, 1967.
Williams, John. "The Subversion of Ancient Governments." *Quarterly Review* (July 1831): 450–471.
Williams, Raymond. *Culture and Society: 1780–1850.* 1958. New Edition. New York: Columbia U. Press, 1983.
——. *Marxism and Literature.* Oxford: Oxford U. Press, 1977.
Wolff, Robert Lee. *Strange Stories, and other Explorations in Victorian Fiction.* Boston: Gambit, 1971.
Wollstonecraft, Mary. *An Historical and Moral View of the French Revolution.* 2nd ed. 1795; New York: Scolar Reprints, 1975.
Wordsworth, William. *The Fourteen-Book Prelude.* Ed. W. J. B. Owen. Ithaca: Cornell U. Press, 1985.
——. *The Prelude, A Parallel Text.* Ed. J. C. Maxwell. Harmondsworth: Penguin, 1971, rpt. 1986.
——. *The Salisbury Plain Poems.* Ed. Stephen Gill. Ithaca: Cornell U. Press, 1975.
Young, Arthur. *Travels during the Years 1787, 1788, and 1789 ... [in] France.* Bury St. Edmunds, 1792.
"Zanoni." *The Athenaeum* Feb. 26, 1842: 181–183.
Zola, Emile. *La Débâcle.* Ed. R. Jouanny. Paris: Garnier, 1975.

Index

Acton, Lord 206
Ashmead-Bartlett, Ellis 209–10
Alison, Archibald 64–71, 102;
  Blackwood's articles 67–68, 117;
  History of Europe 66–71; 84–85, 91
Alison, Archibald, the younger 205
Althorp, Lord 56–57
America, United States of 168, 174–5,
  183, 188; American Revolution
  14–15, 40, 44
Armstrong, Nancy, and Leonard
  Tennenhouse 26
Arnold, Matthew 124, 176; Sonnets on
  1848 119–121; *Friendship's Garland*
  189–193
Ayling, Stanley 37–38

Bahti, Timothy 26, 28
Bastille, Storming of 2, 8, 69, 84, 86,
  150 *see also* French Revolution
Bentham, Jeremy 43, 73, 173
Bhabha, Homi 195
Bismarck, Otto von 173
Bivona, Daniel 196
Blanc, Louis 99, 117, 123, 127–128;
  History of Ten Years 105–106,
  109–110, 113
Bolingbroke, Henry, Lord 16, 29
Brantlinger, Patrick 15
British Broadcasting Company 1
Brougham, Henry, Lord 48, 54–55, 95,
  118

Brontë, Charlotte 116
Broughton, Lord (John Cam Hobhouse)
  29
Browning, Robert 204
Bulwer-Lytton, Edward *see* Lord Lytton
Burdett-Coutts, Angela 160–61
Burke, Edmund 2–3, 23–24, 33–44, 67,
  92, 94, 193; emulations of 45–58, 82,
  102; *Appeal* 38–40, 43; *English
  History* 35–37, 40–41, 59;
  Reflections 9–10, 17, 33, 37–41,
  122, 154; other writings on France
  49, 51
Burke, William, and Hare 67, 94
Burrow, J. W. 7, 11, 28
Butler, Samuel 176, 190; *Erewhon*
  181–183
Butterfield, Herbert 11, 16, 28, 206
Byron, Lord 61, 75–76, 96

Carlyle, Thomas 23–24, 63–93, 100,
  186, 207; and Dickens 144–50,
  161–2; Count Cagliostro" 85–86;
  "Diamond Necklace" 85–86; on the
  Franco-Prussian War 169–74; *French
  Revolution* 77–8, 84–93, 135–7, 173;
  "Latter-Day Pamphlets" 145–6
Cavaignac, General Louis-Eugène 123,
  137
Carroll, Lewis (Charles Dodgson)
  176–81, 184
Chandler, James K. 17, 34

Index

Channel Tunnel 16–18; proposals for 3–4, 23, 159–160; 1882 tunnel 199–208; Eurotunnel 1–3, 8, 206–210 *see also* Thomé de Gamond
Charles X, King of France 46–49, 118
Chartism 24, 99–101, 127–129, 137
Chatham, Earl of (Pitt the Elder) 15, 72
Chesney, G. T. 176; *Battle of Dorking* 187–191, 202–203
Chesterfield, Lord 151
Ciolkowski, L. 107–108
Civil War, English 2, 8, 38–9, 43, 122–24, 150–51
Clarke, I. F. 187, 209
Clive, John 28
Clough, A. H. 100, 118–121
Cobban, Alfred 24
Cole, G. D. H. 128
Coleridge, S. T. 16, 30, 33–34
Colley, Linda 8
Collins, Wilkie 161–2
Comte, Auguste 142–3, 204
Cone, Carl B. 37
Conservative party 1–5, 29, 64, 83, 141, 191, 202, 206 *see also* Tories; Disraeli; Thatcher
Corday, Charlotte 91–2
Coutts, Angela Burdett 142–3
Crimean War 158–161, 168
Croker, J. W. 29, 50–64; *Quarterly* essays 49–54, 57–58, 117–118, 123–24, 129
Culler, A. Dwight 6

Danton, G.-J 70, 77, 87–89
Darwin, Charles 68–9, 170
Daily Telegraph 189–90
Deane, Seamus 9–10
De Certeau, Michel 11, 26
Deleuze, Gilles 179
De Quincey, Thomas 94
Dickens, Charles 23, 135–162; *Barnaby Rudge* 155–56; *Child's History of England* 147, 150–51, 162;
Household Words 145–7, 158–61; *Tale of Two Cities* 135–162, 187
Disraeli, Benjamin 15, 28, 160, 175, 191, 193, 202
Donne, W. B. 122
Dowling, Linda 180
Dumas, Alexandre 108, 131, 132
Dumont, Étienne 73–75, 95

Eastlake, Lady (Elizabeth Rigby) 116–17
Edinburgh Review 48–49, 54–55, 122 *see also* Brougham; Macaulay; Gladstone
Egyptian Crisis 203, 205–206
Elias, Norbert 154
Eliot, George 24, 205
Elizabeth II, Queen of Great Britain 206–207
Emerson, Ralph Waldo 83, 118

Fairbairn, Patrick 18
Farrell, John P. 76, 82, 89
Ferris, David 7
Feuchères, Madame de 109–110
Fielding, K. J. 136
Forster, John 108, 115, 130, 140
Franco-Prussian War 167–193, 204
Freeman, E. A. 170, 194
French Revolutions 89; of 1789 2–7, 15, 24, 37, 46, 51, 55, 57, 64, 69–71, 113, 118, 173, 193; of 1848 99–102, 107, 167 *see also* Carlyle; Dickens; July Revolution; Paris Commune, Terror
Foucault, Michel 6, 11, 26n, 154–5, 157, 161
Fox, Charles James 4, 12
Friedman, Barton 8, 26, 86, 97, 148
Furet, François 10
Fullarton, John 27, 51

Garibaldi, Giuseppe 168–69
George IV, King of Great Britain 12, 46, 144, 151–52

German states   45, 99, 101, 203;
    Germanic origins of English   43, 121,
    183–84; in Franco-Prussian War
    167–74
Gilbert, Elliott L.   86, 97
Gilbert, W. S.   177–78, 199–201
Girondists (*Girondins*)   59, 70, 72, 91–2,
    100; Whigs as   54, 64, 150; radicals as
    119, 126
Gladstone, W. E.   171–2, 175, 181,
    199–201, 204
"Glorious" Revolution of 1688   13–15,
    122–24, 151; comparisons with 1789
    2, 8, 37–38, 40–44, 69, 87; comparisons
    with 1830   54–57
Goldberg, Michael   136, 147–48
Gooch, G. P.   6
"Grip"   203–206
The Guardian   5, 207, 210

Habermas, Jürgen   61
Halévy, Eli   43
Hall, Basil   49
Hall, Stuart   1
Hardy, Thomas   204
Hazlitt, William   27, 62, 66
Hegel, G. W. F.   76–77, 97, 129
History   6–7, 10, 16–18, 39, 83;
    historical determinism   76–78, 89–90,
    93, 189; hypothetical   72–80; study of
    121; and *A Tale of Two Cities*   135–37
    see also progress; tory history; whig
    view of history
Hollingsworth, Keith   111, 117
Hood, Thomas   94
Horsman, Reginald   194
Household Words see Dickens
Hugo, Victor   108
Hume, David   13–14, 17, 29, 30, 35
Hunt, Donald   4, 163
The Independent   207

Indian Rebellion ("Mutiny")   160–61
Inglis, Sir Robert   56

Italy and Italian states   45, 47, 101, 168
Ireland and the Irish   22, 92–93, 150, 170;
    in 1848   99–102, 120, 127–28; Irish
    nationalism   167, 174–75, 205, 207

Jameson, Fredric   103
Jewsbury, Geraldine   79–80, 118
Jouanny, Robert A.   194
July Revolution (1830)   8, 23, 33–54, 73,
    81, 118

Keats, John   51–52
Kemble, John Mitchell   121–25
Kingsley, Charles   169–70
Knowles, James   203–204
Kucich, John   148

Labour movement and party   13, 29,
    174–75, 206–7
Lafarge, Madame   109–110, 116
Lamartine, Alphonse de   99, 126–27, 137
Landow, George P.   17, 28, 30
Leigh, Percival   146–47
Lewes, G. H.   103–4, 109–10, 127–28,
    142
Lewis, Darby   194
Liberal party   12, 171, 190–93, 206
    see also Gladstone; Whigs
Liu, Alan   59
Louis XIV, King of France   85
Louis XV, King of France   84–85; France
    under   69, 72, 84–87, 153, 173
Louis XVI, King of France   51–52, 64,
    66, 85, 87–88, 153; execution of   12,
    39, 91
Louis XVIII, King of France   45–46
Louis Philippe, King of the French   52,
    103–4, 114–15; and the July Revolution
    46–48; overthrow of   99–100, 117–18;
    France under   103–112, 141
Lowe, Robert   191–92
Lucas de Montigny, Gabriel   73–78
Lukács, Georg   129, 136, 144
Luttrell, Barbara   74

Lytton, Edward, Lord   140–41, 152–54, 169, 190; *The Coming Race*   23, 176, 182–87; *Lucretia*   102–11, 119; *Zanoni*   139–42, 162

Macaulay, Catherine   27, 43
Macaulay, T. B. (later Lord Macaulay)   14–15, 24, 29, 44, 54, 57–58, 60, 96; *History of England*   23, 121–25, 149, 162; "Mirabeau" essay   73–77; "Southey" essay   18–21
Mackay, Charles   131
Mackintosh, Sir James   57–58
Maenads (also Menads), women as   22–3, 88, 148
Magna Carta   2, 8, 36, 69, 127
Mahon, Lord (later Earl Stanhope)   55–56
Mannheim, Karl   12, 16, 28, 31, 61
Marcus, David D.   136
Marat, Jean-Paul   87–88, 91–92
Marie Antoinette, Queen of France   39–41, 64, 85–86, 92
Martineau, Harriet   140, 142
Marx, Karl, and F. Engels   100–1
Mercier, Louis-Sebastien   152–54, 165, 166, 177
Mignet, F. A.   70–71, 98, 149
Mill, John Stuart   13, 22, 24, 73, 98, 100, 117; and Carlyle   80–84
Mirabeau, H. G. Riquetti, Comte de   72, 82, 95, 106, 125–28, 177; in the 1830s   65, 71–79, 87, 89–90
Mitterand, François, President of France   206
"Mob," populace as   22, 70, 73, 81–82, 90–93 *passim*, 175, 186
Monod, Sylvère   135–36
Monnier, Sophie de   72, 79
Morris, William   177, 204
Müller, F. Max   169–74, 179–80, 183–84, 191

Napoleon I, Emperor (Bonaparte)   2–4, 8, 45, 49, 65–66, 71, 203–4; Carlyle on 77, 89, 92; in *Vanity Fair*   111–12, 115; Napoleon III and   129, 137–38, 165
Napoleon III, Emperor (Lucien Bonaparte)   129, 137–38, 42–43; and Britain   159–60, 167; in 1870   167–69, 172, 175–76
Newgate novel   105, 111, 117
Newman, Gerald   8
Nicolas, Sir (Nicholas) Harris   63
Nightingale, Florence   158–59
Norman Conquest of England   13, 36, 43, 188

O'Brien, Bronterre   127–28
O'Connell, Feargus   127
Oddie, William   144, 147–48, 150, 153
Odger, George   175
Oliphant, Margaret   152
Orsini Incident   159–60, 201
Outram, Dorinda   22

Paine, Thomas   27, 30, 40, 42
Paris Commune   181–87, 192
Parliamentary Reform Act, First   12, 14, 22–24, 45–48 *passim*, 63, 67–68, 73–76, 100–2, 150
Peel, Sir Robert   15, 46, 58, 61, 64–65, 71–72, 93, 99 *see also* Tories
Pitt, William, the Younger   12
Plummer, Alfred   127
Poison   52, 106–10, 131–33
Polignac, Prince Auguste Jules   47–49
Porter, G. R.   131
Price, Richard   37–38, 60, 122
Progress, theories of   20, 24, 42, 57, 71–72, 75, 118–20, 123–24, 143–62 *passim*, 186–87
Prussia *see* German States
Punch   22, 31, 107–8, 191, 200–1, 205

Quarterly Review   17, 41–42, 48–55, 116–18 *see also* Croker

Radicalism   13, 44, 83, 113

Revolution *see* French Revolutions, "Glorious" Revolution
Robespierre, Maximilien 8, 52–54, 64–75 *passim*, 88–89, 100, 106; in 1848 123–29, 141–42
Roland, Madame 91
Roman Catholicism 56, 159, 168–69; Roman Catholic emancipation 20, 24, 66
Rousseau, Jean-Jacques 40, 55–56, 79, 85
Russell, Lord John 15, 67, 85, 149–50; *Causes* 55–57

Saint-Just, L.-A. de 113, 125
Sambourne, Linley 200–3
Sanders, Andrew 165
Schama, Simon 34–35
Scotland 99, 102, 128, 156
Scott, Sir Walter 27, 48, 65–66, 95, 97, 98, 112–13, 182
"Scrutator" 172–73, 191
Shakespeare, William 203–4, 210
Shanley, Mary Lyndon 196
Shaw, George Bernard 136
Shelley, Mary 78–79
Shires, Linda 31
Smith, Goldwin 193
Southey, Robert 18–20, 51, 134; *Colloquies* 18–24, 67
Stalleybrass, Peter, and Allon White 157–58
Strauss, Leo 59
Super, R. H. 192
Surtees, Robert 94

Tennyson, Alfred, Lord 50, 159, 204
Terror, Reign of 18, 56, 66, 71–72, 90–92, 106; terror as outcome of change 2, 118, 126, 140
Thackeray, W. M. 23; *Vanity Fair* 102–17, 124; *Continuations of Ivanhoe* 112–13; *Four Georges* 114; 151–52
Thatcher, Margaret 2–3, 8, 35
Théroigne de Mericourt, Anne (Josèphe Tewagne) 87–88

Thierry, Augustin 13
Thiers, Adolphe 47, 52, 70–71, 91, 126, 176, 149
Thomé de Gamond, J.-A 4, 117, 138–39, 201, 208
The Times 1, 13, 46–48, 51, 107, 128, 129, 138, 159, 168–74 *passim*, 188, 192–93, 207–8
Tocqueville, Alexis de 56, 126
Tories 3, 12–16, 45–46, 58, 103–4, 175; tory history 12, 19, 38–39, 64, 80, 91, 208 *see also* Conservative party
Tunnel *see* Channel Tunnel

Utilitarianism 21, 43, 57–58, 83–84 *see also* Bentham

Vanden Bossche, Chris R. 82
Verne, Jules 170, 176
Victoria, Queen of Great Britain 138
Voltaire (F.-M. Arouet) 55–56, 79, 189, 192

Wainewright, T. G. 108
Watkin, Sir Edward 201
Wellington, Arthur, Duke of 50, 141
Wells, H. G. 196
White, Hayden 9, 11, 26n
Whigs 12–16, 47, 60, 63, 138; whig view of history 11–12, 22, 100, 128, 138, 206–8
Wilkins, B. T. 59
William IV, King of Great Britain 64
Williams, Raymond 7, 26, 31
Wollstonecraft, Mary 9, 24
Wolsley, Sir Garnet 201, 205–6
Women, roles of 22, 41–42, 52, 110, 148–49, 159, 175, 185
Woodcock, George 152–53
Wordsworth, William 24, 34–36, 141

Young, Arthur 152–4
Young, Hugo 5

Zola, Émile 175–76, 188